SHALLOW GRAVES

Maureen Boyle

SHALLOW

The Hunt for the

New Bedford Highway

Serial Killer

ForeEdge

GRAVES

ForeEdge
An imprint of University Press of New England
www.upne.com
© 2017 Maureen Boyle
Manufactured in the United States of America
Designed by Mindy Basinger Hill
Typeset in Minion Pro

For permission to reproduce any of the material in this book,
contact Permissions, University Press of New England,
One Court Street, Suite 250, Lebanon NH 03766;
or visit www.upne.com

Library of Congress Cataloging-in-Publication Data

Names: Boyle, Maureen, 1956– author.
Title: Shallow graves: the hunt for the New Bedford Highway serial killer / Maureen Boyle.
Description: Lebanon NH : ForeEdge, [2017] | Includes bibliographical references.
Identifiers: LCCN 2017013544 (print) | LCCN 2017027368 (ebook) | ISBN 9781512601275
    (epub, mobi, & pdf) | ISBN 9781512600742 (pbk.)
Subjects: LCSH: Ponte, Kenneth, 1949–2010. | Serial murders—Massachusetts—New
    Bedford—Case studies. | Serial murder investigation—Massachusetts—New Bedford—
    Case studies. | Serial murderers—Massachusetts—New Bedford—Case studies.
Classification: LCC HV6534.N33 (ebook) | LCC HV6534.N33 B68 2017 (print) |
    DDC 364.152/320974485—dc23
LC record available at https://lccn.loc.gov/2017013544

9 8 7 6 5

TO KEVIN *who said the story must be told,*

and to the families of the lost still looking for an answer

CONTENTS

Illustrations follow pages 88 and 188

TIMELINE

1988

April 3 Kenneth Ponte, an attorney, allegedly threatens a man with a gun.

July 3 Debra Medeiros found on Route 140 north in Freetown by a woman who stopped to relieve herself. Debra went missing May 27, 1988, and was identified in December 1988.

July 30 Nancy Lee Paiva found on the westbound side of Interstate 195 in Dartmouth, about one and a half miles east of the Reed Road exit by two men on motorcycles. She went missing July 7, 1988, and was identified in December 1988.

September New Bedford detective John Dextradeur notices a number of drug-addicted women are missing and contacts the district attorney's office to set up a meeting to discuss the cases.

October 10 Kenneth Ponte moves to Florida.

November 8 Debra Greenlaw DeMello found off the eastbound Reed Road ramp of Interstate 195 by a state highway crew. She walked away from a prison work-release program in Rhode Island on June 18, 1988, and was identified in December of 1988.

November 29 Dawn Mendes found on the westbound Reed Road ramp off Interstate 195 by a search dog. She went missing September 4, 1988, and was identified days later.

December 1 Debroh Lynn McConnell found off Route 140 northbound in Freetown by a search dog. She was last seen by her family in May of 1988 and was identified in March of 1989.

December 10   Rochelle Clifford Dopierala found in a gravel pit along Reed
Road, about two miles from Interstate 195, by people riding ATVs. She
was last seen in late April of 1988 and was identified in December of 1988.

1989

January 18   Kenneth Ponte is arraigned in New Bedford Superior Court; a
grand jury handed up an indictment on the April 1988 gun charges.

March 28   Robbin L. Rhodes found along Route 140 southbound in Freetown by a search dog. She was believed to have gone missing sometime in
March or April of 1988. She was identified soon after being found.

March 31   Mary Rose Santos found along Route 88 in Westport by two boys.
She was last seen July 16, 1988. She was identified soon after she was found.

April 24   Sandra Botelho found along Interstate 195 in Marion by a state
highway crew. She went missing August 11, 1988, and was identified soon
after she was found.

1990

August 17   Ponte is arraigned on a single count of murder.

1991

July 29   The murder charge against Ponte is dropped.

SHALLOW GRAVES

PROLOGUE

IT WOULD HAPPEN FAST. She would reach up, clawing at the fingers — or maybe it was a piece of clothing — tightening around her neck. She might try to kick at the attacker, struggling to get free. She might try to hit him as the pressure on her carotid arteries intensified. She might try to bite him on the forearm or bicep. She would wonder why this was happening.

She would struggle to breathe, grabbing at her neck and gasping for air. If only she could loosen the grip. She might even succeed for a brief second, giving her hope of escape; getting free, she would run fast and not look back. But then the pressure would intensify, and the air, and the hope, would be squeezed from her once again. She would hear ringing in her ears, or maybe it was a muffled or gurgling sound as the pressure on her neck increased. Her vision would blur. She would feel everything around her closing in — like being in a tunnel. Things would go black. She would feel a tingling sensation in her lips, arms, and legs. Her head would be hot. Her pulse would be weak.

The pressure on the jugular vein would stop the blood going to her heart. The pressure on the carotid arteries, the major vessels in the neck and deeper than the jugular vein, would stop blood to the brain. The hyoid bone in her neck might fracture. She would do everything in her power to stay conscious, to hang on. She was a fighter, a survivor.

It would take only minutes for the darkness to take over. It would seem much longer.

She does not want to die.[1]

1 MISSING

NANCY PAIVA passed beneath the signs of the two neighborhood bars, tears in her eyes, and walked quickly up the street. It was a hot and drizzly July night, and a few people were standing outside, close to the buildings, catching a smoke and a cool breeze.

Her boyfriend stayed behind, bouncing between the street and the bars; it was near closing time. The two parted just before one o'clock in the morning from a County Street bar in the South End of New Bedford, Massachusetts, down the street from two stone churches, one Catholic, one Episcopal.

This is not how the thirty-six-year-old Nancy envisioned her life would turn out: walking home drunk and high on heroin, penniless and jobless, past inebriated men and noisy bars. Growing up, she dreamed of becoming a nurse, of traveling the country, of having a beautiful home and family. And she had started down that path. She learned the importance of hard work from her father, who labored in local factories to support his wife and kids. She learned the importance of family from her mother, who opened their home to foster babies. She knew education was important and took college-track courses in high school and, later, when college seemed out of reach, enrolled in a local secretarial school, then took courses to become a certified nursing assistant. She grew up in a two-story, single-family home, where food was always cooking, in a quiet middle-class neighborhood in New Bedford, far from the city's noisy tenements and wolf-whistling drunks.

She tried to grasp the American Dream by marrying, working in tidy offices, having a beautiful baby. Then, somehow, it slipped away. Slowly at first. So slowly she didn't realize it was happening until it was gone. First it was a divorce, then the deaths of her parents, both in their fifties, then a failed long-term relationship. She worked in a series of jobs, but the good ones, the high-paying ones, seemed to elude her. The bright spot in her life were her two daughters, one by her former husband, the second by her longtime common-law partner. She loved her girls: loved taking them on trips, loved staying home with them, loved cooking nightly dinners for them, loved hosting birthday parties. Now, as she walked up the street in New Bedford alone, she felt she was failing at even that part of her life.

Others could pinpoint when Nancy's life turned, even when she couldn't. It happened when she met a guy. Then she met his drugs. Then her life unraveled to this point, walking up County Street in the South End in the early morning hours, looking for someone to give her the sixty dollars she needed to pay a fine on bad-check charges at the courthouse forty-five minutes away in Stoughton later that day, money she didn't have. Her boyfriend would later say she was "hitchhiking to go and see if she could get some money." A friend thought Nancy got into a truck parked near a corner that night.

And then Nancy was gone.

It was as if she had vanished into the night air.

Less than forty-eight hours later, her boyfriend, Frankie Pina, nervously walked into the century-old downtown New Bedford police station and tried to get the desk officer's attention. Frankie had a record for drugs, robbery, and street scams. He had done some jail time and, in his world, talking to the police was to be avoided at all costs. But now, with Nancy gone without a word, he didn't care about street code or cred. It had been two days since he saw Nancy walking north, toward the apartment they shared. She never got home and she never called. He had been looking for her ever since.

Frankie was trying to tell the desk officer he was now worried. Nancy wouldn't just disappear without telling someone, without taking her children.

Detective John Dextradeur was passing the front desk and paused when he saw Frankie. His first thought was: What the hell is Frankie Pina doing here?

Frankie, at five feet five, was a muscular guy with a reputation as a tough, streetwise con man. Originally from the Boston area, he was a little rougher, maybe a little tougher, than the others arrested on the streets of this historic waterfront city; but he still blended into the social underbelly the police saw every day.

The detective flipped through the paperwork on a clipboard behind the lobby desk, listening to the conversation, trying to figure out why this guy — of all guys — would be at the station, insisting on talking to a police officer.

He listened as Frankie said his girlfriend didn't come home, that something was wrong, that he needed to report her missing. She didn't take off, he kept repeating. Something happened.

John turned around and nodded to the desk officer — I got it.[1]

The New Bedford police missing-person report at the time was a single-page form: name, age, height, weight, eye color, race, when last seen, address, person making the report. One copy would hang in the outer office of the police department records room on a clipboard. Another copy would remain at the front desk. It was 1988, the days of typewriters, payphones, Bic Wite-Out typing-correction fluid and steel-gray file cabinets.

The missing-person report for Nancy Paiva listed the basics. Age: thirty-six; Hair color: brown; Eye color: brown; Height: five feet three; Weight: one hundred and twenty pounds. Eventually, a small family photo of Nancy smiling would be attached to the report. It was one of the dozens of missing-person reports filed that year in this fishing port known as the Whaling City, where *Moby-Dick*, fishing boats, Frederick Douglass, textile mills, and heroin dealing were diverse threads in the community fabric.

It would take months before the public would see the significance of that single-page report.

By then it was too late.

But on that July day in 1988, John Dextradeur didn't know the report of this missing woman would launch the area's largest murder investigation. He just knew something didn't sit right. The veteran detective had investigated just about every type of crime during his seven years in the detective bureau's olive-drab second-floor office. He could tell when something was wrong. And this was wrong. He could tell by the way Frankie was talking, the way he was moving.

But what was it? Was Frankie, in some clumsy way, trying to cover his tracks by reporting this woman missing? Did she rip him off? Did he rip someone off and did she pay the price? Or was it something else? There appeared to be genuine concern in Frankie's voice as he stood in the police department lobby, even a touch of fear.

For three years John Dextradeur had been tracking what he thought was a growing — and troubling — series of crimes against women in the city. Some of the women were addicts. Some were prostitutes. Some were living on the rougher edges of the city. A few were just enjoying a night out. Three women last seen leaving one of the city's shot-and-beer bars were found dead. A well-known prostitute needed seventeen stitches after she was stabbed in the head, shoulder, and knee, and the attacker told her he did the same thing to other women. Another prostitute was raped so brutally she left a yards-long blood trail as she desperately looked for help. Yet another was taken to a nearby town and attacked. One female addict was stabbed to death and left in a snow bank in 1987; a Cuban who came over on the Mariel boatlift was later charged with the murder. And then there was Dorothy "Darcy" Danelson, the nineteen-year-old woman found raped and strangled alongside railroad tracks by a Sunbeam Bread Baking Company driver starting his shift on July 16, 1986. Her body was so brutalized that even hardened detectives, years later, were still haunted by what they had seen. Her head was covered in blood. Her skull was fractured. She had been beaten with a railroad tie. She had been raped anally and vaginally with a stick and a beer bottle. There was an animal rage in that attack, an anger of the wild.

The detectives tracked the last hours of Darcy's life in minute detail.[2] She made the rounds of four bars known for cheap booze and drugs with a guy she met that night. She shot pool at the Lucky Star on North Front Street and Coffin Avenue. She stopped for an egg sandwich as they waited for a cab because the guy didn't have a car — only a bicycle. She went to the Fisherman Lounge in Fairhaven but the bouncer wouldn't let her in because she didn't have an ID. They went to Paul's Sports Corner about 100 yards away near the New Bedford line where she drank gin and tonics. She danced to jukebox music at another bar — called Alfie's Place — in the city's North End then abruptly left the guy on the dance floor and plunked herself down at the bar. The two exchanged phone numbers. He kept drinking beer; she kept drinking gin and tonic. The guy left to use the bathroom, and when he returned, he said her seat was empty. She was gone. He ordered another beer. No one in the bar remembered Darcy leaving. But that wasn't unusual. Everyone at Alfie's was pretty drunk at the time. Some people outside the bar did remember the guy with a cane who cracked his head on the sidewalk around one o'clock in the morning and went off in an ambulance. The commotion — the cruiser and the ambulance lights — made it hard to miss. Someone saw a woman walking down the street right around that time and get into what looked like a Ford Bronco. It looked like she was wearing a floral shirt. Her hair may have been shoulder length. The person wasn't sure. It was dark, after all. No one could say for certain if it was Darcy. Some people at the bar, though, did remember seeing her inside earlier dancing and drinking. A few "kind of" remembered what she was wearing. Dextradeur's colleagues, Detectives Gardner Greany, Gary Baron, and State Trooper Jeff Gonsalves, tracked down cars, trucks, and drivers who might have been in the area. They interviewed Darcy's family, her ex-boyfriend in jail, her current boyfriend, the guy she was dancing with, bartenders, bouncers, cab drivers. They talked with prostitutes and drug dealers who were on the street that night. They asked people to take polygraph tests. They sent evidence to the FBI. They detailed nearly every minute of Darcy's last day alive. There was just one gap: from the time she left the bar until roughly five hours later when she was found dead. There were at least three possible suspects in the slaying at the time. There was no evidence to arrest any of them.

One prostitute later told police a strange guy driving a green Cadillac tried to pick her up that night. She spotted a knife on the seat, yelled, and he took off. Another woman told Detective Gardner Greany she saw a "spaced out" man driving a Pinto between two and two forty-five that morning trying to pick up a prostitute. The car was loaded with beer bottles, the same brand used to assault Darcy. The driver was never found.

And then there was the phone call to police. One of the prostitutes out on the street that night was brought to the station to listen to the recording to see if she recognized the voice. "We got the girl on Purchase Street and now we're going to get another," the caller reportedly said.[3] She didn't recognize the man's voice. No one did.

That vicious murder fueled John Dextradeur's determination to learn more about the men in his hometown preying on the women who lived or partied on the edge, some of the most vulnerable, and sometimes the toughest, in the city. He wondered if the killer of Darcy would strike again. A year later, when another woman known to walk the Purchase Street area, Margaret Nunes, was found stabbed to death in a snowbank, Dextradeur wondered how many people were stalking vulnerable women on the streets. He found himself talking with the city's prostitutes and drug addicts more often, learning their backstories. One woman came from a wealthy family with ties to Nantucket. Another grew up near Cape Cod. Yet another was lured into the heroin world by a boyfriend who later overdosed. Most of the women were white, from the suburbs, and caught in the cycle of addiction. In his chats with them, he learned about other, unreported and disturbing attacks: women punched, choked, robbed, stabbed. He learned of the men who cruised the streets day and night, looking for sex. Some were factory workers, fishermen, and day laborers, looking for oral sex. Others were lawyers and doctors. Some were in law enforcement. While drug addiction crossed socioeconomic lines, so did the johns who picked up these women. Quick sex for a quick fix.

As he stood in the aging foyer of the New Bedford police headquarters, listening to Frankie Pina struggle to report his girlfriend missing, John Dextradeur tried not to think of those other cases. Maybe Nancy had just taken off for a few days. Maybe she was trying to get away from her boyfriend. Maybe she was getting high someplace, lost in a drug fog in a rundown tenement. Maybe she landed in a drug-treatment program. He knew Frankie was an addict and suspected that was likely the case with Nancy. He saw one too many addicts go missing, only to reemerge days or weeks later. Often, the detectives in the narcotics office tracked them down on the street corners — or in jail. The families accustomed to seeing this rarely reported them missing — and when they did it was often weeks or months later.

This time, with Nancy Paiva, something felt different. Maybe it was the panic in the boyfriend's voice. Maybe it was how quickly he came to the station. This felt bad, very bad.

In the 1980s, nearly all crime in New Bedford was tied somehow to the drug trade: prostitution, drug dealing, robberies, burglaries, bad checks, shoplifting. The two central spots for drug sales were a section of the South End where addicts sought out drugs in a few bars and neighborhoods, and north of the city center in Weld Square, a neighborhood about two miles from the historic downtown where dealers would sometimes pop up on the streets. Many of the women who turned to prostitution to buy heroin paced this historic, rundown neighborhood along Purchase Street. Sometimes the women just lingered on the corners, watching as johns slowly drove by,

annoying residents in the 1911 railway-car barn renovated for senior housing. Most of this sex trade occurred during the day — the busiest time was
right before school got out when fathers would stop by before picking up
their children, the prostitutes would say. At night, some women would work
both the streets and the bars in the city's South End and in Weld Square. The
charge: twenty dollars, enough to buy a single glassine packet of heroin, the
devil drug at the time.

People in New Bedford often recognized the women on the street and
sometimes knew how they got there. More than a third of the nearly 100,000
people living in the city were of Portuguese descent, hailing from large,
tight-knit families. Roughly 7 percent more could trace family roots to Cape
Verde, the African islands colonized by Portugal in the fifteenth century and
that gained independence in 1975. Some tracked their ancestry to the early
whaling ships, a handful to the captains, but most to crews. People in this
city were tight: they put down deep roots and stayed for generations. Families
were intertwined, friendships decades old. The long and narrow city had that
small-town feel, where, like the *Cheers* television show, everyone knew your
name — or at least someone in your family. Most people felt comfortable reporting even the smallest of crimes and talking with police. Some cops said
that openness in the 1980s to report crime was what drove up some of the
crime statistics, such as petty thefts and bar fights. The "no-snitch" culture in
larger cities hadn't yet spread to this community. As a result, most murders
in New Bedford were solved within a year and were tied to either domestic
violence or drugs.

In this blue-collar fishing community, with its close-knit neighborhoods,
the homicide detectives often knew the families of the victim or killer — or
both. Sometimes they had been classmates. Sometimes they were relatives.
Sometimes they were relatives of friends. Even when there wasn't enough
evidence to make an arrest, investigators usually had a good idea who did it.
They would wait, listen, watch. People talked and, even if it was the faintest
whisper, someone always seemed to be listening. When the body of a Vietnam veteran, weighted with cinderblocks, was dragged up from the water
by fishermen, investigators already knew it was a suicide. That's because
months earlier, an investigator overheard two shaken men pounding back
shots at a Fairhaven waterfront bar talking about the guy who paid them

to bring him out to sea. He tied himself to the blocks, shot himself, then toppled overboard.

A defense attorney once described the homicides in the city as assault-and-battery cases gone awry, where instead of going to the emergency room for treatment, the victim went to the morgue. The cases were tragic, yes, but not chilling, the types of deaths seen in other cities throughout the country. Husband or boyfriend kills wife or girlfriend in drunken rage. Crying infant shaken repeatedly by parent, causing brain swelling and death. Man stabbed during fight over spilled drink, a girl, a debt, a wrong word. Teenaged gang wannabe fires gun into a crowd, kills bystander. What police in New Bedford saw were crimes of passion, stupidity, and addiction. These were crimes a community shook its collective head at and pledged to prevent — until the bill for social services was tallied, government funds vanished, a factory closed, fish catches shrunk, and jobs disappeared.

Overcoming adversity, though, seemed to be imbedded in the municipal DNA of New Bedford. Perhaps the historic motto, penned when the whale oil it refined was used in the days before electricity, helped give it strength: *Lucem diffundo* — "We spread the light." Perhaps it was seeing the fishing boats leave the harbor, not knowing if everyone onboard would return. The city had known destruction and had known how to rebuild. As far back as the Revolutionary War, when the British burned 70 vessels and twenty-six warehouses, and the city saw its whaling industry come to a near halt,[4] the community was able, at war's end, to slowly right its economy and send the whaling ships back out so that, by 1857, there were 329 vessels sailing out of the harbor.[5] When the whaling industry finally died in the 1860s, the city transformed itself into a booming industrial city famous for fine cloth and yarn.[6] Politically and historically, the residents welcomed those seeking a better life. New Bedford stood tall as a leader in the abolitionism movement in the United States and became a station in the Underground Railroad, helping slaves escape to freedom.[7] In later years, wave after wave of European immigrants came to the city, filling the mill, factory, and fishery-related jobs.

New Bedford always seemed to be a city of contrast. It was a city of riches in the early to mid-1800s, when the whaling industry boomed. The lofty mansions of the aristocratic vessel owners sat atop the hill, overlooking the harbor. The families of those who were out to sea or worked in the shops labored below, struggling to survive until the boats returned. Along some of the streets, widows like Lydia Russell, whose husband was killed by a whale, made a living running boarding houses in cramped wooden homes.[8]

It was a rough-and-tumble city cloaked in finery.

Throughout the years, the fishing industry and the bustling waterfront remained the economic spine of the city. Fishermen in the 1980s could make up to $4,000 on a single, ten-day fishing trip, and the boat owners would take in much more.[9]

The reliance on the sea also made the community used to death — and always struggling for ways to comfort those left behind. Each year, hundreds of names are read at the Port Society's annual Fishermen's Memorial Service. The walls of the Seamen's Bethel, the downtown chapel opened in 1832, puts names to those numbers. There, memorial plaques with the names of the boats lost at sea — and the men missing with each vessel — are displayed. Nearly every year, a name or names are added. By 1988, there were 235 names memorialized; there were the 11 lost when the Midnight Sun went down in a storm in 1962; the 13 when the scalloper *Navigator* out for a ten-day trip was lost in 1977; the 6 when the trawler *Irene & Hilda* went missing in a storm in the Nantucket Sound in 1980.[10] It is a testament to the power of the sea and the endurance of the fisherman.

"O God thy sea is so Great and my Boat is so Small," reads the inscription for the *Irene & Hilda* at the Bethel.

Death in New Bedford was familiar in that way you know a Catholic Mass will soon end when the priest says "May almighty God bless you, the Father, the Son, and the Holy Spirit," that cemeteries — not makeshift street memorials — are where you honor the dead. The city was built on hard work, perseverance, and the knowledge that some things — such as the rough seas so many died in — are beyond the control of man.

When a person was murdered nearly everyone in the community was touched in the intricate web of pain threading together family, friends, friends of friends, work colleagues, former classmates, neighbors. Finding justice was the one thing in this city on the water everyone believed would happen after a murder, sooner or later. That is why the death of Dorothy "Darcy" Danelson and the unsolved slayings of three other women in the city bothered John

Dextradeur so much. There was no closure, there was no justice. There was just a nagging dread that the worst was yet to come.

After the death of Darcy Danelson, the woman found dead by the railroad tracks, John Dextradeur began reading up on serial-killing cases, devouring articles with "serial killer," "murder," and "criminal profiling" in the title — often while sitting in the stands at a local rink as his youngest daughter practiced ice skating.

What's that you're reading? One mother once asked him.

He showed her the cover: *Sexual Homicide: Patterns and Motives*, by Robert K. Ressler, Ann W. Burgess, and John E. Douglas.

Oh, she answered, flustered, and looked away.

He just smiled and went back to reading.[11]

John looked at his cases with skepticism, taking the word of no one for granted — even that of a cop. When a fellow officer accidentally fired his service weapon struggling with a suspect, John grilled the man for more than an hour — then reenacted the scene sans gun to make sure it was plausible. He would, as the worn adage goes, "think out of the box" and wonder why others didn't do the same. He believed each case could be solved, and when it wasn't he took it personally. On first blush, he could appear aloof and tough. Fools, he felt, had no place in police work, and he wasn't shy about letting people know that. Lazy fools? Don't ask. He excelled on the job, rising to the rank of sergeant, but the job took a personal toll. By 1988, he was already divorced twice. His eldest child from his first marriage, Christopher, saw his father occasionally when he was younger, but as the years passed — and his dad remarried — they drifted apart. It would take the bonds of blue to bring them back together in 1987, when Chris at age eighteen became a New Bedford police cadet. They now could talk about the job; fatherly advice was now career advice.

The job, the elder Dextradeur would sometimes say, stole his family life and put a strain on his relationship with his children, particularly his son. He hoped he could now make it right. He also worried about his health. His father had heart problems, and he had his first heart attack at age forty-five chasing a robbery suspect on Union Street in New Bedford. His doctors warned him back then to slow down. He really tried to follow their advice, but it didn't work out all that well. It was the era of cigarettes, coffee, and fast food for police officers across the country. New Bedford was no different.

After he took down the information from Frankie Pina that July day, John wondered where this investigation into Nancy Paiva's disappearance would lead.

Five blocks away at city hall, Judy DeSantos was hunched over her desk in the election office updating voting lists, unaware her older sister was gone.

JUDY DESANTOS spent the day of July 7, 1988, in a state of aggravation. It was hot outside and it was hot inside the apartment she shared with her husband and four children. She could feel her temper rising. She had to get out of the house. She decided getting a haircut was the best thing to do. It would lift her spirits. Plus, the beauty school was air-conditioned.

Her husband had the car, so Judy did what she usually did: walk. She figured out years ago it was easier, and quicker, to walk the mile into downtown rather than drive. You didn't have to worry about parking tickets either. Today, she thought the walk would "do her good."[12] It would clear her mind, lift her mood, and give her a little bit of exercise.

As she passed United Front Homes, one of the low-income developments in the city, Judy spotted a dark-haired, petite woman on a second-floor, east-side balcony on Morgan Street. Even from across the street she could recognize who it was, her sister Nancy-Lee Paiva.[13]

The two sisters hadn't spoken much in nearly eight months. The issue was Nancy's boyfriend, Frankie. Nancy met him through a mutual friend whose boyfriend had been in jail with Frankie. Most everyone thought Frankie was an odd choice for her, and Nancy herself might have thought the same a few years earlier. Maybe she was lonely, maybe she saw something in him others couldn't. Nancy was the type of person who would look beyond first impressions, who would look into someone's heart, who was always ready to take a chance. For whatever the reason, the two began to date and he eventually moved in. Three years older than Judy, Nancy was outgoing, determined, and fearless. She spoke her mind, had a wide circle of friends, and, from the outside, seemed in control of her life. As a child, she was adventurous — willing to climb trees to thrilling heights while her sister watched safely below. As an adult, Nancy was still the risk-taker — new relationships, new experiences. Judy, the caut something would go wrong. Nancy, the extrovert, she would miss if she didn't try.

Nancy graduated from New Bedford High School at Kinyon Campbell business school in the 1970s, tł young women in the 1970s. She married at age nineteen, moved into an apartment in the city's North End, landed a job at a city business, and had her first child, Jill. "She was happy," Judy would later recall.[14]

When Nancy's first marriage ended in divorce, she stayed on the same track: working, taking care of her daughter. Eventually, she met Freddie, and the two, while not married, were viewed by family and friends as husband and wife. She had a second girl, Jolene, and worked a wide range of jobs in a wide range of places: general office worker, keypuncher, nursing-home assistant, clerk in a video store, bartender in one of the many working-class establishments scattered in the city. She dreamed of becoming a nurse but knew dreams didn't pay the bills. Hard work was something both sets of grandparents, immigrants from the Azores, and her parents, born in the United States, had stressed. Hard work and family.

After fourteen years and one child together, Nancy and Freddie broke up. But Nancy's spirit, while a bit bruised, was not broken. She took her daughters on a vacation to California and, when she returned, kept up the same life pace as before.

Then she met Frankie. Things seemed to be good at first. Then they weren't.

For nearly two years, Judy suspected something was wrong in that relationship. Her nieces were fifteen and twelve when Frankie entered the picture, and they would sometimes tell her of the fights they heard between the couple in the apartment. Judy saw the bruises on her sister's arms. Once Nancy's shoulder was dislocated. Another time there was a black eye. When questioned, Nancy shrugged it off. There was a car accident. She fell. A string of reasons for what appeared to be an increasing number of bruises and injuries.

The tipping point between the sisters came in November of 1987. Nancy wanted to sell her microwave. She needed money. Judy suspected at the time sister was giving Frankie money and knew Nancy must be desperate was selling household items. She gave Nancy eighty dollars as a down payment. She called a few days later so they could figure out when she could swing by to give Nancy the balance and pick up the microwave. On the other end, Judy could hear a man yelling in the background. It sounded like Frankie. She heard what sounded like slaps. She could hear her sister crying.

"You know what your sister wants this money for?" Frankie yelled into the phone, Judy recalled.[15]

Judy could hear her sister in the background, crying. "Please don't tell her."

"It's to buy her drugs. So she can shoot up," Frankie snapped at Judy on the phone.

Judy was stunned.

Her husband took the phone and, in a firm and loud voice, told Frankie to bring back the money or bring over the microwave. Then he hung up.

Judy waited for her sister to call back that day. And the next. And the next.

Shortly after Thanksgiving, Judy learned her sister checked into a Worcester, Massachusetts, rehab center about an hour away. "If only she would stay long enough and get away from Frankie," Judy would later write in a journal. "That was my hope."

Two weeks after checking into rehab, Nancy was back out.

In the 1980s, those struggling with heroin and cocaine addiction discovered inpatient treatment options were few if they didn't have health insurance, and those programs were often just two-week detox programs, often geared toward men. Two weeks was long enough to get the drugs out of the system but not long enough to stop the craving. It was what recovering addicts called "spin and dry." Men filled most of the program beds. Women often waited weeks for a spot.

When Nancy got out of detox, she told Judy in a brief conversation that she went every night to support meetings, such as Narcotics Anonymous, to stay straight. Judy wanted to believe her but, when she later looked back, there were warning signs of serious trouble. When she later called her sister's apartment after that short chat, Nancy never came to the phone. After a while, Judy stopped calling. Some friends told Judy that Frankie wouldn't allow her sister to call or visit. Judy wasn't sure if that was true, but it reinforced her worry that something was going wrong in Nancy's family. She suspected

Nancy was a battered woman. She wasn't sure how she could help her. She wasn't sure if Nancy would even let her.

So, Judy was pleasantly surprised on that hot summer day as she passed the Morgan Street apartment to see her sister on the balcony.

If Nancy had been downstairs, Judy would have crossed the street to say hi. But Judy was in a hurry to get to her hair appointment, her sister was on the second-floor apartment balcony, and there would be another time to catch up.

Judy waved from across the street.

Her sister waved back.

It was July 7, 1988.

NANCY PAIVA's seventeen-year-old daughter, Jill, was living on her own in a small three-room first-floor apartment in New Bedford's South End in July of 1988, a single mom with two children under the age of two. The place wasn't perfect, she knew, but it was better than living in what was becoming a battleground between Frankie and her mother. By the time Jill moved out, strangers were in her mother's life. They were at the apartment at odd hours. Some, Jill knew, were using drugs—likely heroin or cocaine. She hoped her mother wasn't doing the same. Frankie and her mother were yelling. Hiding in her bedroom, Jill could hear things smash. She could hear thuds. She could hear her mother cry. Her mother who was always the strong one, the no-nonsense, don't-mess-with-me-or-my-kids one, the person with the answers, the protector of the family, now seemed broken. She seemed beaten, her laugh silenced, her vigor sapped. Her mother seemed afraid. "They would fight and he would say he was going to tell us what she was really and she would beg him not to say anything to us. She would be crying," Jill recalled.[16] Jill packed up when she was pregnant with her second child, shortly after she got in a shoving match at the top of the stairs with Frankie. She had the safety of her own children to worry about now.

Jill moved to the South End apartment, around the corner from a pizza parlor, in a neighborhood with the type of multifamily homes seen in so many old factory cities. It was cramped, and there wasn't much of a yard, but for Jill it was a safe haven. Years earlier, Jill would have found comfort in her mother's apartment—her home—as she faced raising two children.

Her mother was the mama bear. She would have been there to help raise the grandbabies. Nothing would have come between her and her girls — or her grandchildren. Those days were now gone, though.

Nancy could be tough. When Jill first became pregnant at age fifteen, Nancy wasn't pleased. Angry was more like it. The person she first directed that anger at was Jill's boyfriend, a local boxer who was a few years older. But as the pregnancy progressed, she calmed down and focused on her daughter and soon-to-be grandchild. She made sure Jill ate right, made it to doctor visits and, when the time came, she was there in the delivery room to welcome her first grandson. That was before Frankie and his drugs moved in, before life quickly spiraled downward. By the time Jill was pregnant with her second child, Frankie was firmly ensconced in the household, and life at home was very different.

At age seventeen, Jill was out of the house but tried to stay in her mother's life. She still chatted on the phone with her mom and sometimes they would meet when Frankie wasn't around. Jill harbored the hope that whatever tied her mother to the relationship would snap. Or Frankie would wind up back in jail. For a long time. Long enough for her mother to start fresh and the family to move on. Nancy kept telling people she would leave him. Her daughter hoped it would be soon.

Jill remembered Nancy Paiva the mom as the woman who baked chocolate-chip cookies — the ones with real chocolate chips, the big ones that oozed and filled the apartment with that sweet, lush scent. Who hosted slumber parties. Who took her daughters — and their friends — strawberry and apple picking at the farms of Acushnet. Who cooked every meal, every day. Who insisted on everyone eating together. Christmas with her mom was a festive event, with evergreen trees over the years decked out with homemade decorations by her children, popcorn on a string and pinecones. There was never a lot of money, but what there was she spent on her children.

Jill wanted that mom back. She wanted that life back.

Jill refused to believe her mother was using hard drugs. Other people years later would echo the daughter's conviction. Not Nancy, not ever. Jill, however, was not naive. She knew some people her mother knew — like Frankie — did use hard drugs. She would see them and try to look the other way. Her mother was different, though. She wasn't like the rest. She was smarter, she was sharper, she was classier. She would never risk her health, her family, her life. Her mother knew better. Jill kept repeating that in a silent mantra each day. But she knew, deep down, that something was wrong. It all happened so quickly, these changes in her mother both physically and psychologically. She saw how thin her always-fit mother was getting. She heard the yelling, she saw the bruises and she saw the tears. She could see both the fight and the light in her mother's eyes flickering out.

On July 7, 1988, Jill was outside on the stoop of her apartment in the late afternoon when she saw a figure walk by. The woman was thin, dazed, looking ahead. She could tell, even from across the street, it was her mother. She raised her arm to motion to her. Her mother kept walking. Later that night, Nancy called her daughter from a pay phone from the South End. She told Jill it might be a while before she saw or even talked with her again. She had to go to court the next day and would likely go to jail. She owed court fines on a bad-check case, money she didn't have just yet. Money she likely wouldn't get by the morning. She spent her last dime in the pay phone, on this call. The recorded operator's voice broke in, instructing Nancy to insert more coins to continue. Then the line went dead. Jill waited that night and the hot July days that followed for another call.

THE SEA BREEZES off New Bedford harbor and city beaches a mile away did little to cool Jill's tiny apartment as the summer temperatures reached the mid to high nineties that month. People were calling it one of the hottest summers in recent memory — or at least the hottest stretch.

Jill was trying to figure out the best way to keep the children cool when she saw Frankie at her door.

What's that son of a bitch doing here? she wondered.

She let him in, warily.

Your mother is in a rehab, he lied to her.

Jill was suspicious. This just didn't make sense. She peppered him with questions. Why didn't her mother call to tell her this? What rehab? Where? When did she go?

Frankie paused. He didn't tell her Nancy was missing. He didn't tell her he had no idea where Nancy had gone. He didn't tell the teenager he had reported her mother missing to the police a week earlier. Instead, he lied again.

He insisted her mother didn't want Jill and her younger sister to know she had gone to rehab, that she was an addict, but he couldn't keep it a secret. He would later say he lied because he didn't want Nancy's daughters to worry, that he thought she would be back soon. So, on this day, facing Nancy's oldest child, he spun this rehab tale. Jill wasn't buying it.

Jill repeated her questions. What rehab? When did she go? I need to talk with her.

Frankie picked up Jill's phone and dialed.

I'll call them for you, he told her.

Jill glared as he talked into the phone.

She listened suspiciously as Frankie appeared to talk with a receptionist. He asked to speak to Nancy Paiva. He paused, spoke again and looked up at Jill.

He hung up and told Jill her mother was fine but she was busy. She couldn't come to the phone.

What's the number? she demanded.

Your mother didn't want me to tell you where she was, he insisted.

What's the number?

He jotted a phone number down and left.

When Frankie was out the door and out of sight, Jill picked up the phone and dialed the number.

Doo. Doo. Dee.

Check the number and dial again.

Doo. Doo. Dee.

Jill replaced the receiver, puzzled.

Maybe mommy finally left him, Jill thought. *Maybe she is in hiding. Maybe he was trying to see if she was here. Maybe he was trying to see if I knew where she was.*

Maybe now she is finally safe.

BY THE THIRD WEEK of July, there was still no word from Nancy. Frankie finally broke down and told Jill and her sister he had no idea where Nancy was. He had been trying to buy some time, hoping Nancy would show up.

Jill called her aunt.

"What do you mean your mother is gone?" Judy DeSantos asked her niece on the phone.[17]

Time is important when someone goes missing, Judy knew from television and newspaper articles; the sooner a search starts, the better. As she listened to her niece, she hoped time hadn't run out for her older sister already.

"Let me call the police," Judy said. "Let me find out what's going on."[18]

She hung up and called the downtown police station and was transferred to the front desk.

"I understand there is a missing-person's report on my sister," she told the officer on the line. She heard a scoff.

"You have to understand, junkies go missing all the time," the officer answered, she recalled. "I wouldn't worry about it. She'll show up."

Judy went silent. She didn't question what cops said. She rarely questioned what anyone in authority said, even if it was the counter clerk at Dunkin' Donuts. She didn't like to argue or rock the boat. She kept her voice soft and tone even. Her life was simple, uncomplicated, nonconfrontational, risk free, just as she liked it. What was she supposed to do now?

She thanked the officer and hung up.

The next day, police came to her door with a message: call Detective John Dextradeur. She called right away. The detective first apologized. He told her he had taken a missing-person report for her sister from a man named Franklin Pina, who claimed he was Nancy's common-law husband. He never mentioned any other relatives, and Mr. Pina gave the impression he was the only next of kin, the detective said. This type of follow-up on a missing-person report in 1988 was unusual. At the time, New Bedford police did not launch intensive investigations into reports of adults who went missing unless there was evidence of foul play or an indication the person might be in danger. Police officers at the daily roll call at the start of a shift would be made aware of the reports but rarely would it go much further than that. In nearly all of the cases, many involving teenagers, the person reported missing would show up safe. However, the disappearance of Nancy Paiva nagged the detective. He didn't like the tale he heard her boyfriend told Nancy's children and he was now bothered by how quickly Frankie reported her missing. He wondered: was Frankie hiding something? He didn't share those concerns with Judy just yet. Instead he tried to learn more about Nancy Paiva's life, her relationship with Frankie and, if possible, her last days.

He asked Judy what she thought of Frankie's decision to report her sister missing so quickly. Did she think that was strange? What did she know about her sister's boyfriend? About Nancy and Frankie's relationship? Did she think he would hurt Nancy? The detective didn't like what he was now hearing about the relationship between Nancy and Frankie. Did Frankie have something to do with Nancy's disappearance? Was he no longer the worried boyfriend? Should he be a suspect, instead? John kept the suspicions to himself as he spoke with Judy. He asked for more information about her family and jotted down Judy's home and work numbers. It would be best to call at work, she told him. Judy thanked him. He thanked her. She promised to do whatever she could to help. But Judy still wasn't sure what that was.

As disturbing as her sister's disappearance was, Judy discovered the conflicting information she was getting from people about Nancy's whereabouts was even more troubling: Nancy was at a bar last night. She was walking along a street in the South End. She was at a pharmacy, a grocery store, a coffee shop. She was paying a bill. She took off. She was hiding out. She was everywhere and, when Judy checked, she was nowhere.

By the end of the week, Judy found herself at the front door of her sister's Morgan Street apartment with a friend's son fiddling with the key. Her stomach felt hollow. Her hands trembled as she opened the door. Her heart raced. Her instinct was to turn and leave. She took a deep breath. *I need to do this for Nancy.* She stepped inside. It had been more than a year since she had been in the place and she wondered — no, she worried — what she would find. Her youngest niece, Jolene, was fourteen and now living with her paternal aunt, Linda Spinner, around the corner, a place where she stayed when things got bad at home. Both of Nancy's daughters had dropped hints about what had been going on in the apartment but didn't tell her everything until after their mother was gone. They told her about the strangers crashing on the couch. Once, someone tried to crawl into the place through a window. There was a lot of arguing. When they were in the bedroom, the girls could hear things crashing to the floor in the other room. People were high. They saw signs — such as burned spoons and needles — that someone was using heroin but never saw their mother shoot up. The girls laid the chaos of their home at the feet of Frankie. None of this happened before he moved in. None of this would have happened but for him, they were convinced. If their mother was using heroin, and that was something the girls still didn't want to believe was possible, it was Frankie's fault, they believed.

As Judy stood in the doorway of her sister's apartment, holding her niece's house key, she worried what she might now see. She looked around. There were no signs of a struggle. No signs of Nancy. No signs of Frankie. Judy felt like a criminal, waiting for someone to order her out. She fought the urge to run out.

Judy scanned the apartment. There were tiny spatters of blood on the telephone. There were the boots and clothes of strangers in the closet. The bedroom set was in pieces on the floor. The mattress was ripped open. The dresser drawers were on the floor, broken. She spotted her late father's shoe-shine box on the floor and opened it: there were needles and syringes on the bottom. There were no drugs — at least none she could see. She quickly left, called the police from her home and went back.

The uniformed officers who showed up confiscated the phone and took her father's shoeshine box with her permission.

"What did you expect to find in there?" she remembers one officer asking, trying to hide a wry smile as he raised the box up.

"Shoe polish, what do you think?" she answered.

A week later, she went back to the apartment, this time with her husband. Her nieces — one living on her own, the other still staying with another aunt a block away — had been retrieving clothes, photographs, and mementos from the unit. She didn't know where Frankie, who was not on the apartment lease, was. She suspected he had moved on. She hoped he might be in jail on some type of charge. She prayed he wasn't in the apartment. Judy's hands still trembled as she opened the door again. Her heart still raced. Her instinct was still to turn and leave. Instead, she pushed inside. The apartment still looked as if it had been ransacked. Judy opened the kitchen cabinets, the refrigerator, the stove, looking for anything of importance hidden there. She went into the bedroom, where the mattress was still overturned, and looked through the clothes strewn on the floor. She recognized the gray, metal lock box — roughly the size of a piece of notebook paper — near the dresser. Her mother, who died four years earlier of a heart attack at age fifty-seven, used it as a recipe box. Judy placed it on the dresser top and opened it. She recognized the tight writing of her mother's hand, detailing the dishes of her childhood. She lifted the first recipe card then saw *it*.

She froze. There, on the bottom of the two-inch-high box, was a gun. It was gray. It looked big. She wasn't sure what make or model. She knew nothing about guns. She had never touched one. She'd never even seen one up close. Guns scared her. This one scared her. She picked it up and carried it gently with both hands like you would a tray of brimming water glasses then placed it on the washing machine. *I'll come back for it with the police.* Then she bolted out.

Judy's heart was still pounding by the time she got home but she had talked herself out of reporting the gun to authorities, at least for that night. She tried to tell herself she didn't want to cause trouble for Nancy. The apartment lease was in her sister's name, and having an unlicensed gun might be cause for eviction, she tried to reason. It could even lead to an arrest. Her hesitation, though, was deeper than the worry about the apartment lease. She was afraid. What was really going on in that apartment? Who was involved? What if someone came back for the gun? What would happen to her? What would happen to her children? Did she want to get involved? She would wait before she said anything. She needed to think. But by the next day, Judy changed her mind. She returned to the apartment to find the gun. It was gone.

Judy knew things were now out of her control. She couldn't try to do things on her own. She couldn't try to hide whatever problems her sister had. She called the detective who talked to her about the missing-person report. He in turn told her he wanted to get into her sister's apartment. Would she let him in? I can do it after work, she told him. They agreed to meet outside the daycare center near Nancy's apartment. Later that night, Judy realized they had only spoken by phone. She had no idea what he looked like.

At 4:15 that next afternoon, weeks after her sister went missing, Judy stood at the corner of Maxfield and Cedar Streets in the West End of the city, waiting for a stranger to meet her. She saw a sedan circle the block once, twice, three times. Then it stopped. A fortyish sandy-haired man behind the wheel rolled down the window. Another detective was in the passenger seat.

"Are you Judy?" the driver asked, she recalled.[19]

"Yes."

John Dextradeur introduced himself.

The two detectives and Judy were at the Morgan Street apartment a block away minutes later: Judy walked, the detectives drove. This time the apartment key wouldn't work. The detectives said it appeared someone had jammed the lock. Judy walked over to the apartment management office and asked for help getting in. No, she was told. She wasn't the tenant. She couldn't get in. It didn't matter that her sister was missing. Judy's name wasn't on the lease and the police didn't have a search warrant. The three left, frustrated.

In the weeks and months that followed, John Dextradeur groused about not getting into the apartment that day, about not knowing about Nancy's extended family when she was reported missing, about what evidence might have been in the unit. When he went there with Judy, he didn't have a search warrant to get into the apartment and he likely couldn't have gotten one even if he went to court and asked a judge for it. He didn't have any legal grounds. There was no evidence of an abduction. There was no evidence of a homicide. There was no evidence any harm came to her at the apartment. All he had was a missing mother, likely addicted to heroin, last seen walking in the South End of the city. All he had was a gut feeling she might be dead.

Frankie later credited the detective with being the first to take seriously Nancy's disappearance, to believe she wasn't an addict who just went off with junkie friends to get high. He would say John Dextradeur was the first to believe him, the first to suspect a deadly pattern might be emerging in the city. Frankie didn't realize back then the detective also considered him a possible suspect. When Nancy went missing, city detectives and the state police homicide investigators assigned to the district attorney's office were working on another case taxing resources: the drowning deaths of four people, including two children, after an overloaded boat with fifteen people capsized in the city's harbor following the Fourth of July fireworks display. Investigators were building a manslaughter case against the man helming the boat. There was little time to spare on a city detective's hunch.

By the end of August, Judy would see the contents of her sister's apartment piled outside in the trash. Friends would tell her they saw mail scattered on the ground. The apartment was emptied out, ready for a new tenant. Nancy was still gone. Judy feared any evidence that might have been inside the place was now gone too.

2 BODIES

WITH TEMPERATURES HOVERING IN THE EIGHTIES, it was a perfect day for boating.

It was July 3, a Sunday, and Alan Alves had waited weeks for this day when he could kick off the Fourth of July weekend cruising his spanking-new blue twenty-foot Bonito through the waters of Long Pond in Freetown, Massachusetts. He had been waiting years to finally buy this boat and, about a month earlier, he had convinced his wife, Donna, to let him spend the $18,000 to do it. They had three children, two still at home, and as a police sergeant in Freetown, population 8,500, he was earning just $38,000 if you included overtime and paid details. Alves grew up in Freetown and, as one of the few Cape Verdeans in town, was one of just a handful of people of color in the rural community sandwiched between the mill cities of New Bedford and Fall River. He knew every corner of the town. He could describe the dark corners of the expansive state forest where he believed a satanic cult worshiped in the early 1980s. He could rattle off the names of the families who had owned acres of land for generations. He loved the cool breezes across Long Pond, the shallow warm waterway nestled in one corner of town. His family, like others in town, went back generations in Freetown. Most of his extended family lived within walking distance from his house.

He knew from age ten that he wanted to be a cop. He remembers at age seven seeing Superman on television and telling people he wanted to be a crime-fighting superhero. But he didn't see any Cape Verdean cops in his hometown growing up. He didn't see any cops of color anywhere. Go to technical school, he remembers a high school counselor telling him. Being a black cop just wasn't going to happen.

He started as an auxiliary officer at age twenty-three in 1971, a volunteer job he juggled with a full-time job as a union drywall carpenter. He thought he would land a full-time spot pretty quickly, like most auxiliary officers did. He was a townie through and through. Townies got the town jobs.

He took the town's police test and aced it, twice. He would later say he scored so high the first time — the highest of those vying for the Freetown slot — that someone accused him of cheating. A black guy couldn't beat out all of those whites, he was told. So he took the test again — and again scored high. After two and a half years as an auxiliary, he was finally appointed a full-time cop. For his first assignment on the midnight-to-eight shift he said he was ordered to wash and wax the cruisers in between calls. He would drive a cruiser from the police station to the elementary school three miles away, clean it then drop it back off. None of the other new guys did that, he recalled.[1] He would be assigned to the cruiser with the bald tires, with headlights that would heat up and short out. At first he complained privately to a friend who was a town official. He didn't want to cause trouble. He just wanted to be a regular cop on his hometown force.

Then he was passed over for promotion to sergeant, even though he had seniority. He filed a complaint with the Massachusetts Commission Against Discrimination, the state board handling civil rights and discrimination cases. The town was forced to promote him. Then he was passed over for a second promotion. He filed another complaint and won. By 1988, Alves was known as a cop who wasn't afraid of challenging the town. He would eventually win, years and a third complaint later, a total of $750,000 once it was all settled.

But he didn't have any of that money when he first spied that boat in Captain Bub's Marine. When he went for a ride with his wife a month earlier, the first spot they went to, the only place he really wanted to bring her, was to Captain Bub's.

"Isn't it beautiful?" he told her. "Wouldn't you just love being on it?"

"We're not getting a boat," she said. "We don't need a boat."

She made up her mind, he knew by her tone. So they hopped back into their fiberglass black two-seater Pontiac Fiero and headed home.

Less than five minutes into the ride, she turned to him. "You really want that boat, don't you?" she asked. "Turn around. Let's get it."

Within an hour, Alan Alves was the proud owner of a brand-new blue-and-white inboard/outboard Bonito. Everything was special about the boat, from the two captain's chairs in the front to the name on the side. It had an eight-foot-wide beam, a cuddy cabin, a porta-potty, and a canvas top. The registration ended with AA, his initials. He named it *Mr. Meanor* and painted a pair of handcuffs on the side. Some people dreamed of the perfect car. Alves dreamed of — and had — his perfect boat.

He put it in the water at a buddy's dock on Long Pond a week or so before the Fourth of July holiday and planned to spend a couple of days on it, tooling around the water there, making sure there weren't any problems before trailering it to open waters in Fall River later in the month.

Alves had packed a cooler and a small bag that Sunday morning and was looking forward to a relaxing weekend and, hopefully — using some vacation time — taking off part of the upcoming week during this unseasonably hot summer.

He pulled down his buddy's driveway around noon and was getting out. Alves could feel a slight breeze. This would be a good day, he thought.

Eeep. Eeep. Eeep.

Alves heard the annoying sound and felt the vibration of his Motorola beeper. As the sole detective on the department, he was on call 24-7, even on holiday weekends.

Crap.

He took a deep breath. Maybe it was something minor, he thought hopefully. He reached down and pulled out the bulky cell phone he kept in a suitcase-like box in the car. He liked gadgets, and this phone was the ultimate of gadgets. It was cool. *Miami Vice* cool.

There was a body northbound on Route 140, just over the Lakeville town line, the dispatcher told him. Head over there. State police will meet you.

He went home, picked up his unmarked cruiser, and zipped up to the highway where two Lakeville officers waited.

About thirty feet off the road, in the brush, lay the remains of what appeared to be a partially clad woman, a bra wrapped around her neck. A woman who stopped along the roadway to relieve herself in the brush had discovered the body, he learned.

"It's all yours," one Lakeville officer said, before eventually taking off in the cruiser.[2]

Finding bodies along a highway happened sometimes. A few years earlier, the skull of a man was discovered on Interstate 195 in a nearby town. The skull was examined, and eventually an artist crafted a model of what the man might have looked like. Police circulated that image nationwide. He was still unidentified. But Alves was pretty certain this would be different. The area was pretty close-knit. If a woman were missing, someone would know. This woman would not be nameless long, he was convinced.

To seasoned investigators there wasn't anything unusual about the scene. Classic "body dump" is how several would later describe it: a vehicle would pull over; someone hauls a body out and flips it onto the ground then takes off. Far enough from the road to stay hidden, close enough to the highway so someone wouldn't have to walk too deep into the woods and risk getting caught by a state trooper passing by.

That's what State Trooper William Delaney first thought when he stepped gingerly through the brush that day.[3] In Massachusetts, whenever there is an unattended death, such as a homicide, state police investigators assigned to the county district attorney's office are required to respond to scenes in all but the three largest cities in Massachusetts — Boston, Worcester, and Springfield — where local departments have larger detective and specialty units. At the scenes, they work with the locals and coordinate crime-scene efforts. Technically, the state police are in charge of the cases. In practice, they often share the workload — and credit — with the locals. In the days, weeks, and months after a homicide, the state police officers interview witnesses usually in coordination with the town or city detectives, and hopefully identify the killer or killers. When one of these cases came in, the troopers would take turns going out. This holiday weekend, it was Delaney's turn to be on call.

The troopers assigned to the Bristol County District Attorney's Office, on average, went out to fifteen to twenty homicides a year in the 1980s and more than double that in what are called unattended deaths — overdoses, drownings, accidents, and a wide range of other deaths outside a hospital setting where a doctor isn't present. Most of the cases were in the main cities of the county: New Bedford and Fall River to the south, Taunton to the north, and Attleboro to the west.

Delaney walked up to the Freetown detective standing at the side of the highway to get the rundown on what was there, gave the scene a quick look then backed away, making sure he didn't disturb any potential evidence. He could tell, though, it was not a recent death. The body was unrecognizable. The skin, to his eye, looked leatherlike, as if the person had been there for months. The medical examiner, he hoped, would be able to give him more information about how this woman — if it really was a woman — died and how long she had been out here. The state crime-scene investigators, he hoped, might be able to give him a lead on who put her there.

It would take hours before the medical examiner would remove the body, enough time for someone from the state police photo and fingerprint unit to get there to memorialize the scene in photographs. These were the days before DNA collection was the norm, before crime-scene collection became a widespread law-enforcement art. These were the days of television shows like *Magnum, P.I.* and *Murder, She Wrote,* where quick-thinking detectives reigned, not the scientific wizards of CSI and *Bones.* Old-fashioned interviews, street work, and searching records by hand were what cleared most cases in Bristol County in 1988.

The troopers in the district attorney's office were pretty versatile. All had spent time on road patrol. Some worked in other investigative services before coming to the Bristol County office. They knew how to get stuff done and who could do it quickly. They were specialists who also had a good general knowledge of other areas and other jobs. If needed, they could step into any investigation confidently. The state police units assigned to district attorneys in Massachusetts are split into two sections: the body side, where troopers investigate deaths, and the drug side, where the major narcotics investigations are done.

On this holiday weekend, when folks were heading to Cape Cod on other highways or to family cookouts, it was the uniformed troopers from the Dartmouth barracks who were on hand to wave the few ogling drivers on, stop others from walking to the scene, and offer whatever help Delaney needed.

The uniformed state troopers stood guard at the scene as the sun set along what is normally a quiet highway leading to New Bedford, waiting for the medical examiner to arrive.

There was nothing unusual about the case to cops accustomed to death.

AT THE SOUTHERN MORTUARY in Boston, a state trooper watched as the medical examiner made the distinct incisions on the body as the autopsy began. Troopers — and longtime detectives in local police departments — had long gotten used to the sights and smells of the procedure. Well, maybe not quite used to it, but they knew what to expect. Cops early in their careers learned the tricks to observing autopsies. High on the list of necessary accessories was Vick's VapoRub under the nostrils to deaden the smell of decomposition. "Decomp" is a smell police say is unique. Once you smell it, you never forget it. It is harsh, pungent, and permeates the senses. The scent sticks to your clothes, your skin. Some say it gets into your head. Death does not let go easily.

But there were few of those smells on this day. The woman had lain dead along the highway in Freetown for months, more than enough time for the bulk of death's scent to dissipate. What investigators hoped was not gone was evidence telling them how this woman — classified as Jane Doe for now — died and how long she had been exposed to the elements.

The troopers got some of those answers, or at least thought they did.

Cause of death: Strangulation.

Manner of death: homicide.

Time of death: About nine months earlier, prior to winter.

Based on decomposition and the skin condition, the body had been out there before winter came, the medical examiner reported to police, anywhere from September to December of 1987. The woman also had been treated for a broken jaw, which was still wired.

Billy Delaney later went to the newly formed missing-person unit at the state police barracks in Middleboro, a brick building along what was once the main road to Cape Cod before Interstate 495 was extended through the area. There he was given a computer list of 1,724 missing women in Massachusetts who matched the description and death time frame. He went through it. Nothing matched.

He then checked missing-person reports for January. Then February.

Nothing.

The information would eventually be entered into a state and national system with the same results. He put the file for Jane Doe on his desk, a daily visual reminder of a lost, unnamed woman and waited.

It would be five months before he would learn how wrong the medical examiner had been in estimating time of death. By that time, other bodies would be found and investigators would be on the hunt for a suspected serial killer.

IT WAS THREE O'CLOCK, on July 30, 1988, more than three weeks after Jane Doe was found in Freetown. Trooper David Wordell was in the Dartmouth state police barracks, about twenty minutes southwest of where that body was found. It was a Sunday, the start of his shift, and he was itching to get on the road. It was hot outside and it was hot inside. It had been unseasonably hot for all of July, and cooler weather wasn't in the forecast. There was air-conditioning in the state police barracks in Dartmouth — barely. It consisted of a couple of air-conditioner boxes hanging from the windows, blasting cold air in a few corners of the old house. It was best to hit the road in the air-conditioned cruiser.

First, though, he needed to read the roll-call items: who was wanted, what to be on the lookout for, what major crimes just happened in the area. He exchanged a few words with the trooper working the desk for the evening, and then he headed out.[4]

David Wordell wasn't one to hang around the barracks. There really wasn't much going on in the white clapboard building on Route 6, down the road from the mall. It was once a house, complete with china cabinets and a fireplace, and it tended to get cramped very quickly — such as when troopers brought in more than one prisoner at a time to be booked and had to handcuff a suspect to a hook attached to the wall in what used to be the dining room. Or on payday when everyone stopped by to pick up his or her check and stayed a few extra minutes to chat.

David expected a quiet Sunday shift on the road. It was 95 degrees, it was late in the afternoon, and the Cape Cod congestion didn't really hit the section of Interstate 195 he patrolled. Most of the attention — and traffic — for the day was in Fall River for the Coors International Cycling Pro-Am where a contingent of eight troopers, including four on motorcycles, were covering the race. And that was just fine with him. A few weeks earlier, he had wound up parked in his cruiser for hours in Freetown, guarding the spot where a woman's remains were found. He watched as the medical examiner pulled the body — now in a body bag — out of the brush. Then he waited until someone came to relieve him at the end of his shift. That was the most excitement he had had on his shift this summer. Days on the road for a road trooper — at least in D Troop — meant endless loops on the highway, helping disabled motorists, stopping speeders and drunks and keeping an eye out for the occasional wanted criminal.

He was getting ready to head out when he heard the trooper working the desk tell him to head over to 195 westbound, between the Hixville Road over-pass and Reed Road exit. Two guys on motorcycles say they found a body.

Minutes later, he and another trooper were standing by the side of the road with two motorcycle riders. The riders, Arthur Denham and Francis Carreiro, both of Fall River, pointed into the brush. David walked about fifteen feet down a narrow worn path. Then he saw it — the remains of what appeared to be a woman. Her features were unrecognizable. There was no smell, no flies. No one would ever know she was there, even if they walked a few feet to the right or the left. He remembers thinking it was amazing she was found at all.

The bikers told the troopers they stopped to take a quick leak by the side of the highway and saw the remains. Fearing they wouldn't find the spot again, the men flagged down a driver and asked the person to call police. The troopers stayed with the pair, keeping the scene secure, until the detectives from the district attorney's office showed up. Wordell looked at the path, thinking it looked like one of those narrow "cut-through" trails a person might take to avoid a longer walk. An investigator noticed the worn grass and later wondered if someone had come to the spot before, possibly lin-gering over the body, raising the possibility the killer returned to the scene to mentally relive the crime.

Troopers Jose Gonsalves, Kenneth Martin, and state police sgt. Natale Lapriore, all assigned to the district attorney's office, were there pretty quickly to search the area for evidence as they waited for the medical examiner.

It all looked eerily familiar when Trooper William Delaney, the official on-call trooper from the district attorney's office, pulled up and looked around.

Two women found dead in the brush off two highways in the same month, less than twenty minutes and thirteen miles apart. What were the odds they were related?

THE THREE KIDS were laughing in the back seat of the station wagon as the DeSantos family drove home from a day at a public pool in Fall River, about twenty minutes away from New Bedford. Even with the windows rolled down to fight the ninety-plus July temperatures, Judy DeSantos could smell pool chlorine and suntan lotion from damp swimsuits and towels. It was one of the hottest Julys she could remember, with temperatures hovering some days in the high nineties. There were days, as she walked to work at New Bedford City Hall, that it seemed higher. The heat was making her youngest three kids cranky. It wasn't doing much for her mood either. And even though they lived in a port city, with a public beach, she wanted to get out of the city, and away from the worries about her missing sister, to cool off. The public pool in Fall River's Kennedy Park was the perfect spot, she thought.[5] So, early in the day, she had packed up the car, roused the kids out of bed, and handed her husband the keys to the family's station wagon, telling him he was driving them to the pool.

It had been three weeks since her sister, Nancy Paiva, had disappeared, and she couldn't shake off a feeling of dread. Her sister was devoted to her two daughters. Nancy wouldn't just take off without them. And if she did have to go someplace, she would have taken pains to make sure the girls were taken care of. Nothing about Nancy's disappearance made sense. But neither did Nancy's taking up with Frankie Pina, Judy thought.

Squished in the back seat next to her children, Judy gazed out the window as they drove east along Interstate 195 around four o'clock heading back home to New Bedford.

She saw the medical examiner's van and state police cruisers ahead on the opposite side of the road, parked on the grass. She felt a knot in her stomach.

"Pull over," she yelled to her husband, Tony. "Pull over."[6]

Her husband reflexively slowed down and glanced up at the rearview mirror at her, puzzled.

"Pull over. They are taking my sister out of the woods. That could be my sister," she cried.

Tony shook his head and kept driving.

I'm losing it, Judy remembers thinking to herself that day as the family headed home. Of course, that's not my sister.

TROOPER WILLIAM DELANEY was stymied. By the luck of the on-call shift — or was it the misfortune — he now had two, back-to-back tough cases: two bodies, both women, both found in the brush along a highway on their backs. Both were white, with brown hair, and both were five feet two inches tall. There were no obvious signs of a struggle at the scenes. What were the chances they were related? What were the chances they weren't?

This last body, the one found on Interstate 195 in Dartmouth by motor- cyclists on July 30, was "weathered," meaning it had been exposed to the elements, and little more than a skeleton was left. He was told the woman was likely killed in the spring, before the warm weather struck.[7] He checked missing-person reports for that time period, just as he had for the first body, with little luck. He now knew he needed more assistance. His state police colleagues would soon enlist the help of experts at the Smithsonian Institute in Washington, which was working with the FBI, to conduct a microscopic examination of the bones. They would look for knife wounds, signs of bullet wounds, bone cracks — including slight breaks in the hyoid, the U-shaped neck bone that suggested strangulation — as well as anything that might help lead to an identification. The district attorney's office had used one of the Smithsonian experts in previous cases to examine human remains; calling them for help this time wasn't unusual for the prosecutor's office.

This was a tough case in a tough and busy year for the state police in Bristol County, which included four cities and sixteen towns in the southern part of the state. There were fourteen homicides by early August of 1988, and nine of them had already been cleared with an arrest. One that was not cleared was the murder of a twenty-seven-year-old mother last seen at a New Bedford bar and who was later found dead on a beach in Dartmouth. Another was the shooting death of a man in New Bedford. A third was a Taunton man found dead in Fall River. There was a starting point to those cases and, hopefully, an end. Knowing the name of the victim was always the first step: How else can you learn where they had been, who they knew, what they did, who would want to kill them? Justice started with a name. With the bodies found on the highways, the trooper didn't have that detail just yet. Based on the condition of the bodies, he suspected it could be a long time before he would.

William Delaney was an easygoing guy who worked hard but didn't let the job frustrate him. He had been with the state police for six years already but was fairly new to the investigative unit, with just one year under his belt. He had handled a number of murders and other cases so far, but these two were the most difficult. He first needed to learn the identities of these two women so he could retrace their steps and have some hope of finding out who killed them. Two weeks after the second body was found, a front-page story ran in the New Bedford newspaper, the *Standard-Times,* on August 13, 1988, detailing the efforts to learn who the women were. He hoped someone who hadn't yet filed a missing-person report would read the article. He hoped that person would call the police. He told the reporter what he had learned from the medical examiner's office: one woman likely died just before cold weather set in, and the other woman likely died in the spring, before the warm weather. Weeks after that story ran, though, he still was no closer to knowing who the women were.[8]

ON A HUNCH, John Dextradeur flipped through the missing-person reports in the New Bedford police department record room and saw a pattern emerge. It was September, two months after Nancy Paiva went missing, and he could see there were now at least four women gone, all from similar backgrounds, all similar in height. He made a note of the other names: Mary Rose Santos, Sandra Botelho, and Dawn Mendes. Then he learned their stories.

MARY SANTOS hopped out of her husband's car at the bus station, across the way from the Quarterdeck bar in New Bedford. It was a Friday night, disco night at the downtown lounge, and the place would be jammed once the sun set. Mary was a semi-regular at the Quarterdeck, but not so regular that the bartenders would remember what she drank. When she did go, it was on disco night where she would often stand near the railing close to the music or sit at a table, talking with people. She loved to talk and she loved to dance, a barmaid said.[9] On this Friday night, July 15, 1988, though, she told her husband, Donald, that she would walk from the downtown bus station to her friend's apartment nearby. She would just be hanging out with the girls, she told him. It was only seven thirty and still light out as she stepped onto the sidewalk. She had change for the payphone for a ride back, and Donald returned home to wait for her call.

Donald and Mary had met while working at a fish-processing house in New Bedford nine years earlier. Three weeks after they met, they married, and now, in a few weeks on August 4, they were planning to renew their vows. The couple had two boys, ages five and seven, and seemed happy. Donald was a big guy — weighing in at well over 250 — and Mary was what some called a little bit chubby with a round, angelic face. She was his world, his life, he would say. He adored her. "She was the only one who would give me a second look and liked me."[10]

As his wife walked away from the car that night, Donald was already looking forward to when she would be back home.

Mary walked the few blocks to her girlfriend's apartment where she did some cocaine with one of the two women there. It was dark out when she eventually left; no one remembers the exact time. One of the women at the apartment later told police she told them "she was going to work."[11] They knew what that meant. Her husband, several people later told police, had no clue Mary was making money on the street as a prostitute. It was quick, easy money, she once told one friend; it helped pay the bills. No one pressed her further. Mary was new to the work and the street. She was not a hardened or seasoned girl. One person called her naive and said she went with the guys others would ignore. She thought nearly everyone was nice and good.

At the Quarterdeck, things were hopping. It was wall-to-wall people, so many that it looked like close to five hundred were crammed inside even though the bar could only legally fit just under one hundred. One of the bartenders who served Mary thought she was there for a few hours.[12] She didn't remember seeing Mary leave. It was likely she may have left around one in the morning, no one was quite sure.

By five thirty that morning, Donald was worried. His wife hadn't called, and she hadn't come home. He put the boys in the car and began to drive around the city, stopping at the apartments and homes of anyone he thought might have seen his wife. He stopped at the friend's apartment Mary had gone to, the bartender's house, the Quarterdeck. No one knew where she was. He finally reported her missing to New Bedford police and, in the days that followed, he called the local newspaper and made up flyers with her photograph. A lawyer the couple knew, Kenneth C. Ponte, helped him make the copies.

Donald left one of the flyers at the Quarterdeck and it was posted on the mirror behind the bar. The owner of the Quarterdeck, Faith Almeida, later told authorities it was taken down after two months when a woman who claimed she was Mary's "sister" spotted the flyer and laughed. She told the barmaid Mary had left with a boyfriend and "said they were fools."[13] No one in Mary's family believed she had left voluntarily, and no one identified the woman who claimed to be her sister.

CRAIG ANDRADE was in bed around eleven thirty at night on August 11, 1988, when his girlfriend, Sandy Botelho, twenty-five, hollered from downstairs. About an hour earlier, she had been dropped off by a john at their Malden Street apartment, had done a bit of coke, and was now headed back out, this time to her girlfriend's house a few doors down in the Brickenwood housing project in New Bedford to get some bread. She would be right back, she yelled up.[14]

Craig, twenty-seven, and Sandy, had been together for thirteen years. They shared the apartment with their two young sons. They also shared an addiction to cocaine. Things were getting so out of control with the drugs that Craig split for a few months — from January to July — to "dry out" at a treatment program in nearby Fall River. But Sandy didn't stop. She was still home in New Bedford, shooting up about a gram of coke a day and hitting the streets to make money to pay for it. She worked the area between Hathaway and Nauset Streets and spots in the Weld Square area. Sometimes men would call her directly, and she kept their names and numbers, along with those of her family and friends, in an address book that she kept in the bedroom. One of the johns listed in that book would later describe Sandy as "a very nice person caught up in a real bad situation,"[15] who was trusting and would get ripped off by clients on the street.

"Sandy looked like somebody you would see coming out of a shopping mall."[16]

Sandy wasn't home when her boyfriend woke up the first time around three in the morning. He thought she was still over at her girlfriend's house. When he woke up a second time at seven, he was worried.

He called the neighbor's apartment. Sandy had never arrived.

DAWN MENDES left her Bluefield Street apartment in the southern section of the city wearing a white dress and white gloves. Her plan was to walk to a christening party across town where her family and, most importantly, her five-year-old son would be. At age twenty-five, Dawn already had a fairly extensive record of drug and prostitution charges both in New Bedford and elsewhere. Her mother, Charlotte, a deeply religious woman, was raising Dawn's son. Allowing Dawn to have custody of the boy was out of the question. Her addiction was too severe, her inability to care for the boy too great. Dawn's mother, though, was still hopeful things might eventually change, and she encouraged supervised visits with the child. The people at the christening party weren't sure if Dawn would show up high, but they were confident she would show up. If she couldn't, she would call. She always did. "If she wanted to just take off, she would call me to make sure her son was okay," her mother would later say.[17]

By the time the family party broke up, Dawn still wasn't there.

It was September 4, 1988. Her mom would report her missing soon after.

DETECTIVE JOHN DEXTRADEUR took a drag from the Marlboro then mashed it into the ashtray at his steel-gray desk in the cramped New Bedford police detective division. He was frustrated. It was mid-September and the number of missing women in the city who had similar backgrounds and characteristics was now officially at four, and he was convinced there might be more. Most were likely dead, he suspected. But without any bodies in his city, or any solid evidence of foul play in the disappearances, each case was still officially classified as a missing person. That meant the missing-person cases fell to the bottom of the investigative pile in his department. But he suspected — feared was the right word — there was a serial killer in his city; he just needed to prove it. He knew the investigation, done right, would need manpower. His department didn't have it. He wasn't sure his department would even know where to start. He was sure nothing would be done based on just his hunch.

Two bodies had already been found in July along two highways outside the city, but, based on what he heard from the state trooper handling the cases, it appeared both remains had been out there for months — ruling out, to him, Nancy Paiva as one of the victims. But if there were two, could there be more? That was something John couldn't answer. That was something he would need to prod the district attorney's office to look into. At the Bristol County District Attorney's Office, headquartered a few streets from police headquarters, there were two distinct plainclothes investigative units. One was the state police Crime Prevention and Control Unit, known as CPAC, made up of two divisions: homicide and drugs. State police lieutenants, sergeants, and staff sergeants supervised the trooper-investigators. While the state police officers worked out of the district attorney's office and served there at his pleasure, they didn't take orders from him. They all answered to the state police brass. However, the second investigative unit in the office, the Bristol County Drug Task Force, was more closely aligned with the district attorney. It was made up of local police detectives on "loan" to the DA's office who worked on narcotics investigations that crossed city and town lines. A captain or lieutenant from a local department was also "loaned" to the district attorney's office to supervise the task force. In 1988, that man was Capt. Louis J. Pacheco, a self-taught computer whiz from the Raynham police department, a bedroom community thirty minutes north of New Bedford. The task force had started four years earlier and was credited with seizing tons of marijuana off-loaded from commercial fishing boats in the mid-1980s. Each of the local detectives in that unit were sworn in as Bristol County deputy sheriffs to give them arrest powers in communities other than their own; salaries and overtime were picked up by the DA. Sometimes the task-force members got along with the state police narcotics unit and sometimes they didn't.

Robert St. Jean, the chief investigator for the district attorney and a former state trooper, was tasked with making sure everyone played nice. Technically, neither of the other groups answered directly to him. He answered to the district attorney. He was often caught in the middle of internal squabbles while trying to play the diplomat.

John figured he would go right to the top, or at least close to the top, at the district attorney's office to get support. Bob St. Jean had the ear of the district attorney, Ronald A. Pina, and had daily access to the state police investigators in the office. John hoped he could convince him to create a special task force, or at the very least launch a deeper investigation into the disappearance of Nancy Paiva. In his pitch for the task force, he could tell Bob there was a similarity in the descriptions of the missing women, where they were last seen, the drug connections, and their addictions. By putting faces and names to the suspected victims, he could give them a starting point for identifications if any more bodies were found. He could rattle off the cases with ease. First, there was Nancy Paiva, age thirty-six, last seen walking home from the South End in the early hours of July 8. Then Mary Rose Santos, age twenty-six, a mother of two, on July 16 was dropped off by her husband near the downtown bus station and was seen dancing at a bar about five hours later. Another young mother of two, Sandra Botelho, who had a history of heavy cocaine use, left her Malden Street apartment around 11:00 p.m. on August 11 and never returned. Then, finally, Dawn Mendes, twenty-five, missing since September 4. He believed there could also be three more at risk: Robbin Rhodes, a New Bedford woman who hadn't been seen since the spring and was reported missing by her mother on July 28; a Cape Cod woman named Rochelle Dopierala whom he planned to use as a witness in a gun case; and a New Bedford teenager by the name of Christina Monteiro, whose mother was engaged to a Dartmouth cop. The teen hadn't been seen for months.

As he prepared what he would say, he couldn't shake the feeling that the remains of the two women already found along roadways outside the city would eventually be on his expanding list of the missing. He dialed the district attorney's office to make an appointment to share his suspicions, face-to-face, with state troopers and Robert St. Jean, the man who had the district attorney's ear. John worked with most of the troopers in the prosecutor's office on murder cases and had a good relationship with them. Whenever there was a murder, a local detective would be paired with a state trooper in the prosecutor's office to coordinate the investigation, even though he always felt his department did the lion's share of the work. John also felt comfortable talking with Bob St. Jean, whose brother, Laurent, was also a New Bedford cop. John planned to suggest a task force be created to see how many more missing women in southeastern Massachusetts and nearby Rhode Island there were, to exam- ine commonalities in the disappearances, and to see if any of the cases were related. He wasn't sure what type of reception he would get with the call. He worried Bob St. Jean would shrug off his suspicions. So, he was pleasantly surprised when Bob listened to his brief synopsis of the case by phone then asked him to stop by the office to chat. "Let's see what you have," Bob said.[18]

A few days later, in the conference room of the Bristol County District Attorney's office, John met with the chief investigator, a couple of troopers, and two New Bedford detectives assigned to the drug task force. He laid out what he had, what he suspected, what he feared. Then he tossed in two names: Franklin Pina and Kenneth Ponte. Frankie, he told them, was the boyfriend of one of the missing women. He suspected the man might know more than what he first told police. The second person, Kenneth Ponte, was a lawyer with a bad coke habit who knew all of the missing women and had some strange dealings with local hookers. He also knew Frankie. Kenny had worked on the Bristol County sheriff's election campaign and was later sworn in as a deputy sheriff. Being a deputy in Kenny's situation was largely considered an honorary title but, in practice, it allowed the lawyer to serve court papers, such as eviction notices. He could make a little extra cash doing that. The detective discovered Kenny also sometimes used the badge to do more than serve court papers. He was getting reports that Kenny flashed his deputy sheriff badge to drug dealers and then stole their drugs. The lawyer also brought prostitutes to his home. John also told them about the Cape Cod woman, Rochelle Dopierala, who was not on the official missing list but who had been staying with the lawyer. He had been looking for this woman since May because she was a witness in yet another case he was investigating.

John gave them more details about the case Rochelle was to testify in: Rochelle had claimed a guy in the Weld Square neighborhood named Roger Swire had raped her. Later, Kenny was driving along the street with Rochelle when they spotted the man. Kenny pulled over, pulled out a gun and threatened him. Kenny was charged in connection with that gun incident. Since then, Dextradeur had seen Rochelle walking around Weld Square — he even saw her with Frankie Pina — and discussed the gun case with her. She had already recanted the rape allegations but promised to testify against Kenny Ponte. It had been months, though, since the detective had seen Rochelle around. Months since anyone had. She could, he told the group, be one of the missing. She could be dead.

John Dextradeur knew what he was suggesting: there may be a serial killer in the city. It was not a popular idea in a city trying to bring in tourists and new businesses, he knew. City leaders were trying to shake New Bedford's image as an aging, downtrodden mill city with high unemployment, an image damaged further in 1983 by a barroom gang rape at a local tavern called Big Dan's. Six men of Portuguese descent were accused and four convicted in that case. Five years after the rape, which generated national headlines, city officials were working to turn New Bedford into a funky, possibly artsy, community drawing people from throughout the region to the historic downtown landmarks and humming working waterfront. But now some feared a new fictionalized account of the attack, a film called *The Accused* starring Jodie Foster set to premier in October 1988, would reinforce that old impression and hamper the revitalization efforts.

Bob St. Jean knew the politics of the city and the pushback that can occur when bad news hits the front pages and airwaves. None of that worried him. The district attorney had always told him not to worry about the politics. Just do good police work. As he listened to the New Bedford detective talk, Bob was intrigued and knew he was onto something and it likely *was* big. He also knew he would first have to take it up with the district attorney, Ronald Pina, before making a commitment.

"Let me talk with Ron," Bob told the New Bedford detective. "We'll see what we can do."[19]

After the hour-long meeting, John Dextradeur headed back to the New Bedford police station. He had made his point. Everyone told him the right things. But would anything be done? Were they just blowing smoke? He wasn't sure.

He waited a couple of weeks then decided to add some public pressure. He called the local newspaper, where a reporter had also noticed the cluster of women gone missing and had been asking if the bodies along the highways could be linked.

"Fears Build for Missing Women," read the front-page article in the *Standard-Times* on October 3, 1988. The story listed four of the missing women, their similarities in appearance and lifestyles. It also quoted a heroin addict saying two more were likely gone. Relatives of the missing women were worried. The missing women had troubles but stayed close to their families, despite their drug problems, and visited or called regularly. A day, maybe a week, might go by without contact but not months. The women, the families insisted, wouldn't leave without telling someone. It was out of character. Nancy's sister, Judy, still nervous about stepping into the public spotlight, was quoted anonymously at the end as a "relative." "I think something has happened to her. I don't think she's alive."[20]

3 SEARCHING

BY LATE OCTOBER, the official list of the missing women considered endangered was officially six. After additional investigation, John Dextradeur noted that two more New Bedford women reported missing fit the criteria of the others: Robbin "Bobbie Lynn" Rhodes, twenty-nine, and Christina Monteiro, nineteen, who John earlier had suspected was a victim of foul play. Both had a young child, both were heroin and cocaine addicts, both stayed close to the New Bedford city limits and would check in regularly with relatives, usually their mothers. Both just vanished. John Dextradeur wondered how many more were gone and not reported missing, such as the Cape Cod woman he was trying to find for one of his cases. How high could this number go?

Bob St. Jean shared John Dextradeur's fear that the missing women were likely dead, and he convinced the district attorney that the prosecutor's office needed to step in. The case would not be easy to navigate, he knew. Bob needed to pull in the right people from different agencies to work on the case. He needed people who thought broadly, who were not territorial, who cooperated with others, who worked across different law-enforcement agency lines. He needed people who worked hard and played nice with others. He needed smart people without egos. He had a few in mind. He just needed to find a way to convince the chiefs in those already short-staffed departments to cut them loose for this case.

Bob had been a state trooper for thirteen years before the district attorney, Ronald Pina, convinced him to join his office as a civilian investigator. It was right after the district attorney won reelection in the 1982 primary with 49 percent of the vote against Patrick E. Lowney, a Fall River attorney whose brother was a state trooper. Two days after winning reelection, Ron Pina booted out all the state troopers working in his building, forcing them to work one town over in the Dartmouth barracks where road troopers were dispatched. "I know that there were a number of people down there (in the state police office) who were actively supporting Lowney. They made it quite clear where they stood. They were out to get me. They lost," Ron said at the time.[1]

Kicking the troopers out strained the already tense relations the district attorney had with the state police. At the time the troopers were evicted from the downtown New Bedford offices — and that's how the cops described it — Bob was out of town. He returned to a political hurricane. He also faced a choice that changed the trajectory of his career as well as his friendships with longtime colleagues. The district attorney took him aside and asked him to stay as his special investigator in the office and help rebuild the unit. It would mean, Bob knew, leaving the state police. The new job was enticing; it paid $20,000 more than his trooper's salary, but he was forty-eight, just two years away from the mandatory state police retirement age at the time. "I had no intention of leaving the state police," he recalled. "I told him I'm not going to do that."[2] The district attorney refused to take no for an answer. He called the governor who called the state police who told Bob to take a leave of absence as a trooper for a year and take the job to smooth things over between the agency and the prosecutor's office. They needed someone in the office who knew the state police, Bob remembers being told. His state police job would still be waiting. Bob took the job. He was stunned by the swift and vicious backlash. Troopers he counted as friends called him a traitor and shunned him. Other troopers used much stronger language. The state police family he knew was gone. The rift and hard feelings ran deep and lasted for years. "I really didn't expect it," he recalled. "It was a very difficult time."

During that first year, Bob tried to develop closer ties with local departments, strengthen a regional drug task force, and promote long-term investigations, including ones using wiretaps. When the year and leave of absence was up Bob was faced with a choice: stay or return to the state police. He had six children at home and was now earning $62,500, the equivalent of a captain's pay, working for the district attorney. If he went back, he would be taking a huge financial hit with the much lower trooper's pay. Bob resigned from the state police.

Younger men and women coming up the state police ranks had heard about the maelstrom that pitted trooper against trooper, but by 1988 it was fast becoming history, and new investigators coming into the unit saw it as a blip in law-enforcement relations and politics. Bob knew there were still some in the state police who held a grudge, but he tried to move on, finding ways to help the diverse law enforcement groups in complex investigations. The investigation into the disappearances of the New Bedford women was one he felt he could help coordinate.

By early November, Bob was on the phone taking one of the first steps in trying to solve the case. He was asking the Connecticut State Police if one of the country's best search-dog handlers in its department could help with the case. The handler ran dogs that looked for the dead.

IT WAS A SUNNY and comfortable November afternoon in 1988 as the state cleanup crew trudged along the highway ramp off Interstate 195 in Dartmouth, picking up cans and garbage. The trash along the highway was a jumble of road life: tires, paper cups, bags, shoes, cans, diapers. Four months earlier, two men riding motorcycles stopped to relieve themselves across this same highway and found a body. From where the crew now stood on the eastbound Reed Road exit ramp, they even might have been able to see that spot about a mile and a half away. But that wasn't on the workers' minds around two o'clock on Tuesday November 8, 1988. Getting to the end of the workday was. The crew kept moving along the tree line, clearing the trash.

Then they stopped. There, in the center strip of the Reed Road cloverleaf, on the eastbound side of the highway, were human remains. About twenty to thirty feet away, scattered in the woods, there were some clothes: A London Fog jacket, a pair of pants, socks, underwear, shirts. The crew supervisor radioed the District 5 office in Taunton. The office called the Dartmouth state police barracks. Get your people down there now. They found a body.

Staff Sgt. Paul Fitzgerald, who was the supervisor in the Dartmouth barracks five minutes away, was one of the first to arrive. There he could see remains along the tree line. Nothing immediately identifiable was his first impression.[3] Dick Phillips, a Dartmouth police officer who arrived soon after, thought it might be a woman.[4]

Paul Fitzgerald ordered the state troopers to keep people away from the scene and keep any gawking drivers moving. He shut down the on and off Reed Road cloverleaf ramps on the eastbound side of the highway. He knew what needed to be done. He joined the state police at age twenty-two, working the road and later intricate criminal investigations. For five years, from 1976 to 1981, he was in the district attorney's office — one of the first members of the state police assigned to the Bristol County office — and was close to the troopers who were later kicked out by the prosecutor. He worked homicides, drug cases, white-collar crime, bank robberies — what he would later describe as "pretty much everything you can dream of."[5] He knew the intricacies of what it took to solve a case, and a good part of it started right here, at the scene. The first step: keep people, civilians, and fellow cops alike away until the state investigative-police team from the district attorney's office arrived. Today, he figured that between the state police and the Dartmouth police officer, they had that part covered pretty well.

When the unmarked cruiser pulled up, he recognized the trooper behind the wheel: Jose Gonsalves. Tall with thinning dark hair, Jose was soft-spoken and conscientious. He was a family man who stayed out of the politics. Troopers who worked with him on the road, before he transferred into the detective unit in the district attorney's office, praised his even temperament. He was, everyone agreed, a good guy.

Jose and Maryann Dill were the troopers on call that week to cover any unattended deaths in the county. Human remains found off a highway ramp definitely fell into that category. A tanned Maryann arrived a few minutes after Jose pulled up. It was her first day back to work from vacation in Aruba.

As Jose scanned the scene, he felt a sense of déjà vu. It was eerily similar to the crime scene he viewed just four months earlier on the same highway: the remains of a woman, on her back.

He turned to Maryann. "This isn't good."[6]

A few days before this discovery, the prosecutor's chief investigator, Bob St. Jean, had already finalized the plans to bring the search dogs to the area. A couple of people in the office scoffed at the idea at first. No one would question the decision now.

By the end of the month, the three cases of the dead women would be merged into one: Case file 0515. Troopers Maryann Dill and Jose (pronounced

"Joe-sey ") Gonsalves, who was one of the senior troopers in the unit, were told by their state police supervisor that they were now the primary investigators in the case.

BOB ST. JEAN spread the map out on the conference table in the downtown office of the district attorney and pointed to the three spots where the remains of three women were found: Route 140 northbound in Freetown; Interstate 195 westbound, just short of the Reed Road exit; and off the Reed Road exit on the eastbound side of Interstate 195. The three were all within a twenty-minute drive.

Andy Rebmann, the Connecticut state trooper considered the premier police canine handler in the region, nodded.

A few minutes earlier, Andy had walked into the lobby of the fifth-floor prosecutor's office after driving one and a half hours from just north of Norwich, Connecticut, to meet with Bob St. Jean. At the top of the agenda: Where would someone likely dump a body? Andy's dog, Josie, was one of just a few canines in the Northeast trained exclusively to find bodies. Andy trained nearly all of those so-called "body" dogs, and Josie was considered the top dog in the pack.

This was the second time he had been in New Bedford. About a year earlier, Andy was called to search a cemetery in nearby Acushnet where police feared a missing young woman had been killed then buried in an open grave by her ex-husband. Andy and his dog didn't find the woman — she was eventually discovered in a water-filled quarry a few years later and two towns away by a group of divers practicing — but the Connecticut trooper found the region rich in ethnic culture and food. Especially the food. The small Portuguese restaurants scattered throughout New Bedford rivaled anything he had tasted before. The people he met — both in law enforcement and on the streets — were warm and welcoming. This is a nice area, he remembered thinking at the time, one he wouldn't mind going back to.[7]

So, when the call came asking if he could help find several missing women who were presumed dead, possibly at the hands of a serial killer, he didn't think twice.

When Andy arrived in New Bedford that mid-November day in 1988, the chief investigator greeted him warmly. It was the first time the two had met, and Bob was struck at how unassuming the Connecticut trooper appeared. Andy was wearing coveralls, boots, and a broad smile. "He looked like a hunter," Bob recalled. "He just came across as a regular guy."[8]

Bob ushered him into the conference room where, along with state police investigators, they went over the case. The remains of three women, still unidentified, were found roughly thirty feet into the brush off two local highways. Several more were reported missing, no suspects. Could there be more bodies along the highways? Could his dog find them? Bob asked. Andy knew the answer: Yes. Hopefully.

After first reviewing the maps, Andy was brought to the highway crime scenes to get a feel for the search area. He noted the traffic patterns, the way the guardrails were spaced, where the brush was. He was out at the scenes for about an hour and a half before returning to Connecticut. Back home, he looked over the maps again, calculated the distance from the road to the bodies, and tried to estimate how many cars were on the road and how many were going over the speed limit for search safety. He also needed to determine how many miles could he safely search with his dog, Josie. "Are we going to cover a mile? Ten miles? We had to just come up with a basic search plan and a safety plan," Andy recalled.[9] A plan to keep Josie motivated during the search if she didn't find anything was also crucial.

Work and reward are two key elements in police-dog training. Some trainers use treats, others use play. Play always seemed to work with Josie and several other cadaver search dogs that Andy trained. Cadaver dogs are the elite in the police-canine world. It takes weeks of initial training — and only if the dog is "right" for the job — followed by months of reinforcement and fieldwork.

The best dogs in the cadaver field are the ones who are not cross-trained, who specialize in the search for bodies. Give them just one job, just one, and they will excel. More than one, the dog's skill set can be diluted. In the late 1980s, specialty police dogs were rare. Most police departments with canines, largely for budget reasons, wanted dogs to do general police-dog work: search, rescue, find drugs, and help catch suspects. That meant Andy was the first call when communities along the East Coast needed a good dog to search for a person. He was usually the only call. His bosses on the Connecticut

State Police knew how important it was to find the missing, alive or dead, and rarely turned down any out-of-state request if Andy was available.

Before joining the state police, Andy had worked at a lumber company after returning home from the U.S. Army, where he worked in military intelligence. He was looking for something different to do at the time and joined the volunteer Auxiliary State Police in Connecticut. In that capacity he rode with troopers and got a taste of state police life. He liked the pace, the excitement, and the idea he was helping people. Eventually, he was accepted as a full-time trooper at age thirty, went through the rigorous academy and, after working as a road trooper, joined the state police canine unit. One of his search dogs, a bloodhound named Clem, had a good nose for finding people and received an award in 1977 from the National Bloodhound Association. But Clem had a big problem when it came to searches. Clem didn't like dead people. Since a number of missing individuals turn out to be suicides, Andy trained his next dog, a German shepherd named Rufus, specifically to find the dead. As the years passed, he would train more dogs.

Training a cadaver dog takes time, patience, and a working knowledge of scent. The handler needs to know how scent moves through the air, comes up through the ground and how best to guide the dog at the scene. Handlers use the chemical equivalents of decomposing bodies, cadaverine and putrescine,[10] to reproduce what the dogs need to find in the field. Sometimes they use soil samples from sites where bodies were found. Early on, some handlers used bones or pieces of decaying flesh. (The son of one Massachusetts state trooper once said he learned as a child to always read the labels carefully on the Tupperware containers in the refrigerator because you never knew what was inside.)

How much of a smell a dead person gives off depends on the level of decomposition. The freshly dead likely won't be detected by the human nose, but an animal, such as a search dog, even one not trained to find cadavers, may react to the scent as if it were a person very much alive. But as time passes, the body changes. It bloats and decays. You can smell the stench from a distance. Eventually, the dead begin to liquefy as part of the decaying process and the body finally dries out. A cheesy or musty smell lingers in the aftermath. By the time a body is skeletal or mummified, you may still catch that musty whiff near the remains.[11] For the search dog, it is what is left behind that is crucial. The chemicals from a decomposing body seep into the soil, leaving a telltale scent for the well-trained dog. A body, even skeletal remains, can leave clues for these highly trained dogs. The handlers are the ones who make sure the dogs can find those clues.

By the time he came to New Bedford, Andy had already spent eleven years training search and cadaver dogs using what was called the play-reward system. When his dogs found something, they ran to him, nudged a tennis ball in his pocket then led him to the body. Andy would then bring the dog to a safe area and play ball as a reward.

Josie, the German shepherd Andy planned to use in New Bedford, was about two years old when he first got her. Originally, she was undergoing training as a guide dog for the blind and visually impaired at the Fidelco Guide Dog Foundation in Bloomfield, Connecticut. She flunked out. "They couldn't break her of stealing food off the plate," Andy later joked.[12] One thing Josie was good at was finding bodies. She was one of the best — and she loved to play.

Less than a week after returning home from that first meeting with investigators in New Bedford, Andy was back in Massachusetts with a search plan in a folder and Josie in his suv.

The first area he picked was Interstate 195 in Dartmouth, where two bodies had already been found. He searched for five hours that first day. All he found was litter and discarded bald tires. A lot of tires.

On the second day, November 29, 1988, he slowly walked along the westbound section of the highway in Dartmouth just before the spot where one of the bodies had been found. He was looking at areas where a car or truck could easily pull over, where there were no guardrails and where there was heavy brush or a gully.

Secluded entrance ramps — like the one where one body on Interstate 195 was found earlier that month — were also on his list.

It was a warm day for November, and an unmarked cruiser, driven by Trooper Kevin Butler, stayed a safe distance behind Andy and his dog, Josie, making sure no one bothered the searchers. After passing the area where the second woman had been found in July, Andy moved on to the exit and entrance ramps.

The pair searched the brush by the exit ramp then moved onto the adjoining westbound entrance ramp and the small clump of woods between the two.

Twenty-five feet in, Josie bolted to a drainage ditch and came back, nudging at the ball in Andy's pocket.

"She found something," Andy called out.[13]

State Trooper Kevin Butler got out of his unmarked cruiser a few yards away and walked up the entrance ramp.[14]

"Over there," Andy told him, pointing.

"Where?" the trooper asked.

They walked through the brush.

"Right there," Andy said, pointing to the drainage ditch.

Kevin Butler looked down. He saw muck.

"I don't see anything," the trooper said. "Andy, there's nobody there."

"The dog says the body is right there." Andy pointed straight down. "Right there."

Kevin straddled the ditch, bent down and reached into the mud with his gloved hands.

He felt something and pulled it out.

It was what appeared to be a skeleton.

He put it gently back down.

Body number four was found.

This was now a crime scene.

NATURE WILL CHANGE and reclaim a dead body over time. Exposed to dry heat, the skin can take on a leatherlike or mummified appearance. Exposed to the freezing cold, the body can look ashen. Exposed to the water, the body will bloat, and algae may be found growing on it. Sometimes the environment can shield the body from the elements. Sometimes it can give conflicting clues. Sometimes what you see on first sight can be misleading; sometimes it is spot on. There are no quick or simple answers, only questions to be answered through detailed examination in laboratories. That first sight, though, can give a direction. These are all the things police in the field and forensic experts in the lab know from years of work. In 1988, many investigators still relied heavily on what they could see in the field rather than what could be seen under the microscope or in the laboratory. The use of forensic DNA science in law enforcement and in the courts was still evolving. To get a good DNA sample from a suspect, police merely obtained a blood sample. To get good DNA from a scene, however, the sample size often needed to be fairly large and sometimes was destroyed in the testing process. Some cautious judges demanded prosecutors prove DNA testing was not "voodoo science." Defense attorneys challenged the science as confusing, misleading, and unreliable. Juries were often confused by the scientific verbiage and statistics used to explain the testing and results.

State police in Massachusetts were also working to catch up with the latest technology in 1988. There was no official "crime scene services" division yet — that wouldn't come until 1993 — and gathering evidence was a fragmented process. At that time, four different units could be at a scene: the primary investigator assigned to the DA's office, someone to collect ballistics evidence, chemists to collect blood or fluid evidence, and yet another person to photograph the scene and check for fingerprints. The closest thing to a crime-scene unit was the Bureau of Photography and Fingerprints and its five units headquartered in the state police barracks in Middleboro, Yarmouth, Boston, Northampton, and Leominster. While those in the photography and fingerprint unit primarily photographed the scenes as well as checking for fingerprints, some of the troopers in 1988 also looked for such things as tire tracks and the type of evidence the civilian chemists could test in the state lab. However, for the most part, taking charge of evidence often rested primarily with the trooper in the DA's office investigating the case. This was a system that worked for years in Massachusetts and in other states across the country. But things were changing quickly in the forensic field, and investigators discovered they needed to keep up.

In the state police investigative unit in the DA's office, one trooper, Kenneth Martin, was fascinated by the latest advances in the forensic field.[15] He first considered a career in the sciences but instead joined the Massachusetts State Police in 1980 and started in the Bristol County DA's Office unit three years later. He wasn't a scientist back then — the biology degree at Bridgewater State University would come later — but he understood science and knew the importance of finding the type of evidence someone might not realize was viable, the evidence those in the lab could analyze, the evidence that could be crucial in a case. He eventually approached the district attorney and Bob St.

Jean about doing more forensic crime-scene work in the unit to supplement what the other state police evidence units were doing. It was considered a cutting-edge and growing field back then. They said yes.

He went to seminars, workshops, joined professional forensic organizations, and talked with anyone he could about advances in the field. He met people who could analyze things he didn't realize could be helpful in an investigation. Most of all, he found people in the sciences who were willing to help if needed. By 1988, he was looking at crime scenes with a different eye.

In the field, he looked for bugs, dirt, bird nests, spider webs, and eggs, the tiniest of blood droplets. He dug up blocks of outdoor crime scenes and sent those sections, intact, to laboratories. He looked for the footprints, the tire prints, and fingerprints as everyone did. But he was also aware that there were clues that forensic science could find that might point to a suspect or a cause of death or information about a crime.

The woman's body found by Josie in the muck-like dip off the entrance ramp to Interstate 195 could yield a wealth of information. So could the area around her. Part of the woman's body was sunk into water and dampness; a small part, a hand, was not. Kenny Martin bagged and gathered the bugs and dirt and sticks and rocks and anything he could find at the scene, hoping it would help in the investigation. But he, like the other investigators, knew it was sheer luck that this woman's body landed on the ground in just the right way, with her hand clear of the wet. This might give them a break in the case. Unlike the earlier cases, where the bodies were essentially skeletal, the hand and fingers were protected somehow from the elements by a twist of fate. They could get a fingerprint. They might get a name.

Today, thanks to advances in technology, just about every law-enforcement agency in the country can electronically scan a fingerprint from a human finger and enter it into the computerized Automated Fingerprint Identification System (AFIS), where millions of prints are searched and compared. It can take minutes to do a search. In 1988, it wasn't that easy. The AFIS system was introduced just two years earlier in Massachusetts, but only a handful of local police departments in the state were entering new fingerprint cards into it. Even entering the prints into the computer system was time-consuming, compared to the process today. Latent fingerprint images from crime scenes were first enlarged five times, then a technician had to trace the image by hand to identify points in the print. Then that tracing was reduced and scanned into the AFIS computer where it was converted into data for classification and comparison with other prints. The process could take one to two hours. It was a little bit easier to enter the fingerprint cards of people who were arrested. Those prints were first scanned into the system, a technician would then review the prints for quality control and make annotations on them before finally entering the information. On a good day, the process would take roughly ten minutes.[16]

Most fingerprint comparisons, even if they were entered into AFIS, were ultimately done by hand at the time. That meant spending hours poring through fingerprint cards to visually compare prints to find a match. "You had to do every fingerprint by hand and a lot of the fingerprint cards were not good. Most of them weren't good," recalled Richard Lauria, a retired Massachusetts state trooper who worked in the fingerprint and photo unit in the 1980s.[17]

A large percentage of fingerprint cards done by officers in the field in the 1980s were smudged, unreadable, and unusable. Sometimes police officers rolled the fingers wrong on the cards or didn't get a clear imprint or did it so fast the print looked like a blur. "At least 50 percent were not legible [enough] to do anything with," the retired trooper noted.

In most cases, police had a suspect in a case and compared the prints on the cards with those lifted at a crime scene. In the case of the dead, authorities had a possible name of the victim and used the fingerprint cards to confirm it. Early identifications through fingerprints were time consuming. For example, the 1984 slaying of a seventy-four-year-old Holyoke woman was solved thirteen years later through fingerprints when state police lt. Brian O'Hara, who felt the AFIS system at the time was missing some prints, asked a young state police technician named Christopher Dolan to manually examine 40,000 prints from the Holyoke police department after authorities theorized the killer likely was local. It took more than four hundred hours over three months to do. The lieutenant later verified the final comparison and discovered the suspect was in the AFIS system, but the computer originally failed to make the match.

The investigators in Bristol County knew what they were up against as they waited to see if the prints from this latest victim could be matched. The chances they would quickly get a hit on this woman's fingerprints depended on so many factors: If she had ever been arrested. If she gave her correct name when she was booked. If her fingerprints were taken when she was arrested, since not all departments printed everyone who was arrested. If those fingerprints were clear. If that police department entered the prints into the statewide system. There were a lot of ifs.

All they could do now was wait.

IT WAS GETTING LATE in the afternoon, and Andy Rebmann figured he could wrap up the search along this last stretch of Route 140 in Freetown about three hundred yards from the New Bedford line by sunset. Two days earlier, his dog had found the remains of a woman off a highway ramp on Interstate 195 in Dartmouth west of New Bedford, the road to the south T-boning Route 140, and now they were continuing the hunt for more bodies. It seemed unlikely he would find another body in this last area to be checked on this fourth, and final, search day. And it seemed even more unlikely something would be found in this final hour before he drove home to Connecticut. He and Josie spent the day of December 1, 1988, looking, along with Massachusetts trooper Kathleen Barrett and her dog, Syros.

Three Massachusetts troopers — William Delaney, who worked the first two bodies, Leonardo Solana, and Michael Harding — were keeping an eye on the dog handlers throughout the day. If the dogs found a body, the three would secure the scene and call for more help. In the meantime, if Andy needed anything, anything at all, they kept telling him, just ask.

Just one more hour — or less — and Andy figured he would be done. He watched as Josie trotted along the side of the road before heading toward the woods. Then she came back. Her tail was up. She nosed the ball in his pocket. He knew she found something. He followed Josie thirty feet off the road, into the thick brush. There, two miles from where the first woman had been found in July, were the remains of what appeared to be a partially clad woman. As he stared into the tall grass and brambles, Andy knew he wasn't heading home early.

This was now body number five.

By the time Jose and Maryann pulled up to the scene, road troopers were already there to keep what would be a growing number of reporters, photographers, and remote-broadcast trucks back. As word spread about the discovery, people began to gather on a nearby overpass and motorists slowed to catch glimpses of the scene. Troopers lit road flares for safety as night fell.

Bristol County district attorney Ronald A. Pina was fifteen minutes from New Bedford on Route 140, returning home from a meeting in Boston when he saw the cluster of police cruisers. This was now a familiar sight to him. Another body.

Pina pulled over and was ushered to the body. There, he would see the remains of a woman on her stomach, jeans at mid-thigh and the upper body unclothed.[18] He emerged a few minutes later, grim-faced. "It's just crazy," he told reporters. "It's the same thing, a body off the side of the road."[19]

It was becoming a pattern, he said. It was one he hoped would end soon.

They needed to find this killer but first they needed to know who this latest, fifth victim was.

Investigators had some records of missing women and were getting more. They hoped one might match this woman. If not, the district attorney told reporters the FBI or another agency might have an expert who could reconstruct the faces of the dead to help them in the identification process. An autopsy performed the next day at St. Luke's Hospital in New Bedford revealed the woman died four to six months earlier. She weighed between 130 and 140 pounds and stood between five feet two and five feet four.

Outside experts at the FBI and the Smithsonian Institution in Washington needed to be called in again, the investigators knew.

Someone was missing these women — but yet again the haunting question was: who?

JOSE GONSALVES slit open the nine-by-nine manila envelope in that day's mail from the Worcester police and stared at the mug shot on the arrest card inside. Then he slid it over to Maryann. Two more bodies had been found within two days, and the troopers were hopeful they could positively identify one of them today. The troopers already knew a partial fingerprint lifted from the first body found by the dog on November 29 along Interstate 195 in Dartmouth was a match to a woman arrested in Worcester: a woman named Joanna Marie Rose. Just getting that match had been a long shot since so few police departments in the state were in the AFIS system, and if the woman had been local, they would be out of luck. New Bedford wasn't in the system. Neither were the two cities to the north and west, Taunton and Fall River. Troopers Richard Lauria and Kathleen Stefani, both in the photo-and-fingerprint unit, had been able to lift a fingerprint from the woman's right thumb, enter it into AFIS, and then confirm the match to the Worcester print. This fingerprint identification was just the first step, though. They had been waiting for this mug shot to help confirm the identification before taking the next step to obtain dental X-rays.

Maryann and Jose stared at the arrest card dated July 23, 1982, on the desk. They recognized the face in the picture. For more than a month, they had been looking at a family photo of this same woman who had gone missing in New Bedford. It was Dawn Mendes, age twenty-five, a tough New Bedford woman and one of ten children in the Mendes family. Dawn, the mother of a five-year-old boy, was a drug addict with a history of prostitution arrests who disappeared September 4 while walking from her South End apartment to a family christening party.

By the time the identification was confirmed on December 2 through dental records, the searchers were already out on the road, looking for more victims.

There were still four other unidentified bodies, and Maryann and Jose weren't sure how many more would be found before this was over. That was what the search dogs — and their handlers — were trying to find out.

WHILE MARYANN AND JOSE were finalizing the identification of the body of Dawn Mendes, Andy Rebmann was prepping for yet another search with his dog. After an early breakfast at the hotel in New Bedford's North End, he got back on the highway again with Josie. If his dog found two bodies so quickly, maybe a third or even a fourth could be found today. Andy planned to keep looking, but he was getting a little concerned with the media attention the search was attracting. He could see a still photographer across the highway ramp, the camera keyed on his dog. He could see the swiveling heads of the motorists as they drove past. Right, left. Left, right. Traffic on the wide ramps onto Route 140 from one of the city's main North End streets was steady but not heavy. However, Andy was worried Josie was getting distracted by the man with the camera. He could keep the dog's focus away from the cars but keeping her away from people could be harder. Andy looked again across the road and saw the photographer inching closer. This is not good, he thought. This was a situation Andy always worried about during high profile searches: reporters and photographers distracting the dog.

After Josie had found the second body on the highway, media attention on the search and the dog intensified. The plus side to it: investigators might get more tips in the case. Andy was now dealing with the downside of publicity. The reporters had been warned about getting too close for just that reason — repeatedly. There always seemed to be one person who didn't listen. He briefly considered putting Josie on a leash during searches like this along busy roads but she did her best work without one, and he wanted her to do her best work today.

Andy could see the photographer across the way raising his camera, focusing on his dog. He motioned to one of the troopers in a nearby cruiser and pointed at the photographer. Josie perked up. She looked across the highway and started forward. A car sped by. Then another. "Stop," Andy yelled. The dog froze and turned back to her handler.

The trooper shooed the photographer away with a stern warning. Andy snapped the leash on Josie and led her back to the truck.

Three hours into the search, it was over for the day.

A few days later, more than an hour away in Newport, Rhode Island, a sixty-year-old former Navy cook was watching the news. It had been months since James McConnell had seen his youngest daughter, Debroh Lynn; that last time was at a Rhode Island cemetery on May 3, 1988, as they buried his wife, her mother. His daughter was "real hyper" at the time, James McConnell later remembered. When Debroh didn't call or show up for her daughter's tenth birthday, he was a little concerned but knew his daughter would often disappear for long periods of time. This was just another one of those times. Then the bodies began to show up on the highways in Massachusetts, and by December 1, the date when the search dog found the fifth woman's remains, the second to be found on Route 140 in Freetown, he began to worry. Debroh's boyfriend also called him, saying he feared this body was hers.

First, the elder McConnell called the state police and was put off, he would later say. "He got mad at me because I said I-95 instead of I-195," he said.[20]

When he called New Bedford police, the detective was busy and couldn't take his call.

He never spoke to any of the investigators at that time and never reported his daughter missing.

NEW BEDFORD DETECTIVE Bruce Machado, a member of the Bristol County Drug Task Force, knew how to blend into a scene — a major plus working narcotics. He could sit on a barstool or at a restaurant table anywhere in the city, a beer he barely sipped before him, and listen to the idle chatter. Some of it was drunken bragging. Some of it was the stuff major cases were made of. He was always surprised by what people would say in public, and he was always surprised so few people recognized him. He grew up in the area. He testified in court. His picture had been in the newspaper. But he had that everyman look of a hard worker just trying to make ends meet. He wasn't flashy, he wasn't loud. He was quiet, serious, and cautious. From his four years in the U.S. Navy, including time in Vietnam, he learned the importance of working as a team. He wasn't looking for glory; he just wanted to do a good job. That's what he learned from the military, and that's how he approached working narcotics in the New Bedford police department. He joined the Bristol County Drug Task Force in 1980 while still working in the city's narcotics unit. He was then "loaned" to the district attorney's office in 1985 where he worked on the task force full-time along with another city detective. It was a good assignment, but it caused some occasional rifts within his own department. His bosses worried he and his partner, Paul Boudreau, had been away too long. They worried the two would forget they were New Bedford cops first. Bruce tried to reassure them that wasn't the case; after all, his brother was a New Bedford patrolman and so were some of his closest friends. He knew he was just on loan to the district attorney's office a few downtown blocks over. To stay in touch with city life and to check the pulse of the community, he would stop in to different bars across New Bedford, quick check-in stops, after the DA's office closed at five o'clock. He wanted to keep getting the feel of the city, to keep an open ear for potential trouble, to be accessible to some of the people who recognized him and wanted to slip him information.

Bruce knew about the missing girls, the found bodies, the course of the overall investigation from the papers.[21] It was hard to be in the office, or the city for that matter, and not be aware. But the drug task force didn't do murder cases. That was the purview of the state police and local police detectives; his job centered on the drug traffickers. But that didn't mean he didn't hear other things, or notice things in the city. Bruce always noticed what was going on. What he noticed now was a face that *wasn't* behind the old Burt's Pub bar, now renamed and under new management, on Union Street in the city's downtown: Marilyn Cardoza Roberts. It had been a while since he had seen her, he realized. He knew her because her dad had been a New Bedford cop. In recent years, he knew she was using heroin and had been arrested with one of the main heroin dealers in the city, a Cuban with ties to New Jersey who came over on the Mariel boatlift.[22] He would see Marilyn sometimes, just out and about on the streets, and hoped she would eventually get clean.

He motioned to the bartender and asked: Whatever happened to Marilyn?

She just vanished, he was told. That happened sometimes with addicts, Bruce knew, but with the bodies of women discovered along the highways he wondered if she might be one of the victims. No one, he learned, had seen Marilyn in months. No one knew where she was.

He wondered: Could Marilyn be dead? Could she be one of the unidentified?

Marilyn's father, Robert, retired from the force in 1982 and was now working security at the Claremont building near the district attorney's office downtown. Bob had been a top local soccer player in his younger days, serving as captain for the semi-pro Salty's Cleaners team and scoring the only goal for the 25th Signal Battalion Blazers in the Seventh Army Soccer League Championship game in 1958, before settling back in his hometown and joining the police department. He and his wife, Bernadine, raised two children and lived quietly in a modest home in the South End of the city. Bruce liked Bob and his wife. They were a nice couple who put their children first. He hoped his hunch was wrong.

Bob and Bernadine Cardoza spent years — and thousands of dollars — trying to get their daughter off drugs.[23] It started when Marilyn was in her mid-twenties and began dating the son of a business owner from the neighboring town of Dartmouth. Initially, they thought he was a nice match: smart, good-looking, and from a good family with means. What they didn't know was that he was addicted to heroin. It was a tumultuous time for the family as they searched for ways to get Marilyn help. By her late twenties, and after considerable effort, Marilyn seemed to settle down and put her drug issues behind her. She married a fisherman from Virginia at the historic Seamen's Bethel in downtown New Bedford, had a reception in the function room at Burt's Pub where she worked, and moved into an apartment behind one of the city's fire stations. She kept a nice house and seemed to enjoy her new life. But the marriage fell apart when, while her husband was out fishing, she met a man named Raul M. Yero whom narcotics detectives considered one of the largest heroin dealers in the city. He was once imprisoned in Cuba and bore a crude prison tattoo on his hand signifying a drug dealer, said former New Bedford narcotics detective sgt. James Sylvia.[24] He had been arrested in the city in four separate drug raids with thousands of dollars' worth of heroin and cocaine and, one person told police, kept Marilyn well supplied with drugs.[25] On December 4, 1985, both Marilyn and Raul were arrested during a drug raid at the Whaler Motor Inn. By that time, her marriage was over, she was living with Raul, and she was back using drugs.

Marilyn's parents had already sent her to one of the few inpatient drug-treatment programs for women in the state, escorted her to the methadone-treatment program, and underwent a series of counseling sessions with her over the years. They tried to force her into additional treatment but, at the time, she refused. They sought help as a family — and for her individually. Resources at the time were few and answers even fewer. The family felt alone in their battle.

By early 1988, as Marilyn's life spiraled downward, her frustrated family pleaded with her to change her life. You need to get help, they told her during her last visit home looking yet again for money. You have to get help. She stormed out of the house. When she didn't call on her mother's birthday in March, her parents were nervous. When she didn't call for Mother's Day, they tried not to be scared. Her father asked New Bedford police if anyone had seen her on the street. One person later said she might be in New Jersey; another told police that Sandy Botelho, who also went missing, once confided that Marilyn stole $25,000 worth of jewelry from Raul and fled south.[26] Others weren't sure where she was. While some New Bedford police officers kept an eye out for Marilyn, her name was never posted on the missing-person's clipboard in the record room. She was never on the official missing list.

As 1988 neared a close, Bruce swung by Bob's work one night to discreetly ask if there was a chance his daughter's dental records were available. They both knew what was left unsaid. Bob got the records to investigators a couple of days later. Bruce hoped they wouldn't need to use them; he hoped Marilyn would return home safely.

THE FIRST COMPARISONS of Marilyn's dental records with the remains were disappointing: it wasn't her. None of the other records they had of known missing women matched that of the person found along Route 140 by the search dog on December 1. There was some good news, though. By the end of the month, they did know more about this latest Jane Doe thanks to an examination at the Smithsonian by the noted forensic anthropologist Dr. Douglas Ubelaker. They knew she had long, light brown hair; she had what the anthropologist said were "protruding front thighs" (although investigators weren't quite sure how to describe that to the people they interviewed on the street), and had surgical staples, indicating she may have had abdominal surgery at some point. She was between twenty-two and thirty years old and stood between five feet one and five feet two. Based on her bone structure, she may have been racially mixed. An earring with two gold leaves was found near her body. Photos of the earring and the description were circulated to the media.

But no one came forward to say they knew a woman matching that description.

The investigators were back on the street, trying to get names of women who hadn't been seen in a while as well as the names of the odd or violent men who were picking women up. The list of the men was starting to get very, very long.

THE NEW BEDFORD WOMAN telling the story remembered it clearly: It was August 1987, a year before the women began going missing, before the bodies started showing up along the highways. A guy with dirty blond hair, scars on his face, behind the wheel of a white pickup truck pulled up alongside her as she worked the streets of Weld Square. She got in. She liked to stay local, just in case there was a problem. She had her favorite spots to take her johns. Then he hit the highway. *What's going on,* she recalled asking him. He wouldn't hurt her, he insisted. *Just do what I say.* She wasn't so sure once she saw the point of what appeared to be a fillet knife stuck up his sleeve.

The man, she would recall a year later, got off a highway exit in Dartmouth — one exit short of the area where three bodies were later found — and tried to turn onto a dirt road. She jumped out and ran. The man chased her in the truck. She hid in bushes. She ran to a business nearby. No one helped her. She ran again, this time on to the highway toward New Bedford. The man was hiding in a ditch, she would tell a reporter. He had been waiting for her. She was dragged into the ditch, ordered to strip and then was raped. His knife was stuck in the ground where she could see it.

"I'm thinking in my mind . . . he's going to stab me," she later told a reporter. "I knew that knife was going to find a hole in me."[27]

She fought back, grabbed her clothes and ran again. "I never came so close to death in my life," the woman would later say.

Months later, she would see the man again in Weld Square. She was convinced he was stalking her. She never reported it until the bodies started appearing on the highways. After the story about her attack appeared in the *Standard-Times,* on December 3, 1988, she saw him again. He glared at her. She jotted down his license plate number. She then turned the information over to authorities.

The woman's story intrigued investigators. Could this be the killer? Could this be the break they needed?

Less than two weeks after the woman came forward, a team of state police officers assigned to the district attorney's office arrested a thirty-five-year-old man by the name of Neil Anderson at his home and charged him in connection with the attack. Neil Anderson, who lived not far from Weld Square with his mother, had an arrest record for breaking and entering, drunken driving, disturbing the peace, and larceny, among other petty crimes. He was once a welder. He was once a fisherman. A day later, he was charged with rape and intent to rape in connection with an attack on a hitchhiker who told authorities she was attacked near Copicut Road in Dartmouth on July 22, 1988. When state police officers searched his home, they seized a wide range of items, including fillet knives, eight rounds of 30–30 caliber ammunition, a round of 45-caliber ammunition, brass knuckles, a hatchet, a switchblade, an ice pick, a whip, and some clothes. A pair of boots — described as "engineer boots" worn by many motorcyclists — matched the description of the ones the woman said the attacker was wearing, according to court papers in connection with the search.

A month later, Neil Anderson was indicted for a third rape stemming from an attack in the eastern section of Fall River known as the Reservation.

He would be the first of dozens of suspects police would investigate — then later set aside — as time wound forward. There was a twenty-year-old New Bedford man who raped a prostitute in a store parking lot; a Rhode Island man who brought prostitutes to his home for weeks at a time; a man named Louis DaSousa who met a woman at a bar and viciously raped her with a pipe at Fort Taber, a rundown Civil War–era military fort in the city's South End, and who was eventually convicted of the attack. There were the men with the weird sexual tastes, the men who turned violent quickly, the men who beat prostitutes, the men who cruised the bars.

Maryann and Jose found it wasn't a case of no suspects. It was now a matter of too many. They knew they couldn't investigate every lead and every suspect alone.

4 THE STREETS

BEEP. BEEP. BEEP. BEEP.

Maryann Dill hit the button on her Bose clock-radio alarm.

Six o'clock.

Less than five hours earlier, she had crawled into bed, exhausted from a fifteen-hour workday. She and her partner, Jose Gonsalves, spent the night circling the streets, searching for people who might give them yet another shred of information. Finding the right people was tough, getting accurate information even tougher. These were not folks with nine-to-five jobs, with neat homes and listed phones. The lives of the people the two needed to talk with were messy: Getting high, getting arrested, going to court, going to barrooms were the four walls of their rough existence. It could take hours for the state police partners to find one person on the street. Or it could take five minutes. Nothing on the street was predictable, just the unpredictability.

And today, Maryann would do it all again.

Unless tests on evidence from a crime scene finally pointed to a killer. Unless an eyewitness came forward. Unless another body was found. Unless someone confessed.

She hoped the proverbial break in the case would come today. They needed to solve this case. The families needed them to solve this case.

Maryann Dill was one of the small but growing number of women on the state police and one of a handful in the investigative units. Tall and slender with short dark hair, her South Shore accent — a blend of a Boston and Rhode Island twang — gave her a down-to-earth yet no-nonsense air. When she graduated from Cape Cod Community College in 1979, the Hanover, Massachusetts, native was considering two career paths: lawyer or state trooper. Her mother, an assistant postmaster in Hanover, spotted a notice about an upcoming state police entrance exam. Figuring this was a good sign, Maryann took the test and passed. As a kid, she babysat the children of a state trooper and, through talking with him, had a vague idea what the job was like. After attending the then twenty-five-week State Police Academy, she knew the job would be challenging, both mentally and physically. By January of 1980, she graduated from the academy and was a full-time trooper, assigned to the Dartmouth barracks on Route 6. That post covered one of the busiest areas in the state.

In 1983, she and Jose Gonsalves were asked to move from the uniform division to the investigative unit at the Bristol County District Attorney's Office. One of her mentors — Corporal Natale "Butch" Lapriore — was already there and told her to give it a try. The DA's office — headed by District Attorney Ronald A. Pina — had an often-strained relationship with the state police ever since he kicked out the troopers assigned to his office who had supported his opponent a few years earlier. But even before that, relations between the district attorney and state police were strained. It had even come to blows. In an old and often-embellished tale, a trooper returning from a grisly double murder in Norton was at the popular watering hole for the office. The scene he had come from was heart-wrenching: A young mother had been stabbed to death in a house, and then the killer went outside and attacked her little boy. The child was stabbed so many times and so deeply the body was stuck into the ground by the knife. The trooper had just dropped off some evidence to the office and was at the small, downtown New Bedford restaurant and bar called Octavio's trying to clear his head of the bloody scene before heading home to his own young children. And it was there he saw District Attorney Ronald Pina. Some snide words were exchanged. The prosecutor questioned the trooper's election loyalties in impolitic terms. The trooper told him to shut up. The prosecutor kept talking. The trooper turned in his bar stool and, while still sitting, punched the DA in the face. His claddagh ring left a tiny slice on Pina's cheek. It became the stuff of police legend, sharply illustrating the rift between those tasked with investigating death and those holding political office. The nuances of what made the judicial system work in a political climate — the lobbying for state and federal money, the cajoling of state representatives and senators for support—were lost in that moment. It came down to two sides. There were those facing firsthand the grit and pain of death; and there were those running for political office. It would take years to break down that wall between them.

Maryann knew what she was facing when she joined the unit. She heard all those stories, knew the deep-rooted resentments between Ron Pina and some members of the state police, but she also knew working in the unit offered a great opportunity, a chance to hone her investigative skills and learn new police techniques. The politics of the past would stay there. She planned to do good police work.

Now, almost five years after joining the unit and earning her bachelor's degree at Northeastern University, she had no regrets. She had already weathered one potential political storm earlier that year in April when the district attorney's fiancée, a Rhode Island television personality named Sheila Martines, was found locked in the trunk of her Mercedes-Benz along a rural town road in Dighton, Massachusetts, about twenty miles from Providence, Rhode Island. Martines had claimed she stopped at a truck rest stop along one of the busiest sections of Interstate 195 in Seekonk in broad daylight after experiencing car trouble and was abducted at knifepoint by a man. She claimed she was forced to drive her Mercedes about a dozen miles away where, she told police, the man ordered her into the trunk. She was found in the trunk twenty-four hours later when a young man looking out his bathroom window spotted the car in a nearby empty lot and went to investigate.

Maryann and "Butch" Lapriore were the prime investigators in the case. They were determined to find the abductor and prove to the district attorney that state police investigators were professional and nonpartisan. But determination and good intentions were not enough. The more the two dug, the more flaws they found in the girlfriend's story. There were no witnesses to the abduction, other than Sheila. There was no evidence of a second person having been in the vehicle. There were no footprints of a suspect in the dirt. There were no fingerprints of a suspect in the car. Sheila had to drive past a local police station to get to the spot where she—and her car—were later found. And the DA's fiancée, who had documented alcohol problems, wasn't available for additional interviews. There were rumors her job was on the line at the Rhode Island television station. Some in the district attorney's office speculated the abduction was an elaborate hoax. But the two investigators still dug in, looking for that single shred of evidence to prove it happened: a button. Martines claimed her abductor ripped her shirt in the car and a button popped off. Butch searched every crevice of the car for that single button. The final report in the case would note there was no evidence to show the abduction took place. While it was a widely accepted determination by nearly everyone in the prosecutor's office, it wasn't quite what the district attorney wanted to hear. To DA Pina, it was just another time state police dropped the ball. His fiancée had been abducted, and they couldn't find the suspect. The case was eventually closed by the state police.

Now, Maryann was again in the center of an investigation in which the district attorney was taking a keen interest. Butch had asked for a transfer out of the unit when the Martines investigation was done, so now, as the murder investigation intensified, Maryann was working with Jose Gonsalves. She and others in the unit hoped this time politics — and the outside pressures it brought — would stay out of the investigation.

The list of things to do in the case grew daily: finding elusive witnesses, finding experts to examine evidence, sifting through tips coming through a hotline, sorting truth from rumor, sorting through a growing list of suspects — all while still keeping track of other, unrelated cases. For the first few months of the investigation, Maryann and Jose were on the rotating on-call list for the unit, heading out to the "unattended deaths" — ranging from overdoses to murders to accidental deaths — throughout the county. They juggled their days between the highway investigation and the rest of their caseload. Everyone in the unit was trying to share the work, though, as the case progressed. Teams were set up to split the pool of suspects, the first step in ruling out — or ruling in — possible killers.

Maryann mentally checked off what she needed to do that day once she got into the office. Check hotline tips. Call the state prison to check one suspect's alibi — he claimed he was locked up. Call the crime lab to see if testing on the evidence was done. Call back the mother and sister of two of the victims — she knew there would be a message from them waiting on the desk. Then, it was on to the streets, searching for more witnesses.

But before the police work could start, ironing clothes — and feeding her

135-pound German shepherd, Beau — took precedent. It was the era of crisp cotton shirts and dress pants. No jeans. Proper dress was business attire — even though everyone on the job knew he or she might have to walk through muck at a scene. She tried to get all her ironing done on Sundays, her day off, but she knew what they said about the best-laid plans. Ironing often went to the bottom of the list on Sundays as she tried to catch up on bills, grocery shopping, laundry, and sleep. So that meant nearly every morning she hauled out the ironing board to press her cotton shirt and put the proper crease in her dress pants. That meant getting up a little bit earlier.

About twenty miles away, in Freetown, one of the towns abutting New Bedford, Jose Gonsalves was sleeping soundly.

"Wake up," his wife, a nurse in a hospital geriatric unit, said, shaking his shoulder. "It's seven."

He could hear his son and daughter in the kitchen, getting ready for school. By seven fifteen, he'd be showered and shaved and ready to go. His clothes were ready to wear, already ironed by his wife. He noticed the waistband on his pants was a bit loose. So was his shirt. Within a couple of months, the six-feet-two-and-a-half-inch trooper had gone from 220 pounds to his high-school weight of 185 pounds. Someone had asked him just the other day if he was sick. He made a mental note: Eat more.

He looked at the clock. It was seven fifteen. Time to go.

See you later tonight, he told his wife, kissing her.[1]

He grabbed the metal Christmas-cookie tin on the kitchen table as he slipped out the door without eating breakfast. Inside was a trail mix of pretzels, raisins, peanuts, and a few other things. His mother, a widow now in her early seventies, lived in an attached in-law apartment and quietly started leaving the tin on the table a few weeks earlier. That was when his workdays stopped ending at five and his weight loss started becoming noticeable. She never mentioned how thin he was getting. She just left the tin on the table, so he could have just a little something to snack on. He appreciated the quiet gesture — and the food.

Jose tried not to think about when he would be back home as he went out the door. For the past several weeks, he would pull into the driveway well after midnight. He missed dinner with his family. Homework with his children. Quiet time in the house. Noisy times watching his four children playing soccer and basketball. All that was replaced with late-night interviews on New Bedford streets, tracking down people in the city as well as the state prisons and jails who might have information, writing reports, reviewing the reports done by others working on the case. Family was important to him, and the long days were tough. When he and his wife built their Freetown home in 1979, he made sure to add an in-law apartment for his aging parents. Just months before the house was done, his father died at age eighty-three, and his mother moved in alone. His father, a merchant marine who had emigrated from Portugal, like many in the area, and his mother, a stay-at-home mom who was born in New Bedford, instilled a strong work and family ethic in Jose. They also made sure their children embraced their American heritage, insisting on speaking English at home to their children.

Jose graduated from New Bedford High School in 1965 then went to Southeastern Massachusetts University — later called UMass–Dartmouth — where he earned a bachelor's degree in business in 1969. He joined the state police almost by accident. A buddy was taking the state police exam and asked him to take it with him. They both passed. When it later came to the physical endurance test, which included an obstacle course and a required six-and-a-half-minute mile run, Jose did it in six. His buddy did it in seven and failed. Jose wound up on the state police, his friend ended up as a successful business owner in the Albany, New York, area.

By 1983, Jose earned a master's degree in criminal justice from Anna Maria College in Paxton, Massachusetts, and, after years as a road trooper, was working in the state police unit assigned to the district attorney's office. He worked hard on the job — often logging fifty-plus hours — but tried to never lose sight of what was important: family, church, and helping the community. He coached youth sports teams when he could and took a keen interest in the youth basketball program at the Boys' Club in New Bedford, helping to raise money for the center and its efforts targeting at-risk youth. Giving back was rooted in his Catholic faith and something he felt honored to do. He hoped working on this murder case, and hopefully helping to solve it, would be a major service to his community and to the families looking for justice.

MARYANN WALKED INTO THE OFFICE, coffee in hand, and saw her partner already at his desk, flipping through sheets of paper.

Each day, every call to the tip line was logged, and the information was given to Dill and Gonsalves. The tips ranged from the plausible to the preposterous:

My ex-husband did it. He was always weird.

It was a trucker.

The missing bodies are in the ocean.

I had a vision about the killer.

I saw something on TV *about a similar case. You should check it out.*

My ex-boyfriend picks up hookers. I think he did it.

There's a white truck that's always around, picking up girls.

There's a guy out there beating up the girls, I heard.

I heard someone talking, saying the killer is a fisherman. Check it out.

I heard the killer is a truck driver.

Jose scribbled "truck" on a legal pad

"Here's another one about a truck," he said, looking up. "We have a couple of these mentioning a truck."

"There was one where . . ." The ringing phone cut Maryann off.[2]

"Yes, we will be right there," Jose said into the phone.

He put down the pen and shuffled the papers to one side. The staff sergeant wanted to see them.

Down the hall, Staff Sgt. Gale P. Stevens, who went by his middle name of Pat, was waiting in his office to hear a daily update on the case.

What did the two do last night? Who did they talk with? How close are they to identifying a suspect? What did they plan to do today? If the DA asked him a question on the cases, he wanted the right answer. He didn't want any surprises. As the supervisor in the unit, Pat Stevens knew he would be asked by the district attorney and Bob St. Jean what was new in the case, were there any leads, how things were progressing. While the district attorney and Bob also went directly to the troopers regularly for updates, the staff sergeant needed to be kept in the loop daily.

The district attorney wasn't shy about asking questions and often ignored the chain of command to get answers. A couple of times a week, Ron Pina would stroll into the office Jose and Maryann shared, plunk himself down in a chair, and chat.

"So what's going on?" the DA would ask, sitting in the chair next to Jose's desk.

The DA listened as the troopers detailed the latest theories, evidence, and would-be witnesses in the case. Then he would give his thoughts: who looked good, who didn't, what more might need to be done.

The troopers felt the prosecutor wanted to do the right thing—they just didn't always agree with some of his theories or his suspects as the case moved on. "Tunnel vision," is what Jose always worried about as talks with the district attorney continued each day. The phrase was now becoming Jose's mental caution light. Focusing on one suspect and making the facts fit was dangerous. There were many suspects—maybe too many—investigators needed to look at. A wide net brings in more fish at sea and more information on shore.

IT WAS WELL PAST TEN at night, and the street lamps cast a yellow glow onto the streets of Weld Square. Maryann and Jose circled the neighborhood yet again, looking for familiar figures. Once. Twice. Three times.[3]

"There," Maryann Dill said, pointing. "She's over there."

Jose pulled up Penniman Street the wrong way and jerked the cruiser to a stop.

"Hey," he yelled as he opened the car door. "Hey, we just want to talk."

Two pencil-thin women bolted up the dark street.

Jose exhaled. *Really?* he thought, then gave chase.

A minute later, one woman paused on the street to look back—then stopped.

"Oh, it's just you," she said, smiling broadly. She turned and yelled down the street. "It's all right," she yelled to her friend. "It's only Jose and Maryann. Come on back. It's okay."

Maryann stood by the unmarked cruiser, chuckling, as the three walked toward her.

They often talked with the two women on the street. The investigators learned about their families, their HIV diagnosis, their T-counts, their attempts—and failures—to get clean. The investigators spent so much time in the area, Jose and Maryann became "JoseyandMaryann," a single name said in one breath, one unit they could trust.

A week earlier, one of the women who bolted down the street had been in the back seat of the cruiser headed to the district attorney's office to look at some photos.

They were halfway into the ride when one of the women piped up from the back seat.

"Can I ask you a personal question?" she asked.

"Go ahead," Jose answered.

"Are you two married?

"No, that's probably why we get along," he quipped.

"Well, maybe you should be," the woman retorted.[4]

Jose and Maryann appreciated the street humor of the women they met through the investigation. The pair knew the women on the street who either worked as prostitutes or sold small amounts of drugs to support heroin or cocaine habits saw things police didn't. These women knew the rhythm of the street. They knew when things were "off." The troopers knew the women might tell them what johns were acting strange, who was dealing what drugs, who was ripping who off, who disappeared, where the women still missing might have been last seen. Some of the information was second-, third-, or fourth-hand. The information might be part fact, part rumor, part fantasy. But it was what was circulating on the street, and street talk was what Jose and Maryann needed to know. The women on the street had just one request of the investigators: catch the killer.

THE INQUIRIES were discreet, of course. As investigators gathered the names and descriptions of the men who bought sex on the street, some people were getting nervous and calling Bob St. Jean, the DA's chief investigator. *My name wasn't mentioned, was it? I know one of the women on the street. I went to school with one of the women. I was talking to one of the girls. One of the girls down there used to live in my neighborhood, and I once gave her a ride.* When Bob started hearing the names and occupations of some of the customers, he expected to get calls — lots of them. Bob was surprised that men of means, men with power, men who should know better, were picking up prostitutes in the city. Didn't they read the news? Didn't they know the women were shooting heroin? Didn't they know some of the women tested positive for the AIDS virus? How stupid could they be?

With each phone call, Bob would assure the men the investigators were looking to identify a killer, not publically expose their sex lives.

Just cooperate, he told them.

He wanted to yell something different: Are you crazy?

NOTHING SEEMED TO SLOW the sale of drugs in the city in 1988. Not raids on stash houses. Not sweeps of street dealers. Not the deaths and disappearances of women.

Along the narrow South First Street in the South End of the city, the street dealers hawked heroin like newspaper boys of the 1920s. They lined the one-way street, sometimes just feet apart, calling out to passing cars the "brand" of the day stamped on the glassine packets of the heroin.

"Hello," one called out. "Power."

"What's up?" another yelled to a driver. "Power."[5]

Cars driven by young white men and women — most originally from the suburbs — stop quickly, slip cash to the dealers then drive off. South First Street is a quick exit off Route 18, a highway built during the urban renewal in the 1960s dead-ending at a stoplight and cutting the waterfront off from the city's center. It is flanked on both sides by stout two-story brick housing-project units. There's a small playground and tiny swaths of dirt sprinkled with grass that pass for yards. Everything is cement and dirt and metal. You can hear the cars passing just yards away on the highway over the catcalls of the dealers. Every day, the city's narcotics detectives — the unit was officially called the Organized Crime Investigative Bureau — drove through the neighborhood. Nearly every day, someone was arrested. In 1987, 974 people were arrested on drug charges in the city; 590 of that number were charged with either selling or possession of heroin or cocaine. Another 110 people were charged with possessing a needle and syringe, the paraphernalia used to inject heroin. In 1988, those numbers were continuing to rise.

In a separate part of the city, young women addicted to heroin and cocaine paced a five-block neighborhood, waiting for middle- and upper-class men to pick them up. The price of oral sex — a blowjob — was twenty dollars, the

price of a tiny glassine packet of heroin at the time. Sex had to be quick —
since many of the women were shooting five to ten packets of heroin a day
and needed more than a hundred dollars to satisfy their habits. Prostitution
seemed the only way to get that amount of cash. While many male addicts were
robbing banks or breaking into houses, the women victimized themselves in
this never-ending devil dance with heroin. Finding treatment, even for those
with the best intentions, was not easy. In 1988, inpatient drug-treatment beds
for women were scarce, and addicts were waiting for months to get into publically funded, outpatient methadone programs. There were three treatment
programs in the New Bedford and Fall River area at the time: two methadone
programs and one twenty-day, inpatient detoxification program. Between
the three programs, 255 addicts throughout the region could be served. But
that clearly wasn't enough, as everyone in the law enforcement and treatment
fields discovered. The programs weren't just serving those in the greater New
Bedford area: addicts were traveling from more than an hour away to the area
to get what little help there was available. There were other programs elsewhere in the state, including the in-treatment program at Spectrum House
in Worcester where a number of the New Bedford women sought help, but
waits for treatment across Massachusetts were also long.

AIDS also hit the intravenous-drug community hard, and people were
worried the virus would spread quickly if addicts — particularly prostitutes —
didn't get into treatment fast. In its first round of voluntary screening, the
New Bedford methadone clinic discovered 25 percent had been exposed to
the AIDS virus. About a third of the fifty tested in the second round were
exposed. Ten of the people who were tested were prostitutes — and eight of
those were still active on the street.

The situation wasn't improving with time. In 1985, there were 30 people
on the waiting list for the methadone program at the New Bedford Area
Center for Human Services. Within two years, that list ballooned to between
120 and 130 people. New Bedford wasn't the only place with a shortage of
treatment options. More than 500 people, including some pregnant women,
were waiting for one of the 750 state-funded slots in a methadone program.

One woman waited two months to get into the methadone program — then
was sent to the women's state prison on prostitution and bad-check charges
a week before she was set to start.

While some addicts struggled to find help, city narcotics detectives were seeing a steady stream of new heroin addicts and dealers on the street. The price of the drug in New Bedford was the cheapest in the state in the late 1980s, and the supply seemed endless. Each week, on average, the narcotics unit raided two houses and arrested close to a dozen dealers, buyers, and users on the street. For each dealer gone, another appeared. The drug business was booming.

Old-time narcotics detectives and cops in the city insisted the seeds of the heroin trade were planted in the 1960s, when an influx of people from the New York City area moved to the city as part of a jobs program. When the program ended, a few people with ties to the New York heroin market stayed and found the area a ripe place for expansion. Well-meaning community advocates tried to find ways to address the problem but, even from the start, it was tough. Few realized the grip heroin could have on a person and, eventually, on the community. By 1970, community leaders launched a twenty-day campaign called "Countdown to Freedom" to raise money "to combat drugs" and take a stand on the issue. There was a fifty-mile hike from Hyannis to New Bedford, pledges from local leaders, and a telethon that drew national celebrities, among them director Otto Preminger, Clarence Williams III of *Mod Squad* television series fame, and David Selby, best known as Quentin from the popular afternoon vampire soap opera, *Dark Shadows*. The *Standard-Times* newspaper, the television station WTEV, and two radio stations, WNBH and WBSM, beat the media drum almost daily promoting the effort. By the time the campaign ended in April of 1970, more than $150,000 was raised to help buy a building and run a drug-rehabilitation program. However, just a few months after the campaign ended, there were major problems. Plans to open a clinic at a former nursing home were dropped when neighbors threatened to go to court, and it looked like the needed zoning ordinance wouldn't be approved. Then people started questioning how the money raised was being spent. A methadone clinic eventually got off the ground in 1972 with the help of some federal money. By the late 1980s, about 400 heroin addicts were being treated daily.[6]

The methadone clinic, though, created a different type of issue for the city and neighborhood. Originally designed to tackle a local drug problem, the clinic was now drawing addicts from across the southern part of the state and

Rhode Island. Dealers, in turn, set up shop near the clinic to lure the addicts back. Police and community activists felt as if they were on a stationary bike, pedaling fast and getting nowhere.

The heroin problem in the area in the 1970s and '80s touched a wide range of families, foreshadowing what was to come when the opioid epidemic hit the nation more than three decades later. There were the children of politicians, doctors, and lawyers shooting up in the suburbs, and the children of textile workers and fishermen shooting up in the city. Heroin addiction crossed economic and town lines, but few families openly discussed it or knew what to do. There was the undercurrent of blame and shame: addicts could stop if they wanted; the families must have done something wrong for this to happen. Heroin addiction was the dirty secret of embarrassed families.

The fishing industry was the backbone of the local economy. It was also a source of one of the largest "cash only" industries in the city. For years, some of the fishing catch was held back from the fish auction, and crews were paid under the table with a portion of that catch.[7]

Commercial fishing could be lucrative, but it was also expensive. Fishermen could pocket thousands from a single trip, but it cost thousands to keep the vessels seaworthy and running. If the haul was low, so was the payout, and by the 1980s the federal government was continuing to develop regulations on everything from how much could be fished, where boats could go, and how many days a boat could be at sea. The fishermen were saying it was strangling their livelihood. In the early 1980s, marijuana replaced fish on several of the commercial vessels coming into port, leading to large amounts of under-the-table cash circulating on the waterfront. More than a hundred tons of baled marijuana, hidden in false walls and compartments in retrofitted fishing boats, were believed smuggled into the harbor from Colombia at the time. One federal indictment alleged that between 1982 and 1983 alone, 160 tons of marijuana worth at least $150 million had been smuggled in. By 1988, with an influx of free cash flowing in some circles, cocaine became the drug of choice for people ranging from lawyers and businessmen to fishermen and bartenders — just as it had throughout the country. Touted as "nonaddictive" by some at the time, cocaine created a new circle of addicts and a bridge to the street life.

This was the world investigators navigated in the search for the missing women. There is an old saying, don't pick up a rock unless you are prepared to see what is beneath it. There were many rocks in the city in the late 1980s, and not everyone wanted to look under them.

ADDICTS AND PROSTITUTES could be found in several parts of New Bedford throughout the day, but in 1988 Weld Square was the hub. The girls on the street didn't look the Hollywood part. They eschewed heavy makeup and high hair. They wore jeans and T-shirts instead of miniskirts, sneakers instead of high heels. From a distance, they looked average and poor. Sometimes they were animated as they walked along the street and sometimes they just looked tired. It was only when you got closer could you see the drug sickness.

Dark-haired and bone thin, one woman huddled in the shadows on the doorway step. Her dark eyes were aged by drugs and sleeplessness. Unlike the other girls who would walk confidently on the street, or sit smoking on the shadowed steps of the Mickiewicz Social Club in Weld Square, she just sat there quietly in the dark, watching the cars pass. She could be easily missed by anyone walking or driving by. If you got close enough to talk, though, you could see the sickness easily in this young woman, in her face, her eyes, her tiny body. Her voice was flat and dull. Drugs had already stolen her life. "I just need money to buy diapers," she is saying, dropping her eyes. "That's why I'm here."[8] She was just one of the desperate women on the dismal street in the spring and early summer of 1988, when the "girls on the street" were keeping a tally of the "weirdos and sickos," the men who wouldn't pay, the men who slapped them around. There was the guy with the knife, the two guys in a van, the guys in trucks, the trick who seemed nice then suddenly "snapped," the guys who stole their money then beat them. The girls were jotting down license plates, memorizing facial features of johns and the vehicles they drove. They were frightened by what they were seeing on the street but stayed out there because they were more afraid of the gut-wrenching heroin withdrawal symptoms.

In 1987, Margaret "Peggy" Nunes had been stabbed to death and left in a snow bank by a man named William Marquette, a Cuban who came over on the Mariel boatlift. Darcy Danelson, the nineteen-year-old Fall River woman, was found brutally raped and dead along the railroad tracks in 1986 (Marquette was questioned in that killing but was never charged). Another woman, Joanne Andrade, was found dead along the waterfront. Then there were two other murders, both unsolved, of women last seen leaving local bars.

It was dangerous on the street, but most of the girls felt they could take care of themselves. They were tough. They were shrewd. They could usually spot the john who might rob them or worse and knew to keep walking when those guys came around. They were also ready to fight back; some carried small knives, others screwdrivers. However, even the most street savvy knew they couldn't predict what might happen in the cars and trucks of strangers.

One woman on the street that year was originally from Wareham, a waterfront town just before the Cape Cod bridges, and had the look of a young Jamie Lee Curtis: tall and lean, her hair often cropped short. Linda tried to cling to her dignity as she hopped in car after car to get just enough money to feed her ever-growing heroin addiction. She would always say she never stole from her family. When another addict she knew once slipped into her father's garage and stole his tools, she pleaded with her dad to believe it wasn't her. She couldn't take what little her middle-class family had. But her father, weary after her years of addiction and wary of her stories, didn't believe her. She had given him enough pain already. She disappeared from the street in the summer of 1988 after one of her close friends, Marilyn Roberts, disappeared. At first, police feared she was one of the murder victims. They eventually learned from a reporter Linda knew and had called that she had hopped a bus headed west when the other women began to go missing. She kicked heroin cold turkey on that ride and never looked back. In later, occasional phone calls to a reporter on the newspaper's toll-free line, she would check in and ask about Marilyn but would never give specifics on why she left so abruptly. Some on the street speculated she crossed someone in New Bedford, that she may have ripped someone off. Whenever she was asked why she left, she would just say it was to leave the drug life behind. Eight years later, she was still clean. "I've seen people high on that shit since I've been clean and it makes me wonder why I was so in love with it. Yuk," she wrote in a letter to a reporter in 1996. Some women, like her, did heroin and moved on, kicking the habit in detox or on their own. Others went to jail, kicked heroin, and returned to the street. Some were infected with the AIDS virus from shared needles and would later die; others would eventually be infected with the virus. The local methadone clinic in the city began giving prostitutes, particularly those who were HIV positive, top priority for treatment in an attempt to stop the spread of AIDS. There was talk of starting a needle-exchange program.

The deadly virus didn't stop the men from circling the streets and prowling the bars for prostitutes. The chance a killer was picking them up didn't stop the women with the overpowering hunger for heroin and cocaine. It was a gamble both sides took.

MARYANN DILL AND JOSE GONSALVES were in their office, examining their notes one more time. They were looking for links in the disappearances, any commonality in the women's lives, evidence from the scenes tying the cases together. They went through the list.

Drug use. Check.

Going to city bars where drugs were sold. Check.

Boyfriends who used drugs. Check.

Prostitution. Partial check. The troopers discovered all of the women were heavy into drugs but several, such as Nancy Paiva, were not widely known as working girls on the street.

Friends in common. The troopers would always pause on that point. Drug users in a small city tended to hang together. Just knowing a person wasn't suspicious, they knew, especially in those circles and particularly in a city the size of New Bedford. However, finding more people who knew the missing girls could help them craft a detailed timeline on the last hours — and minutes — of their lives. The list of missing girls — everyone in the office still called them "girls," even though only one was a teenager — was now likely at least eight. With five bodies already found it was unlikely the rest of the missing women were still alive. This was turning into a massive homicide investigation, and one of the most difficult the troopers had ever seen. Some people they interviewed who might have information were addled by years of heavy drug or alcohol use, able to remember scenes but not the finer details investigators needed. It was like a picture frame without the photo, or the outline of a puzzle on a card table. At times, they felt they were close to finding the killer. Other times they were chasing shadows in a shifting light.

One name kept coming up in interviews with girls on the street, relatives of the missing women, and even fellow cops as a potential good witness:

Kenneth Ponte, a local lawyer. He had represented Mary Santos in a civil case, and when she disappeared he helped her husband print missing flyers. Dawn Mendes, the identified murder victim who went missing in September, was once seen banging on the door of his home. Rochelle Dopierala, last seen in April or May, was spotted in his car and stayed at his Chestnut Street home. Robbin Rhodes, missing sometime in the spring, once told her sister she was "dating" a lawyer, later identified as Kenny. Nancy Paiva, last seen walking away from a South End bar in July, once worked at the neighborhood video-rental store he frequented and had hired him in a bankruptcy case. Maryann and Jose already heard Ponte's backstory: a former heroin addict who kicked the habit then went to college followed by law school. He eventually passed the bar and was picking up lower-level civil and criminal cases, the bread-and-butter cases to pay the bills. He was never a premier lawyer with headline cases. He was just trudging along under the radar, a big guy in a rumpled suit. He had donated to the Bristol County sheriff's election campaign and was one of a number of people who would be designated as a deputy sheriff. It was primarily an honorary title but it also allowed Kenny to serve court papers and earn some extra cash. He got a badge and, despite his drug record, somehow got a gun. He was also a heavy cocaine user and, according to the girls and some cops who dealt with him, a bit weird. The girls on the street told stories about his paranoia, how he would bring them to his house, bolt the doors and wouldn't let them leave. He didn't seem violent, just really strange. But that didn't stop the girls from going with him, and none of the girls considered pressing any charges. He did, after all, give them coke and didn't seem interested in sex.

Kenny had packed up his home and office and moved to Florida on October 10, 1988, about a month after Dawn Mendes was reported missing. He had signed an agreement to buy a duplex in Port Richey, a town about forty miles north of Tampa, on August 27 and was planning to move in in September. But there were some delays in finalizing the move, and he didn't hit the road until October. A friend, Jay Miller, who was newly separated, made the two-day drive south in the moving truck rented at New Bedford's airport terminal, while Kenny in the passenger seat "sat back and ate."[9] Kenny liked to eat — a lot — and was always on the lookout for good buffets. Miller never asked why Kenny, a man he considered "a big-time lawyer," was closing up shop and moving to Florida because "I didn't want to ask him stuff like that. That's none of my business."[10]

A number of people were saying the move was no surprise. Kenny had been planning it for a while; his life in New Bedford seemed to be spiraling out of control between the cocaine use and the girls from the street at his house. He needed a fresh start. Others described the move as abrupt. Here today, then gone. The district attorney and a few others in his office found the move odd. No other women from the streets went missing after Kenny moved out. A couple of people in the DA's office found the move curious and wondered if Kenny could be involved in the killings — or knew who was. Maryann and Jose weren't convinced Kenny was involved in the homicides, but they did want to know what he knew. But as a precaution, in case he was the killer, police searched his old law office in Dartmouth after he closed up shop with the permission of the landlord, avoiding the need for a search warrant. It was a month after the latest bodies were found — two on the dimly-lit Reed Road clover leaf ramps off Interstate 195 in Dartmouth and another on Route 140 — and it was pretty routine, as far as police searches go. One of the search dogs brought in took an interest on a rug in the office but, after additional examination, nothing tying Ponte to the disappearances or killings turned up. The search needed to be kept low-key, Maryann and Jose knew. If news leaked out, it would look like Kenny was a suspect and any chance of getting him to cooperate would be gone.

BOB ST. JEAN, the chief investigator for the district attorney, was talking with Jose and Maryann in their office as he usually did each day when he got a message from the front desk. There was someone on the line for him, a man named Ken Ponte calling from Florida. Did he want to take it? Of course. Put it through to Jose's extension, he said.

Bob knew Kenny Ponte from his days on the state police in the late sixties and early seventies, before he quit and took the job with the district attorney's office. Kenny back then used to hang out in the North End of the city, outside King of Pizza on Acushnet Avenue, with a group of heavy drug users. That's when Kenny was using heroin. Bob arrested him for drugs back then but there were no hard feelings between the two in the years since. Kenny seemed to be, on the surface, a classic success story: overcoming a drug habit, going to school, becoming a lawyer. Bob found it interesting, as he put the call on speaker phone, that Kenny would pick him of all people to talk with decades later.[11]

"Hey, Kenny, what can I do for you?" he asked, as the troopers listened.

"I understand you think I'm involved with those murders up there?" Kenny answered.

"Who told you that?"

"That's the word on the street. People are calling me from up there."[12]

"Hey, Kenny, I'm not accusing you about anything but I'd like to talk to you about the case. I think you could be helpful."

Bob listened as the former heroin addict turned lawyer began to ramble about the case.

Someone said there were some weird johns in Weld Square bothering the girls, Kenny was saying. It could be someone from the Coast Guard. They come and go from the city. Mary Santos was a former client. He had made missing-person flyers for her husband. And Nancy Paiva. She worked at a video store, right? Rochelle? Yeah, he knew her.

Bob tried to steer the conversation beyond the generalities. He needed specifics. Kenny was spouting off theories. He also seemed to be fishing for information. Bob kept trying to get the lawyer to focus on facts: how well did he know the women, where did he last see them. With each question, Bob detected a touch of agitation and anger in the lawyer's voice. Kenny was talking fast. Very fast. Bob tried again to steer the conversation back to specifics.

"I gotta go. I'll call you later," Kenny said. Then he hung up.

Bob stared at the phone and shook his head.

What the hell just happened? he thought.

MARYANN DILL couldn't feel her fingers. It was twenty degrees and, with the twelve-mile-per-hour winds whipping through the gravel pit a few miles from Interstate 195 in Dartmouth, it felt much colder. It was December 10, 1988, and she could swear it felt like mid-February. Mid-February in Maine. She could feel wind slice through her jacket. Her nostrils stung as she breathed in. Her skin hurt. She couldn't remember ever feeling so cold as she stood near the tree line, looking at the remains of yet another woman.[13] Two squirrel hunters had stumbled on the body earlier and notified police.

As she looked into the brush ringing the gravel pit, Maryann knew this would be victim number six.

The secluded spot was well known to the state police: car thieves often dumped stolen vehicles there, and road troopers routinely swung by to check. The remains — all that was left at this point was a skeleton with a jacket around the neck — were found in the heavy brush ringing the area, difficult to see in a casual glance from a passing cruiser. Only on foot could a person see the remains and then only if the person was within tripping distance. Teenagers on ATVs regularly road through makeshift paths to the pit and hunters were known to stroll through the woods, looking for small animals. No one had walked or driven close enough to this corner of the pit to see the remains during the spring or summer. No one until December 10, a date everyone who was there recalled decades later as one of the coldest days of the year.

Word spread quickly about the discovery. Uniformed troopers were stationed at the scene to keep the growing number of reporters at a distance. Trooper David Wordell was now accustomed to the drill: it would be the third time he stood guard at a crime scene in the case. Newspaper, radio, and television reporters chatted in clusters, trying to stay warm. Bob St. Jean, the chief investigator for the district attorney, came to the scene from home, leaving tickets to that day's Patriots football game he now wouldn't see with his sons on his bedroom bureau. Maryann and Jose gathered with other investigators near the tree line covered in light snow, looking at the scene. The sun was setting, they were losing natural light to search, and the temperature was dropping. The decision was made: a state trooper would guard the scene overnight and everyone would return fresh in the morning.

The next day, Maryann and Jose stood to the side and once again watched their colleague, Trooper Kenneth Martin, kneeling in the brush where the remains were found. Kenny Martin was the unofficial crime-scene expert in the state police homicide unit in the office. Over the years, he developed a keen eye for the details others might miss and for finding the type of evidence lab experts could analyze. He looked for the obvious, of course: the footprints, the shell casings, the blood spatter, the fingerprints. But outdoors, he found himself looking around in less obvious places for evidence or items that could be analyzed.

Maryann and Jose were familiar with how their colleague worked. He would step back and look at the wider scene then slowly narrow his focus. He looked at the scene, not the victim, for clues.

Kenny Martin scanned the area surrounding the remains. He looked for indentations in the brush, for obvious footprints, tire impressions. It was an old scene, he knew, and some of the best evidence might be gone or covered over. He would come back, if needed, with a metal detector to scan for bullet casings, knives or other pieces of metal. He also knew animals will carry away things from crime scenes. Sometimes it will be bones. Sometimes it will be clothing. Sometimes birds will take minute items to be used in nests.

As the other investigators stayed back, he moved in closer, finally crouching near the remains. It had been too cold the day before to do an exacting inspection and he was trying to make up for lost time. He looked up, his eyes following the tree trunk about a foot away. Earlier, at another scene, he had pointed to a nest perched in the branches. "We'll take that," he said then.[14] Today, he would be doing much of the same.

For hours, as darkness set and the temperatures dropped, he scoured the scene. Finally, when it got too dark and light snow continued to fall, he left.

An autopsy later determined manner of death was homicide; cause of death was strangulation. It would be up to a forensic dentist, Stanley Schwartz, from the Tufts Medical Center, to try to identify her.

BEFORE AND AFTER the body was found in the gravel pit in Dartmouth, Kenny Ponte continued to call Bob St. Jean in the DA's office. *Hey, did you find out anything about the Coast Guard? How about truck drivers? Someone said a truck driver could be involved. Have you talked with the girls in Weld Square?* And with each phone call, the chief investigator would try to extract bits of information from Kenny before the lawyer would slam the phone down. *When was the last time you saw Rochelle? What was she doing? Who was she with? What were you doing with Rochelle when you last saw her? Was she your girlfriend? Did you date her?* The answers were broad. Rochelle was just a friend. No, they weren't close. They were just friends.[15]

Investigators already knew Rochelle Dopierala, the woman from Cape Cod, was more than a brief acquaintance of Kenny's. She told people she was staying with Kenny, and, they believed, he once called her mother looking for Rochelle (although her mother would later insist she never spoke with him). In April, shortly before she went missing, the twenty-eight-year-old mother of two was seen driving with Kenny in the city. The first time she was seen with him, Kenny pulled a gun on a guy who Rochelle claimed assaulted her. Another time, a woman claimed Kenny was chasing Rochelle, yelling that she stole something from him, then saw them together a few days later. Yet another time, Kenny waited outside a trailer while Rochelle briefly visited a man inside, and then the two drove off. Some people told police they saw them later that day in the Weld Square neighborhood, or at least they thought it was the same day. No one, Bob knew, came forward to say they saw her after that. She never called her mother on her birthday. She never called anyone, as far as they knew, since April of 1988. Bob wanted to know if Kenny could pinpoint when he last saw her, if he could give a specific date, time, and place. Did he know who else she might have gone with? Bob couldn't get a straight answer in any of the telephone conversations with Kenny.

"Kenny, how about we talk face to face?" Bob would eventually ask during one phone call. "I can come down there."[16]

"I'm coming up there in a few weeks," Kenny answered.[17]

"We would like to get together with you when you're up here."

"I'm only talking to you," Kenny said.

When the call ended, Bob St. Jean stared at the phone. Maybe Kenny isn't involved, maybe the guy can be of some help, he thought. This was a good first step forward. Bob discovered that would change quickly.

By the first week of January 1989, before the two could meet, Kenny Ponte was headline material throughout the state: "Ex-New Bedford Man Reportedly Frequented Weld Square," read the *Standard-Times*. "Cops Probe Lawyer in Serial Case," and "Serial Probe Targets Ex-Junkie," blared the *Boston Herald*. "DA: New Bedford Probe Has Fewer Suspects," headlined the *Boston Globe*, where the district attorney confirmed Kenny had a "personal relationship" with some of the victims.

How the hell did this get out? Bob thought. This was not good. They still needed to sit Kenny down, talk face-to-face, to see what he knew or didn't know. They weren't sure if he was a killer or a fumbling, egotistical cokehead. Ken Ponte was a wild card in the investigation. Bob thought about what he would say when Kenny next called to rant. He needed to find a way to calm him down and get some information.

He had asked the New Bedford detectives assigned to the drug task force what they knew about the Kenny Ponte of today. Could they give him some ideas about how to keep him on track?

The New Bedford cops took St. Jean back five years, to January 1984, and detailed what they called one of the most unforgettable — and oddest — visits with Kenny Ponte.

IT WAS JANUARY 1984. The house was dark. That was the first thing the four investigators noticed walking through the door at the Chestnut Street house. Dark and gloomy. In the shadows stood the hulking figure of Kenneth C. Ponte, a local attorney. The lawyer earlier had called New Bedford detective Paul Boudreau, asking for help.

"You know about videos and video equipment," Kenny had said on the phone, the narcotics detective recalled. "I need you to check something out. The film I rented keeps changing. It shows people being killed."

Paul knew a little bit about videos, videotape recorders, and video equipment: he owned two video stores, both called Movies-To-Go, and did plenty of research before plunking down cash for the business. He was surprised, though, by this call from Kenny, an attorney he knew from around the courthouse and who occasionally rented videos at his stores.

Whatever Ponte was talking about was worth checking out.

New Bedford sgt. Ronald Cabral, detectives Bruce Machado and Boudreau, along with Robert Jones, a video and financial investigator in the DA's office, were now at the house to see this film.

From the moment the investigators arrived, Ponte was jumpy, "wired, really wired," Bruce Machado would later say.[18] He was talking fast and he was intense. Someone, Ponte was telling them, taped over a film he rented. Look, he said. Look. Then he turned on his new VCR and ran the film. It was the film *Porky's*. The investigators looked at each other.

After about twenty-five minutes, he turned to them. "Okay, get ready. I'm going to play it in the slow-motion mode."

Look, he told them. It changed into a different movie. Don't you see it? He pointed to the large-screen TV. There, he said, running the film in slow motion. See it? Right there. He froze the frame. See the women being raped? See the women hung upside down and their heads cut off, one by one? He started the film again.

"See it! See them! They are killing the babies."[19]

Kenny moved closer to the television, pointing at the screen. "There," he told the investigators, "right there. Don't you see it?"

Paul moved closer to the television. "Where, Kenny? Where?"[20]

Kenny sat on the floor in front of the television. "See how it comes on? Look at the babies. Look at the babies under the porch," he told them.[21]

Kenny kept pointing. The detectives noticed he was moving quickly. Pointing. Tapping his foot. Looking around. His agitation was increasing. There had been stories about Ponte's cocaine use. It was clear to them he was high, if not on coke then on something else. The other investigators moved closer to the screen. There was nothing. Just another 1980s teenage raunchy comedy. For nearly an hour, they watched as Kenny played and freeze-framed the film, tears streaming down his face. Yeah, there may be something, they told him. We'll take the movie to be tested. It was the only way, they knew, they could get out of the house without a hassle.

Outside, the four looked at each other, stifling a laugh. Paul watched the film again that night. He played scenes in slow motion. He froze frames. Over and over. What was Kenny seeing? Was he missing something? He watched the film four times. It was just another B-grade film. Other investigators watched the film. Nothing. Boudreau filed away the incident in his mind as just another weird day as a cop.

Weeks later, Bruce Machado saw the disheveled lawyer, his tie crooked, prowling the arraignment session in district court looking to make a quick buck on a bail hearing. The detective remembers seeing him in the court, fumbling routine court matters, unsure of basic procedures and protocols. Machado remembers saying to himself, "How did this guy pass the bar exam?"[22]

Kenneth Ponte nearly didn't.

He was a familiar sight on a North End corner in the late 1960s and early '70s where drug users and dealers would hang out. By age twenty-two in 1971, after several heroin arrests and convictions for drug possession, he was jailed in the Bristol County House of Correction, the oldest operating

State Trooper Kevin Butler, far right, on the Reed Road westbound entrance ramp to Interstate 195 in Dartmouth where Andy Rebmann's dog found the remains of Dawn Mendes in November 1988 (*Standard-Times* photo by Jack Iddon)

Connecticut state trooper Andy Rebmann with his dog before starting another search in March of 1989 (*Standard-Times* photo by Ron Rolo)

New Bedford residents joined friends and relatives of the victims in a candlelight march through the streets of New Bedford in December 1988 (*Standard-Times* photo by Ron Rolo)

Chandra Greenlaw, daughter of victim Debra Greenlaw DeMello, leans out of a school bus brought to the courthouse to bring relatives back to the district attorney's office the day Kenneth Ponte was indicted in August 1990 (*Standard-Times* photo by Hank Seaman)

Crowd outside New Bedford Superior Court waiting for Kenneth Ponte to leave after he was indicted on a single count of murder in August 1990 (*Standard-Times* photo by Dana Smith)

Diane Doherty, who claimed Ponte confessed and then recanted her statement, is led from New Bedford Superior Court after testifying before a special grand jury (*Standard-Times* photo by Dana Smith)

ABOVE Trooper Kevin Butler holds a flashlight as Trooper Kenneth Martin examines the ground for evidence where the body of Robbin Rhodes was found on Route 140, this time in March 1989 (photo by Kevin Fachetti)

LEFT Hearse carrying the body of Sandra Botelho, the ninth body discovered, pulls away from the scene on Interstate 195 in Marion, Massachusetts, in April 1989 (*Standard-Times* photo by Jack Iddon)

ABOVE Teams of dogs continued
to search for more victims in 1989.
Here Massachusetts Trooper Walter
Keenan walks along Interstate 195
near Reed Road, the general area
where three bodies were found in
1988 (*Standard-Times* Photo by
Jack Iddon)

RIGHT Judy DeSantos, sister of
victim Nancy Paiva, hugs Chandra
Greenlaw, the teen daughter of
victim Debra Greenlaw DeMello,
after Ponte was arraigned
(*Standard-Times* photo by
Dana Smith)

LEFT Paul Ryley, a friend of Kenneth Ponte, is brought to New Bedford Superior Court in handcuffs to testify before the special grand jury in January of 1990 (*Standard-Times* photo by Jack Iddon)

BELOW Authorities remove the ninth body, later identified as Sandra Botelho, from the woods off Interstate 195 in Marion on April 24, 1989 (*Standard-Times* photo by Jack Iddon)

The homes of Bristol County district attorney Ronald Pina and the mother of suspect Kenneth Ponte, separated by campaign signs in 1990 (*Standard-Times* photo by Hank Seaman)

First Assistant District Attorney Raymond P. Veary Jr. (*left*) and Bristol County district attorney Ronald A. Pina at the scene where the body of Mary Rose Santos was found along Route 88 in Westport in March 1989 (*Standard-Times* photo by Jack Iddon)

The press surrounds District Attorney Ronald Pina during press conference outside New Bedford Superior Court in J 1989 (*Standard-Times* photo by Hank Seaman)

An angry Kenneth Ponte stops on the courthouse steps on his way into the courthouse where the murder charge was to be dropped to swear at a *Standard-Times* news photographer (*Standard-Times* photo by Jack Iddon)

State Trooper Jose Gonsalves walks to the scene with a bag for evidence where other investigators are examining the spot where the remains of Mary Rose Santos were found on Route 88 in Westport on March 31, 1989 (*Standard-Times* photo by Jack Iddon)

First Assistant District Attorney Raymond P. Veary Jr. walks along Route 140 in Freetown in the distance as a state trooper takes photo of the scene in March 1989 where the body of Robbin Rhodes was found (*Standard-Times* photo by Jack Iddon)

Trooper Ken Candeias talks with divers John Garcia and Jay Faulkner as they search a small waterway near Interstate 195 in Marion after the body of Sandra Botelho was found in April 1989 (*Standard-Times* photo by Ron Rolo)

jail in the country. He was sentenced to six months, served three, and was out by 1972.

His family was prominent in the way local people are who stay put and work in the community. His father was once the veterans' agent in the city, his mother worked at local businesses, and they had raised three children. They were connected the way everyone can be in a small city: local politicians were neighbors, high school friends, or members of the same Catholic parish. They were a respectable middle-class family with a son who, as folks would whisper with shaking heads at the time, "was on drugs." Drug addiction — and heroin addiction in particular — wasn't openly discussed in polite society at the time. Few admitted the opiate snared the children of the well connected or middle-class parents in the city or surrounding suburbs. It was still considered a drug of the street, and the difficulty in shaking its hold was still misunderstood by many. Kenny Ponte's family was rooting for him to succeed once he was released from jail, and it seemed to work.

To all appearances, he was turning his life around after getting out of jail. He went to Bristol Community College, and in 1974, while still in community college, he asked the state to wipe his record clean and give him a pardon. "My record represents a barrier towards fulfilling my goal of attending law school," he wrote on the application. His probation officer agreed, noting the conviction was due to Kenny's past drug problems. "During that time he became deeply involved in the local drug scene and ultimately became a very obvious addict," the officer wrote in a letter, supporting the pardon. A state representative at the time, George G. Mendonca, also recommended the pardon be granted, telling the Advisory Board of Pardons in 1974 that Kenny had "done an outstanding job in rehabilitating himself." He got the pardon.

Things in his life were changing. Drug addiction seemed to be in his past. He graduated from Southeastern Massachusetts University in nearby Dartmouth, later renamed UMass–Dartmouth, and earned a master of arts degree in public administration from Suffolk University in Boston by 1977. Two years later, he was working as a law clerk in the office of attorney Norman R. McCarthy Jr. in Westport. By 1980, he was awarded a degree from the New England School of Law and admitted to the bar the following year. Drug addiction and the streets appeared to be receding in the rearview mirror of his life.

Now, less than four years after graduating law school, it appeared this new life was unraveling.

Paul Boudreau, the New Bedford detective, had wondered as he watched the *Porky's* film for the fourth time that night in 1984 how far gone the lawyer was and if he could ever recover.

WHILE BOB ST. JEAN tried to get more information from Kenny Ponte, other investigators in late November and early December of 1988 were still trying to identify the remains found along Route 140 in Freetown and Interstate 195 in Dartmouth. Clothing discovered scattered near the remains found in November by the Department of Public Works crew on the Reed Road entrance ramp on westbound side of Interstate 195 in Dartmouth appeared to match that of Nancy Paiva, the thirty-six-year-old mother who disappeared in July. The height and body frame appeared to also match Nancy's description. The next step was to bring in her family to identify the clothing.

Judy DeSantos and her two nieces, Jill and Jolene, were apprehensive as they were led into the prosecutor's conference room where clothes were neatly placed on a table late one December afternoon. A London Fog jacket. A purple tank top. Underwear. Two jackets. Three stud earrings — one solid gold, two with a chip of blue topaz. Socks.

Is this how you identify the missing, Judy wondered. *Is this how it ends? With a few articles of clothing stretched out on a conference table?*

Troopers Jose Gonsalves and Maryann Dill waited next to Judy and the girls.

"Do you recognize any of this?" Jose asked.[23]

Judy pointed to the London Fog jacket.

It was one her sister used to wear. It had been their mother's.

Jill looked at the earrings and fought back tears. Two of the earrings, the ones with the December birthstones, had belonged to Jill's own young daughter and the gold stud to her mother's grandmother. Her mother always wore them. Jill thought it was her mom's way to always keep her family close.

"My mother used to wear it," she whispered to the state troopers, pointing to the earrings.[24]

The underwear?

"My mother's," Jill answered softly.

The sweatshirt?

"My mother's," she answered again.

Her sister, Jolene, looked hard at the troopers. She wanted to see her mother. Her family and the troopers could hear her voice beginning to crack.

It can't be done, the troopers told the teen.

Jill could hear anger, frustration, and grief in her sister's voice.

"Show me my mother," Jill heard her repeat.[25]

It's not possible, the troopers told her gently.

The investigators knew that the girls needed to hold tight a living image of their mother, not the haunting image of a dead body after four months of being exposed to the elements.

Did your sister have a partial plate? Judy was asked.

"Not that I know of."

The troopers looked at the girls.

"I don't think so," Jill answered.

The troopers pressed them again.

Were they sure?

Judy was puzzled. Why were they asking this? Didn't they have her sister's dental charts?

"No, at least I don't think so," Judy said. "No, I'm pretty sure she didn't."

She told the troopers they should check her sister's dental records. Earlier, she had told Detective John Dextradeur who Nancy's dentist was. The records must be somewhere, she told them. Wouldn't they know right away if the records matched? Isn't that how things were done?

The troopers looked at each other then made a mental note to check if any dental records had been given to the office. Then they quickly explained why they brought the three into the office. The clothing on the table before them had been found on Interstate 195, near one of the bodies, the troopers told them. Judy knew what that meant. Nancy's daughters tried not to. The now eighteen-year-old Jill Paiva could feel her mind go blank as the troopers spoke. This wasn't happening. This is a dream. A bad dream. This is not real. She could hear her younger sister's voice in the background. She couldn't tell if Jolene was crying or yelling or both. The troopers' reassuring voices were verbal Muzak to her.

Jill focused on the gold earrings on the table, the ones her mother always wore. She could see her mother in her mind's eye, the jewelry in her earlobes. She could see her mother's smile. If she thought hard enough, she could imagine her mother's voice.

Jill kept her eyes on the earrings until it was time to go.

TROOPERS MARYANN DILL AND JOSE GONSALVES had wanted to talk with Nancy's girls when they came in to look at the clothes, but it was clear the youngest child was too upset. It was hard when a parent dies, even harder when it is murder. They planned to wait a couple of days to let the children try to process the possibility their mother was dead, check on the dental records, and then ask the family to come back to talk. It would not be easy for the girls, they knew. It was never easy for the children.

It was another late afternoon when Judy and her nieces returned to the state police offices to talk with investigators. Judy went into one room with Trooper William Delaney, the one called to the scene where the first two bodies were found in July: one in Freetown, the other in Dartmouth. Maryann and Jose split up to interview the girls alone. The troopers needed to know who had visited Nancy's apartment, whether the girls recognized the photos of the missing women, whether they saw anything strange, whether they heard anyone make threats. It would take a few weeks before the troopers would be able to learn at least two women who had been reported missing had stayed in or visited Nancy's apartment.

As the three left the DA's office that evening, the body on the ramp still hadn't been identified, and Nancy Paiva's family was still in that state between fear and grief. Judy could see her young nieces were trying to focus on the present, on things they could control. Jolene looked at her aunt and told her she was hungry.

Billy Delaney slipped Judy some cash. Get something to eat, he told her quietly.

Judy knew feeding the children was easy. Healing their hearts would be harder.

MARYANN AND JOSE spent the next days and weeks making sure they now had up-to-date dental X-rays for all of the missing women. A Fall River detective, Bob Miller, called about a woman from his city who was reported missing in the spring of 1988 and was last seen in New Bedford and brought over her dental records. A Falmouth detective, Bob Nolan, tracked down Rochelle Dopierala's records. They also had the records for Robbin Rhodes and for Sandra Botelho, and more records belonging to missing women from throughout New England would eventually be coming in.

At the top of their list was getting the dental X-rays belonging to Nancy Paiva. Handwritten dental charts for Nancy dated 1983 had been forwarded to the state police offices, as Judy believed, but the exact date that was done was unclear. However, a forensic dentist had done a preliminary comparison sometime in October of 1988, three months after Nancy went missing. The finding: there was a possibility Jane Doe No. 2, found on Interstate 195 on July 30, might be Nancy, but the dentist couldn't be positive since, unlike X-rays, handwritten dental charts aren't always accurate for identification purposes and can be misleading: sometimes things are entered on the chart wrong; sometimes a person goes to another dentist and additional, and extensive, dental work is done. When the information about that preliminary identification by the forensic dentist was forwarded to the state police was unclear; neither was it clear why Maryann and Jose were not made aware of the information earlier. However, even if the troopers had been aware of the information, it would not have been enough to make a positive identification. To confirm the preliminary finding from the dental charts, Jose, in the days following when the clothing was identified, tracked down Nancy's most recent dentist to see if he could obtain her X-rays for comparison. The dentist Nancy had gone to in 1983 who had completed those initial handwritten charts had closed his office by that time, and Jose needed to learn if Nancy had gone to a new dentist sometime after the old charts were done. He prayed X-rays were taken — and those prayers were answered. The new dentist not only had Nancy's full dental records — those records also included X-rays taken just three months before she went missing. They would now know for certain if that was Nancy's body that was found on the ramp on November 8, where her clothes were discovered, or if the remains found at the end of July were hers, as the preliminary comparison of the dental charts suggested. Jose was taking no chances. He picked up the records personally.

The body on the ramp, where Nancy's clothing was scattered, was not Nancy Paiva, a comparison of the X-rays and the teeth showed.

What the comparison later confirmed was that the remains found on Interstate 195 on July 30, 1988, the day Judy was returning home from the pool and saw a line of police cars along the highway, were those of Nancy Paiva.

By the end of December, three more bodies, in addition to Nancy's, would have names.

FOR MONTHS, Judy had stayed focused on finding her sister, keeping her family together, and trying not to let the stress influence her performance at work. She felt like a juggler on a high wire, keeping different aspects of her life in the air, trying not to let anything fall. She couldn't fall. She didn't have a safety net below.

Throughout the summer, people had called her to say they saw Nancy. One person claimed to see her in a bar in the South End, another at a club in the North End, yet another saw her walking in the West End. Judy bounced around the city, trying to follow up on the sightings. Judy was surprised at the strength she was finding within herself. She would walk up to strangers, ask them questions and demand answers. She would go into darkened bars she once feared — usually with a friend, of course, she wasn't that brave yet — to follow up potential leads. Now, after seeing the clothing stretched out on the conference table at the DA's office, the chance that Nancy would return alive seemed to be slipping away. Judy couldn't keep the images of her sister's clothes on the table out of her mind. She stared at the typewriter at work and fought back tears. Judy the introvert was slowly channeling her sister's strength.[26]

IT WAS DECEMBER, soon after Nancy Paiva's family had identified her clothing, and New Bedford detective John Dextradeur wasn't feeling well. A year earlier, he was told his heart wasn't in the best of shape and that he needed to be careful. There was a history of heart trouble in his family, he knew, and the stress of the job was getting to him. Smoking also didn't help. He spent months trying to convince people there might be a serial killer in the area after he noticed a number of people had gone missing. The chief investigator for the district attorney, Robert St. Jean, and Trooper Jose Gonsalves seemed to take notice, and he was pleased to see search dogs were brought in to comb the highways. But the case still didn't seem to be moving fast enough for John. More could be done, he thought. In the meantime, he was feeling sort of "off." He felt tired most of the time, even after a good night's sleep. He suspected it might be his heart. He knew he wouldn't live to collect his pension if he continued at this pace and stayed on the job much longer. That's what he told his son, Chris, who was attending the police academy to become a cop. He also told him not to worry if he was rushed from the station with chest pains.[27] Better to have a suspected heart attack on the job rather than at home.

Then it happened, midday on the job in a nearly empty detective-division office, the time when most of his colleagues were out in the field.

Detective Richard Ferreira looked up from his desk in the check-and-fraud division office where he was banging out yet another report on the typewriter and saw his longtime friend in the adjoining, violent-crime office trying to stand. You all right, buddy? Richie asked, walking toward the desk.[28]

John looked pale. He seemed uneasy on his feet and appeared woozy. He was having difficulty breathing. I just need to get out of here, he answered.

Richie loosened his friend's tie and collar and helped him to a nearby conference room. The captain, Carl Moniz, came in, took one look at his detective, and called for an ambulance.

That was the last day John Dextradeur would work as a detective. He would be off the job on sick leave for months and then, on May 28, 1989, he would officially retire with a full disability pension due to his heart issues. He was forty-seven.

On the day the man who helped launch the massive murder investigation left the police department in an ambulance, six bodies had been found. By the time John officially retired, that number would grow to nine.

JUDY COULD FEEL her hands shaking as she took deep breaths sitting at her desk at city hall. The day before, the troopers — Maryann and Jose — told her they would know by today for sure if one of the bodies found on Interstate 195 was that of her sister. She knew part of the answer: Nancy was dead. Nancy would never leave without her children. If she did, she would make sure the girls were safe with family or close friends. She would never miss the girls' birthdays. She would never just *not* call. And then there was the clothing she saw, neatly spread on the table in the prosecutor's office for identification. The clothes were Nancy's, she knew. But the body found a few feet away from the clothing apparently was not, she was told by state police. She was told it was likely the body found in July on Interstate 195 was that of her sister. She wasn't sure why it took so long, but she was thankful she would finally have an answer.

Forensic experts hired to examine all of the remains told investigators, based on a comparison using dental X-rays, there was a nearly 100 percent chance another set of remains found in July on Interstate 195 were those of Nancy Paiva. *But what if it wasn't her?* she wondered. *What if they still didn't know?*

Judy didn't know whether to throw up or cry. She was nervous. She was scared. She was sad. Today she would have an answer. Maybe. But first she needed to get through this day at work in the election office. The work-day — in at eight, out by four — gave her a sense of normalcy. There would be lunch, there would be a break, there would be people coming in. Work to be done. It could be just another day. Her coworkers knew Judy's sister was missing and knew she considered the office her refuge from the reporters looking for interviews. The office — and work — created a protective blister for eight hours, five days a week. Today, though, she didn't tell her coworkers why she was so anxious. To do that, she would have to face a truth she still didn't know. And she was afraid she would cry. Judy was a stoic type. Tears are best kept hidden and fears confronted. But today, she wasn't sure she could do either.

She told the troopers to wait until she wrapped up work and then meet her at the office at city hall to talk. There were too many people at her house, too many children, too many reporters circling the neighborhood waiting to see if her family is one of the unlucky — or is it the lucky? — ones to be visited by the state police.

Judy was dreading this day. For the last five months, in her mind at least, her sister was alive. She could imagine Nancy popping up on her doorstep, asking where her kids were. Jill and Jolene would run up to their mother and hug her. They would cry, then laugh. Judy would ask where she had been. She would yell at Nancy for taking off — maybe. She knew it was an unlikely scenario. She knew her sister would never leave her girls like this. But she didn't want to think of her sister as dead. She had to pretend the unlikely had happened. She could pretend Nancy was coming back. All this was possible yesterday. All this was possible this morning. All this was possible as Judy sat at her desk, waiting for the end of her workday. Part of her wanted to stay at work. Here, at her desk, there was a routine. She knew what to expect. When she left today, she would be stepping off an emotional ledge. She just hoped there was something to catch her.

Nine people had been living in Judy's five-room apartment since her sister disappeared: Judy, her husband, her four children, and Jill and her two children. At one point it briefly had been ten, but two months earlier Jolene moved back in with an aunt on her father's side.

Her niece Jill, however, was getting tired of the cramped living. After searching for an apartment, the young mother finally found one in the city's South End. Jill was determined to be in her own place for her daughter's second birthday and insisted on moving out the day before. *Stay one more day,* Judy asked her. *Just one more day.* She didn't say why. What if the troopers told her they still hadn't found Nancy? What good would it do to put her sister's children through more agony?

Judy looked at the clock. It was four o'clock. Time to leave.

Maybe it wasn't Nancy. Maybe it really was a big mistake. Maybe she really did just take off. Maybe.

Judy grabbed her purse, bolted from the office, and then out the front doors of city hall. If no one says Nancy is dead, then she isn't. If the troopers hadn't come to city hall, if they weren't even waiting outside, it will all be good. She will yell at her sister for putting them through these months of hell. She will yell after she hugs her. She walked faster through downtown. One step closer to home. One step closer to life staying in limbo. One step closer to believing Nancy was alive.

The unmarked cruiser pulled alongside her. She stopped, afraid to turn.

It was Maryann Dill and Jose Gonsalves.

Judy pulled open the rear door and got inside.

We're so sorry, Maryann began.

The forensic dentist made the final confirmation using the dental X-rays Jose tracked down. The body found on Interstate 195 in Dartmouth on July 30, that hot day Judy drove by with her family and saw police on the side of the road, that day she insisted her sister was found, was officially identified. It was Nancy-Lee Paiva, thirty-six, mother of two. The intense heat of that

July summer had left Nancy's body so decomposed it appeared she had been out there for months, not weeks.

Judy sat quietly in the back seat. She couldn't cry.

"Where do you want us to take you?" Jose asked. "Who do you want to tell first?"

It was important to notify everyone in the family and close friends quickly. The district attorney planned to officially announce news of the identification the next afternoon. No one wanted relatives to find out through media reports. First on the list were Nancy's two girls.

The troopers spent the next two hours with Judy, making stops at two apartments: one in the South End to notify Jill, the second to United Front Homes to notify Jolene.

Jill remembers how surreal it was to have Judy and the two troopers standing in her apartment, saying her mother's body was officially identified. "I was a little bit relieved and confused. I was like not thinking it was real," she recalled.[29]

An hour later, Judy and the investigators pulled up to the apartment where Jolene — then fourteen — was living with her paternal aunt, Linda Spinner.

The three spotted Jolene getting out of Linda's red Mustang.

Linda didn't give it much thought when she saw the unmarked cruiser out of the corner of her eye as she drove into the parking lot. An unmarked state police car was a common sight at United Front Homes. Then she saw the cruiser stop. Then she saw the two troopers she knew get out. Then she saw Judy. And she knew.[30]

A day earlier, Jolene helped string Christmas lights around the living room window with her fifteen-year-old cousin, Jon, and her aunt Linda. It was something Linda encouraged her to do to get in the Christmas spirit, to forget her mom was missing. For that moment, as they strung lights, it was just a Merry Christmas.

"Jolene, I need to talk with you," Judy called, as she walked from the cruiser.

There, in the parking lot of United Front Homes, the teen was told her mother was dead.

Maryann Dill would later describe the scenes as heartbreaking. "I remember the girls as just being so young," she recalled.[31]

Throughout the night, calls went out to family and friends.

The next day, the district attorney would announce it to reporters.

"Then the floodgates opened," Judy recalled.

Reporters camped out in front of Jolene's school, and outside the homes of Linda Spinner and Judy. They tracked the women to their workplaces. The phone calls were incessant. It was hard to grieve amid the news noise.

IT WAS LIKE MOST of the tenements in the close-packed Broad Street neighborhood in Fall River: well kept and freshly painted, with the storm windows that pinch the fingers when you open them. It was a neighborhood of people who worked hard in the shops, who went to the neighborhood church, where families gathered for Sunday dinners. It was an ordinary neighborhood with ordinary people living ordinary lives.

Night had already fallen when Maryann and Jose walked up the stairs and knocked on the door. They were recently given the name of yet another woman who went missing and, with the name, were able to match her fingerprints with one set of remains. For five months, the first victim found along the highway had remained unidentified. Until now. Debra Medeiros, twenty-nine, of Fall River, left the New Bedford home she shared with her boyfriend and his family in May after an argument and never returned. Her mother reported her missing to Fall River police a month later. Her body, like that of Nancy Paiva's, was skeletal when found, erroneously leading authorities to believe she had been dead much longer than she was.

The troopers knew the background of Debra Medeiros. She had been arrested for drugs, was in jail at one point, and had been in and out of local rehab programs. Freetown detective Alan Alves would later say she was once one of his informants. She had been staying on Liberty Street in New Bedford, within a three-block radius of where two other victims lived. She likely knew some of the other missing and dead women. She could have known their friends. She could have known her killer. All this, they would be looking into later. At this moment on December 8, 1988, however, they had a more important task.

The door opened.

"I'm sorry," Jose told Debra's mother, Olivia Medeiros.[32]

In the apartment, another daughter was there to comfort her.

"If she had died from a heart attack or overdose I think I could handle it," the mother later told a reporter, Carol Lee Costa-Crowell from the *Fall*

River Herald News. "But this, this, it's amazing how many sick people are out there. I hope she didn't suffer."[33]

IT WAS A WEEK before Christmas, and most houses along the street paralleling Route 28 in South Yarmouth glimmered with holiday lights. Jose and Maryann pulled the unmarked cruiser onto a side street and into the darkened driveway of the small Cape Cod–style home. The two had spent the few days after the most recent body was found in the Dartmouth gravel pit talking with an ever-growing list of people with snippets of information that went nowhere. The medical examiner determined the cause of death of the woman as strangulation, and a forensic dentist had positively identified the remains as that of Rochelle Dopierala.

All that was left was notifying loved ones, in this case Rochelle's mother, and this was the hardest part of the job.

In this moment, before the knock at the door, the troopers knew that, for the family, the missing woman was still thought of as being alive. The months-long purgatory of uncertainty provided a shred of hope. This potential nightmare of not knowing could give way to an implausible dream. The family of someone who went missing faced a desperate need for an answer mixed with the dread of learning the truth.

The troopers paused in the cruiser, the engine idling in the cold Cape Cod air. Then, the two got out and walked to the front door.

Jose got there first and knocked. The door opened. He could see the look of recognition and pain in the eyes of Rochelle's mother. He had seen it too many times in his years on the state police.

State troopers know from experience what to say when they notify someone about a death. Too many times they've had to knock on doors to tell a family about a fatal crash. They learn quickly. Prepare for the unexpected. Be gentle. Be caring. But in that moment, before the door opens, before a parent of one becomes childless, before a wife or husband becomes a widow or widower, there is often that flutter of unease. Troopers often try to figure out how a family member might react and come up with a plan to console them. It doesn't always work.

Some people collapse. Some wail. Some yell. Some are angry. Some are quietly still. But that deep, aching agony is always there in the eyes. That was what Jose could now see as he looked at the mother of twenty-nine-year-old Rochelle Dopierala on this night.

He began to talk.

I'm sorry. . . .

The woman's eyes shifted to a figure behind him.

Then she froze.

He saw her face change for a second, her eyes slightly brightening.

Maryann crossed the dim threshold behind her partner, the light from the interior finally illuminating her face.

The mother began to cry.

I thought you were Rochelle. I thought you brought her home. I thought you found her, she told Maryann.[34]

I'm so sorry, Maryann answered. I'm so very sorry.

The troopers told her Rochelle was identified as the woman found in the gravel pit in Dartmouth a few days earlier. They expressed their condolences. They asked: who could they call? Who would she like to be with? What does she need?

No one, she told them, shaking her head. No one.

The troopers knew the only person Rochelle's mother wanted on that night — no, needed that night a week before Christmas — was gone.

WAYNE PERRY opened the front door of his South Plymouth home three days before Christmas and saw the two troopers.

He knew, before they said a word, that his sister was dead.

He heard them say they were sorry. He heard them offer condolences. His sister, Debra Greenlaw DeMello, they were telling him, was positively identified as the person found dead by a cleanup crew on the eastbound Reed Road ramp in Dartmouth on November 8. It didn't come as a surprise. He knew something was wrong months earlier when his sister first missed her daughter's sixteenth birthday, a worry that increased when she didn't call on their mother's birthday.

"You hear from Debbie?" he had asked their mother several times. "It's been a while."[35]

She would shake her head. It wasn't unusual for Deb to drop out of sight for weeks but this was longer than usual.

Deb was serving time in Rhode Island on a prostitution charge in June of 1988 when she had walked from a Rhode Island prison work-release program. She was now officially considered a prison escapee, and her brother didn't really expect her to pop up at home after that. But no phone calls? No cards? Not even a quick call to ask for money?

And then those bodies kept cropping up along the highways outside New Bedford, about forty-five minutes from Providence. One after another. He worried — no, he knew—one would be his sister. That was why he called the district attorney's office a few weeks earlier to see if anyone had checked to see if one of the women might be Deb. He hoped someone would dismiss the idea right off. We know who they all are, he wanted them to say. We know it is not your sister. The trooper on the phone — Jose Gonsalves — was polite when Wayne called that day to give Deb's description.

Wayne was ready to hang up when he remembered something else. The trooper had asked earlier if she had any broken bones or anything else that could identify her. Wayne at first didn't think so. But now, as he prepared to end the conversation, it came back: that time when his sister was in the women's prison in Framingham, Massachusetts, she got hurt in a fight or a fall.

"There was another thing," Wayne told him. "She broke her wrist when she was in Framingham."

He heard the trooper's voice change.

Did he know which wrist? Wayne was asked.

Wayne knew at that moment, just before he hung up the phone, his sister would not be coming home.

FLASHING BACK A YEAR to December 1987: Christmas was less than a week away, and Debra Greenlaw DeMello felt a crushing emptiness. Debra was spending the holiday in a women's prison in Rhode Island, serving a twenty-one-month sentence on a charge of loitering for the purpose of prostitution. Two of her children were living with her mother; a third was living with the extended family of a former lover. Her mother, brothers, and sisters lived more than an hour and a state away. She made, then broke, promises to her family and disappointed her children — all to chase the high that had first snared her more than a decade earlier. It was a high that was never as good as the first time, an elusive high she could never quite "catch" again. There were just the lows. This is what a life of heroin got her: a cell in a state prison and a fractured family. She knew how she got there. She now wished she could have chosen differently so many years earlier.

Debra once tried to explain to her mother how tight a grip heroin had on her, how hard it was to stop using. "I hope you see in your heart that I am just a weak person who couldn't seem to take control of her life," she wrote in a letter dated August 5, 1982. "Herion [*sic*] is a dangerous enemy it makes you completely helpless in life even after the withdrawals are gone. The anger part starts again it's the need to be high that destroys all thoughts all good intentions of wanting to stay straight."

Debra knew her addiction led to missing so many milestones in her children's lives: the first day of school, school plays, birthdays, reading a bedtime story. There were times she wasn't even sure what her children looked like. Five years earlier, when her son, Justin, was two, and daughter, Chandra, was nine, she was in the women's state prison in Framingham, Massachusetts, the only lockup for women in the state. It had been a while since she had seen the children and wondered how they were faring. She wrote a letter to her mother, asking about her toddler son. "Is he talking a lot? Is he fat?" She added a p.s. at the bottom: "Ma, does Justin still remember me? HUG Chandra for me!"

Debra tried, really tried, to stay straight at different points in her life. She went to Narcotics Anonymous meetings, she cycled through detox programs, she turned to God. Each time, heroin was always stronger than she was.

Now, at age thirty-five, after testing positive for the virus causing AIDS, she feared she was seeing the end of her life before she could make amends, before she could really live, before she could prove she really loved. The month of December 1987 had started on a high note in prison: she got new glasses and, after some teeth were pulled, she was finally getting fitted for dentures. "All I wanted for Xmas was my two front teeth and got them all. Ha-ha!" she wrote her mom. She drew a smiling face beneath the note in teenager-like flowery handwriting. Deb was trying to stay upbeat, despite her medical issues. She expected to be paroled in four months and had repeatedly promised her mother that this time, really, things in her life would be different. Her outward optimism, though, began to crack as the weeks stretched on and the side effects surfaced from the antiviral drug AZT, or azidothymidine, she was taking to stall the advance of AIDS. She first worried how she would be able to pay for this cutting-edge and expensive treatment — which cost between $8,000 and $10,000 a year at the time — once she was paroled. Then she noticed her hair falling out. She began to forget things. She was frightened. She didn't want to die. There was a strong chance she would — and it likely would be in the next two years. In the 1980s, the death rate for those with AIDS was high as researchers scrambled to find "drug cocktails" to combat the virus and increase lifespans. Just 15 percent of people with AIDS survived five years after being diagnosed, New York City researchers found in 1987. The average intravenous drug user lived about a year and a half after being diagnosed.[36] Debra likely wasn't aware of the death-rate numbers but she could feel her body wasting away behind bars. "I've killed time, squandered it, lost days, weeks, years. Now, I know there is a limit, an end, and I'm just reaching out now to save the very life I've destroyed," she wrote in one letter.

As Christmas neared, she finally told her family she had been put on AZT. "Not to be a downer at all. I'm OK really. Just a little scared," she wrote in one letter.

She tried to downplay her fears of dying as she reached out from behind bars. "I am alive, I am here now and want to have some kind of family again," Debra wrote. "I'm trying, I really am, and I am afraid whoever doesn't know I love them may never know."

Her gifts to her family for Christmas 1987 were poems and expressions of love, hope, contrition, and thanks. "I never meant to cause you sorrow or pain and when I did I caused myself even more but my dear family I do love you, all of you, if I could give you anything for Christmas this year it would be just some of me and to tell you to look around at each other and see how much you truly have. Nobody ever knows how much they have till it's no longer there," she wrote in a December 17, 1987, letter sent to her mother and addressed "Dear Family."

She included in the envelope individual letters to her siblings, written in flowing cursive. "You are: someone I'm delighted (always) to see. Someone who is welcome to what I have," she wrote to one brother.

To another, she wrote: "You've sheltered me from the cold when need be and I hope you see I'm the same little sister in heart I always was." To a sister, she asked for forgiveness: "At this holiday season I wish for you wonderful things and the big one a little if not a lot of forgiveness. I'm not always able to give 'cause sometimes I'm empty inside and even when I want to give to say, hey, I love you, sometimes I can't find the key to the door and then when I do, sometimes there's nothing there."

In four months, she expected to be paroled and planned to return to Brockton, Massachusetts. She would be in a drug-treatment program for women, she would be near her children, and she would finally have the life she promised her family for so many years. She would make it all up to everyone, especially her mother. She would prove her mother's faith in her all these years was not lost.

"You are my mom . . . My friend . . . My buddy . . . My Lifeline . . . I throw the rope you've never thrown back and anchor!" she wrote her mother in an early Christmas letter.

While others counted down the days to Christmas in 1987, Debra Greenlaw DeMello was counting down the days to her parole date.

For her children, Christmas of 1987 was a time of new beginnings and hope.

Seeing mom in the time leading up to Christmas of 1987 meant a long car ride to a different state and sitting in a prison visiting room with lots of other people. The visiting room was nice, as far as a prison visiting room could be. There were long tables and chairs, and fourteen-year-old Chandra Greenlaw could sit next to her mother if she wanted. That was a good thing about the women's Adult Correctional Institution in Rhode Island. If she looked at the room a certain way, Chandra could almost convince herself they were meeting in a school cafeteria. Except for the guards at the doors. And the security checkpoints to get in. Overall, though, it wasn't too bad. As far back as she could remember, Chandra and her little brother, Justin, trekked to county jails and state prisons to visit their mother. She suspected her grandmother was relieved when her mom would get locked up. At least then her mom wouldn't be on the street, wouldn't be using drugs, wouldn't be at risk of overdosing. They would know where she was. It wasn't ideal, of course. After all, who wants to go to a prison to see your mom? But that was what Chandra and Justin always did with their grandmother. It was just part of life.

Chandra's grandmother, Madeline Perry, got custody of two of her three grandchildren once it was clear Deb was using drugs heavily — and heroin in particular. Madeline Perry was a strong, no-excuses woman. A widow, she raised six children, took care of her terminally ill father for more than a year and was intent on making sure Deb's children didn't get lost in the foster-care system. When she first got word all those years ago that Deb was holed up in a decrepit Brockton apartment on North Warren Avenue with four-month-old Chandra, doing drugs 24–7, Madeline Perry stepped in swiftly. According to family lore, Madeline and her son, Brian, crept up to the back of the house and Brian crawled through a window, snatching the infant from the back room. No one in the apartment noticed until much later, and by that time Madeline had her infant granddaughter safely at home.

Chandra believed her mom tried over the years to get straight — and a few times she briefly succeeded. She remembers her mother's wedding at St. Edward's Church in Brockton when she was about eight. Her mother looked like a princess in the beautiful white veil and gown of satin *peau de soie* accented with lace and seed pearls.[37] That's what she would always remember: that soft-focus image. The wedding portrait would hang for years in the hallway of her grandmother's apartment, a daily reminder of what might have been.

As a child, Debra was a mischievous blonde with pigtails and never one to back down, her older sister, Gail, would later say. She began hanging around with what her brother, Wayne, called "the wrong crowd" in her early teens, but when the family moved from the city of Brockton to the suburbs of Raynham about fifteen minutes away, everyone thought things would improve. Instead of doing drugs with kids in a city, she was doing drugs with kids with money, her mother once said. "She got started on drugs with the people that some would call the better-class families," Mrs. Perry recalled.[38]

Debra's mother would track her down and bring her home. They went to counseling sessions and she searched out programs — any programs — that might help her daughter. Over the years, Debra was in and out of halfway houses and the few treatment programs available for female addicts at the time. Mrs. Perry sought out meetings with other parents, hoping to find a solution. It always ended the same: Debra would get clean then would use again. It was a heart-wrenching cycle.

By the time Chandra was born, the family had moved back to Brockton and settled into one of the low-income housing developments in the city. Chandra called the development "the projects." Her grandmother, who was very active and respected in the tenant association, preferred the term "housing development."

Over the years, Debra tried to stay in her children's lives as best she could, but drugs always seemed to pull her away. Sometimes she stayed with the children at her mother's house. Sometimes she would come by for a quick visit. Sometimes she came looking for money. Sometimes she just vanished from their lives. Madeline Perry mothered her daughter's children, just as she mothered her own. She soothed their disappointments when Deb didn't show up. She was their anchor.

Shortly before Christmas of 1987, Madeline Perry loaded the kids into her blue Chevy Cavalier and drove the fifty miles to the women's prison in Cranston, Rhode Island. It was visiting day, and it was a chance for the children to see their mother for the holidays. Mrs. Perry hoped, maybe, this time it would be different when her Deb was released. She was on a work-release program, was doing well, and there was the hope she might be paroled to Massachusetts in a few months. But there was a major hurdle to be cleared first: she needed to get into a residential treatment program in Massachusetts, and the openings for women in those programs were few. She might have to stay in prison until there was an opening.

Chandra wasn't aware of any of those intricacies of her mother's life as she sat there in the state prison, staring at her mother in the visiting room. Her mother's long hair was cut short and she had put on some weight. She looked healthy, Chandra remembers thinking as she listened to her mother talk that day.

Her mom was clearly proud. At age thirty-five, she was finally a high school graduate. She passed the General Education Development test — or GED — during her latest stint behind bars and was clutching the high school equivalency certificate in her hands.

It's an early Christmas present, her mother was saying, handing it to Chandra's grandmother.

Chandra could tell her mother was pleased with what she had accomplished and so was her grandmother. Her mother was also chatty this visit. Deb told her daughter not to do drugs — ever. She made dumb choices, Debra said. Don't make the same mistake. If she made parole, as she expected in the upcoming months, she would eventually live with them in Brockton. They could start fresh. She would do better. She would do it this time.

Chandra heard some of those promises before. She'd heard a lot of promises from her mom over the years. This time, though, it felt different. *Wow,* she thought. *This time I'm actually going to get a mom.*

Chandra kept that thought in mind on the hour-plus ride back from Rhode Island and for the months that followed — *it will be different.*

Six months after Christmas, it all changed.

Madeline Perry tried to steel herself when the collect call came from the Rhode Island prison. There would be no parole, her daughter was telling her through tears. She would not be coming home. She tried. She tried so hard. She studied and got her high school equivalency diploma. She followed the rules. She worked hard at her work-release job at a Providence warehouse. Why wasn't it enough? Why wouldn't they let her come home? The Rhode Island parole board had agreed to parole her and let her move to Massachusetts if authorities there supervised her. But the Massachusetts parole board refused, saying Debra needed to come up with a better plan for life outside. The big stumbling block was drug treatment: she needed to first get into a residential treatment program in her hometown of Brockton before she could be paroled. There were no openings.

Madeline consoled her daughter. It will be okay. There will be an opening at a treatment program. Don't worry. You will be home soon. Don't worry, she told her. But, deep inside, Madeline was worried. Her daughter had seemed determined to finally get clean, to change, to finally be a mother. This last time behind bars seemed to be the turning point. Maybe it was age. At thirty-five, running the streets had lost its allure. She was tired of the drug life. It destroyed her relationship with her children, her mother, her siblings. It destroyed her health. It destroyed her looks. Debra Greenlaw DeMello had once been a long-haired stunner, with a bright smile and an easy laugh. But that was before drugs, before the rough life running the streets. By the time she was arrested in Providence and sent to prison, her cheeks were sunken, her eyes dark, and her body rail thin. Her lips folded in, giving her a toothless appearance. She looked like a hag in her mug shot. Even Deb didn't recognize herself.

Madeline Perry tried to stay upbeat as she talked with her daughter on the phone. It will work out, she kept saying. It will work out. She wasn't sure Deb believed her. She wasn't sure she believed it herself.

A few days later, Debra Greenlaw DeMello went to work as usual at the Providence warehouse. Then she walked away.

It was June 18, 1988.

In the weeks that followed, Debra would make her way to New Bedford, Massachusetts, a city she knew from the days when she was married and lived in the neighboring small town of Acushnet. One woman said she met Deb on Hazard Street in New Bedford right after she escaped. They talked about going to Florida, she said Deb called her "sis," stayed with her at an abandoned Mount Pleasant Street house, and used the ID belonging to a friend named "Anne." Deb bounced from house to house during that time, borrowing clothes from other women. One person remembers seeing her in New Bedford in late June or early July. She likely crashed at an apartment on Morgan Street. She likely spent time with Nancy Paiva. She most likely started using drugs again.

Her family learned she was an escapee a few weeks after she walked off. They never heard from her while she was on the run.

Now, six months later, her family would know why.

ARMED WITH DEB'S NAME and description, the state police working out of the district attorney's office were able to obtain dental records from the Rhode Island state prison to positively identify the remains that had been found in Dartmouth on November 8. The dental X-rays had been taken one year earlier, shortly before Christmas. The X-rays detailed what Deb had once called her Christmas present: her new front teeth.

Just days before Christmas in 1988, two troopers — Maryann and Jose — were standing at Wayne Perry's front door to tell him that his sister was dead. Wayne wondered how he was going to break the news to Deb's kids and his mother. The district attorney's office was holding off releasing the news of the identification until Monday, December 27. He had four and a half days to figure it out. He called his older sister, Gail, who had posed the question after seeing news reports about the bodies of the women found along the highways: Do you think one could be Deb? He now had the answer.

CHANDRA GREENLAW could feel the excitement growing as her grandmother drove from their inner city apartment to her aunt's raised ranch home along a rural road in East Taunton on Christmas Day. Chandra Greenlaw figured it was going to be a great Christmas. Holidays at her aunt Gail's home were always the best. There would be a house jammed with aunts, uncles, and cousins, talking and laughing. There would be dish after dish of meatballs, pasta, turkey, and chicken wings. Some people would grab a chair at the kitchen table, others balanced plates piled with food on their laps in the living room while a few braced the winter chill in the sunroom. She loved going there, and her aunt loved hosting those big, sometimes loud, always-fun family bashes.

Her maternal aunt, Gail Hardin, was one of the eldest siblings in the family. She had six children of her own and believed getting everyone together — even just for a holiday — was important. Chandra's mother was always invited and most years showed up or called, unless she was locked up. At those holiday parties — Thanksgiving and Christmas at Gail's, Fourth of July usually at Wayne's — Debbie was just a member of the family, not someone battling addiction, not the ghost in her children's lives. There was just one outburst at a party at Wayne's home in Plymouth: Debbie's son, who was a toddler and had been staying with Gail, called his aunt "mom" at a Fourth of July cookout. *He's my son,* Deb hissed at her sister. *Maybe if you were around he would know who you are,* Gail snapped back. Their voices rose, then cracked. In tears, the sisters later embraced. They had never fought like that before, Gail would later recall, and never did again.[39]

Gail put a bright smile on her face when her mother, niece, and nephew showed up for Christmas dinner. Her brother had called three days before, breaking the news of Deb's death. They agreed not to tell their mother or the kids until the day after Christmas. They would tell the rest of their siblings later on Christmas Day — after the party — or early on December 26. Everyone had kids. Bad news could wait. Gail hugged her mom, Chandra, and Justin, as the three walked in. She would not think about the next day. She would enjoy the moment. She would enjoy the living.

Gail and Wayne knew, though, that they needed to make plans for the next day. Huddling in the corner whispering, they swapped questions. Where should they be when they break the news? Who should be there? Should they tell mom alone? Who should tell the kids? How should the kids be told? How much do they say?

What are you two whispering about? Madeline Perry asked the two suspiciously.

"Nothing, mom. We're just joking around," Gail recalls answering.

For more than a month, Gail and Wayne feared their sister was one of the murder victims. They watched news reports, listened to detailed descriptions of the dead, and knew no one in the family had heard from Deb since June. They were prepared — or at least thought they were — to learn Deb was dead. Their mother had no clue.

Chandra bounced from room to noisy room Christmas Day. Each time she got closer to her aunt and uncle, they stopped talking.

Wow. There must be a big surprise coming, she thought. *I must be getting a pretty awesome Christmas gift this year.*[40]

Not seeing her mother at the party was a disappointment but not unexpected. She would probably call later, Chandra thought. Chandra had tried to shrug off that odd question her aunt Suzanne had asked a couple of weeks earlier. Did her mother have a broken wrist and did she remember which one? Chandra thought it was weird. Why would she want to know that? She recounted that exchange with her best friend in high school. Then she wondered aloud: *I think there's something wrong with my mother.* But Chandra didn't think much more about it as the days passed. Teenagers, she would later say, didn't think beyond their own little world.

As the holiday party wound down, Chandra turned to her grandmother and asked her the same question she had asked on Thanksgiving Day: Mom didn't call like she usually does. Don't you think that's strange?

THE FOLLOWING DAY was another traditional family Christmas bash, this time on Cape Cod. The family packed into the car and drove to Bourne where Chandra's uncle Brian, who didn't make the first Christmas party, would play host. Maybe that's where they'd get the big surprise gift, Chandra thought.

They had barely gotten in the door, though, when Wayne's wife, Suzanne, suggested Chandra and her cousin take a ride with her to the beach a few minutes away. *Why not?* Chandra thought.

The winter sea air was sharp as the three sat in the car parked along Monument Beach. "I have something to tell you," Suzanne Perry started. "Remember when I called you that day and you thought something was wrong. Well, there was."[41]

Suzanne continued, telling the teenager her mother was dead, one of the women found along the highways outside New Bedford.

Chandra was confused. Her mother? Dead? It didn't make sense.

Back at the house, Debra Greenlaw DeMello's brothers and sister called their mother into the living room.

Sit down, her son, Brian, told her. We have some bad news.

Madeline Perry began to cry. Was it Larry? Did something happen to Larry?

The siblings looked at each other and realized their other brother, Larry, who lived in nearby Wareham, wasn't there.

"No, it isn't Larry," Wayne recalls telling her. "It's Deb."

Madeline Perry's children surrounded her, and heard the high-pitched cry of a heart now broken.

5 THE INVESTIGATION EXPANDS

THE CONFERENCE ROOM at the Bristol County District Attorney's Office was crammed with cops. Jose recognized most of the faces: detectives from New Bedford, Dartmouth, Freetown, Providence, and, of course, the Massachusetts State Police. It was mid-December in 1988, and the case, they knew, was getting big — too big for the state police unit assigned to the office. They needed more investigative boots on the ground. They needed to tap into every source, delve into every lead, talk to both the reliable and the unreliable people who claimed to have information. And they needed to do it quickly. Most homicides are solved within forty-eight hours, when memories are fresh and evidence fresher. This was an ice-cold case in ninety-degree temperatures before anyone even knew it existed. The best witnesses were drug addicts with a hazy sense of time. The crime scenes were weathered by rain, heat, and age. Identifying the victims was difficult and laborious. If there was ever an investigative nightmare, this was it.

Bob St. Jean, the former Massachusetts state trooper who was now chief investigator for the district attorney, was sitting at the table, making the introductions, outlining what information they had — and didn't have. Could this be part of a bigger case, Bob asked the group.

He turned to the Providence detectives — Stephen Springer and Timothy O'Brien. Eight women, all but one a prostitute, had been killed in the Providence area since 1978.[1] Some were strangled. Could it be the same killer?

Four other women were killed in New Bedford, all seen leaving local bars, between 1986 and the spring of 1988. Could it be the same killer?

The men arrested for picking up prostitutes or suspected of beating, raping, or stabbing them in years past. Could one of them be the killer?

The men released from the state's treatment center for the sexually dangerous. Could one or more of them be the killer?

There were serial killings across the country, such as the Green River killings in Washington State, where forty-one women were found dumped in the woods, or the White River Junction killings on the Vermont–New Hampshire border, where nine were found dead. What about the bodies of prostitutes found near Route 8 in Waterbury, Connecticut? Could any of those cases be linked?

Is the killer a fisherman now trolling for other victims in another port? Is he dead? In jail? A truck driver picking victims in another state? Is he someone with a badge — a security guard, a prison guard, a deputy sheriff, a cop?

How should they move forward? What should be the next step? How should they coordinate what would likely be the largest, most time-consuming, and frustrating investigation in the area?

Bob St. Jean knew coordinating the investigation — and the different detectives — would be a challenge. As he looked around the room, he knew who the shirkers and the workers were. He knew some disdained the district attorney, Ronald A. Pina. He knew some of them didn't like him. He knew some police agencies played nice with others in the field and others worked in law-enforcement silos. He also knew a big part of the investigation would come down to money. The local police departments didn't have extra manpower to spare. The district attorney's office would need to come up with some overtime cash both for those working on the case and those filling in for those detectives. To solve these murders, they needed cooperation, cash, and a lot of political finesse. He hoped he could pull it off.

The biggest challenge, Bob knew, would be the district attorney. Ron Pina had a knack for picking the best and the brightest young prosecutors and investigators for his office. He had a "take no prisoners" approach to investigations, taking on high-profile drug cases that webbed through the community and state. He was funny, personable, and media savvy. But he could also have a dismissive attitude some found insulting. And he liked to talk. Some thought the district attorney talked too much and to too many people. Investigators privately worried he would turn the intricacies of an investigation into cocktail or dinner chatter. They worried who at the next restaurant table would be listening. In New Bedford someone was always listening when Ron talked.

Today, though, Bob St. Jean was staying upbeat. There might be a few on the team who wouldn't work hard, but there were other investigators who were good — no, great. They could solve this. They would solve this.

The first step would be to see what they had: what was fact, what was fiction, what was a mix of the two.

In the meantime, more information kept coming in. One woman told Freetown police that she saw a man dragging something from a vehicle parked in the breakdown lane on Route 140 northbound. Another woman told Rhode Island State Police a man driving an eighteen-wheel tractor-trailer picked her up as she walked along Belleville Avenue in New Bedford then tossed her out on Interstate 95 in Warwick, Rhode Island, just north of Route 117. She told police the man, who said his name was "Jimmy," claimed to be the highway killer. A teenaged girl claimed she was abducted, punched, and then thrown out of a car on Interstate 195.

When there was a question during the meeting, people turned to Trooper Jose Gonsalves who had some, if not all, of the answers. He had been at all but the first murder scene, had talked with most of the families, and had been spending hours each night with Maryann interviewing potential witnesses. In a level tone, Jose filled in the details about the current case, the difficulties tracking the last hours of the victims, who had been interviewed so far, what evidence — or lack of evidence — was found, the number of possible suspects. There was just one question he couldn't answer: who did it.

New Bedford detectives Richard Ferreira, Gardner Greany, and Gary Baron listened intently, scribbling an occasional note. Working with the state police on homicides was routine for them. However, this case, they knew, would stretch their investigative talents.

"We knew this was something big," Ferreira would later say. "There was a sense of excitement in the room."[2]

By the end of the meeting, each detective had a task. Look up a record, check a suspect, interview a witness. Some local detectives paired up with state troopers, a signal of interagency cooperation. They all agreed to formally meet again to go over what they found. In the meantime, each would keep in touch and share what was learned. It would be the first of what would be weekly meetings of Massachusetts investigators working the case.

Bob St. Jean left the meeting feeling encouraged. He liked the way most of the group interacted. *We can solve this,* he thought.

JUDY DESANTOS clutched the candle as she stood outside city hall, the place where she spent her working days. Tonight, she would walk with 150 others in a candlelight march through downtown to remember her sister and the other women found dead or still missing. She would walk past the district attorney's office, past the police station, and then sit for a community service in the 150-year-old Norman Gothic–style First Unitarian Church built near the top of the Union Street hill on Eighth Street.

It was a few days before New Year's Eve and her sister's remains, which had been identified before Christmas, were now being examined by an expert at the Smithsonian as part of the murder investigation. This vigil was the closest to a funeral Judy and her nieces would have for now. It was cold and it was damp outside. Judy wondered what her sister would think about all of this, whether she would have gone to a similar vigil for someone else. Would Nancy, ever the teasing big sister, be proud of her tonight?

Judy scanned the crowd. She recognized most of the faces: some were community and religious leaders, some were community activists, some were city officials. The faces she needed to see were the ones like hers, the faces of the families of the dead and the missing. There is strength in numbers. She sat back in the church pew and listened to the speakers. She was hoping for comfort; she was hoping for answers.

"I am here to say that no one deserved to be brutalized or killed," the Reverend Ulises Torres told people gathered at the service. "Some have suggested that the victims lived dangerous lives. Even if we make this assumption, we must ask the questions: Why is it so many feel compelled to resort to drugs? Why are we in the United States one of the most violent societies in the world?"[3]

Judy left that night with more questions.

NANCY PAIVA's immediate family met at the gravesite, a half dozen relatives, in the January chill at Pine Grove Cemetery in New Bedford about a week after the downtown vigil. Maryann and Jose stood a discreet distance away, watching to see who else might drive in. There had been no wake, no funeral Mass; just a cremation followed by this simple gathering with little fanfare. It was what Nancy would have wanted, her sister knew. Even this was probably more than she would have wanted. Nancy embraced the philosophy of laughing loudly, dancing freely, seeing challenges as opportunities. She didn't think of death, only life. That was the Nancy her sister would always remember. That was the Nancy she would celebrate. This service wasn't really for Nancy but for her children.

A small box adorned with a crucifix held Nancy's ashes at the grave. The gravestone of her parents was a few inches away. It had been six months since Nancy went missing and was likely killed. It had been one month since she was officially identified. It had been a long process getting to this place in the cemetery. As they stood in the cold, listening to the minister, Judy and Nancy's children felt the waves of grief they thought had long subsided.

They listened to minister from the Methodist church in Fairhaven read 1 Corinthians 13:4–7 and cried.

"Love is patient, love is kind. It does not envy, it does not boast, it is not proud. It does not dishonor others, it is not self-seeking, it is not easily angered, it keeps no record of wrongs. Love does not delight in evil but rejoices with the truth. It always protects, always trusts, always hopes, always perseveres."

MOURNERS PAUSED before the photograph of Dawn Mendes atop the silver casket at Burgo Funeral Home. Flowers surrounded the smiling image. Some made the sign of the cross. Some bowed their heads. Some wiped away tears.

Forty people gathered in the first floor of the funeral home that January 21, 1989, day as the Reverend Z. L. Grady of the Bethel African Methodist Episcopal Church spoke.

"The ordeal is now over. The body has been found and our hopes for survival have vanished," he told them.

Faith in God can help overcome the pain, he said.

"The light shines in the midst of darkness and the darkness will not put it out."[4]

THERE WOULD BE NO WAKE; Madeline Perry was adamant on the issue. Throughout her daughter's life, she had struggled to keep Debra away from drugs and drug users. Faced with her death, Madeline did not want to see the people whom she blamed for indirectly killing her child. "I don't want *those* people to show up" her children and granddaughter remember her saying. "I don't want them there."[5]

So, instead of gathering at Conley Funeral Home to say a final goodbye before the funeral, the family was sitting the morning of January 25 in the pews of St. Colman's Catholic Church on Wendell Avenue in Brockton, the same church where thousands gathered thirty years earlier for Mass after boxer Rocky Marciano was killed.

Debra's brothers escorted her simple casket into the church. Chandra and her little brother, Justin, sat stunned next to their grandmother. After Mass, the twenty-plus family and friends drove to Melrose Cemetery where Debra's final resting place was in an area of tiny flat stones. Her daughter called the spot nondescript and sad.

THROUGHOUT JANUARY the funeral rituals continued for the families of those found. In Fall River, the family of Debra Ann Medeiros gathered at Oliveira Funeral Home, while in Falmouth, the family of Rochelle Clifford Dopierala grieved. As five families buried their dead throughout the month, the families of six missing women were still waiting for answers.

Even before the fifth body was buried, Bob St. Jean was making plans to bring the Connecticut trooper Andy Rebmann and his wonder dog back to the state to look for others. Andy was also making plans to bring in additional search dogs and police handlers from throughout New England to help him. The dogs would search on the highways for victims as the state police and local investigators continued to search the streets to learn who put the women there.

MARYANN grabbed a bag of sour-cream-and-onion potato chips from the convenience-store rack and a bottle of Diet Pepsi from the refrigerator as

Jose snatched a bag of pretzel rods and a diet A & W Root Beer. It was eight o'clock, and this was what would pass for dinner tonight: junk food from the 7-Eleven on the bottom floor of the six-story brick building housing the district attorney's office. Just as they did every night, the two had a list of people to talk with and an open notebook tucked in a pocket to write down names and nicknames of anyone else who might be able help. They pushed open the glass doors and stepped into the chilly downtown street.

It was the beginning of January and, for the first time since the bodies were found along the highways, the troopers were officially on the case full-time. For months, they had still been on the on-call list, taking turns with other troopers in the homicide unit responding to murders at all hours of the day. Taking Maryann and Jose off the list meant others would have fewer weekends off, more late-night calls to murder scenes across the county, and a bigger workload. Bristol County was already a busy and diverse county—556 square miles stretching from the coastline and Rhode Island to the south and from bedroom communities less than an hour from Boston to the north. It included four cities and sixteen towns, including farming communities and wealthy suburbs. If there was an unattended death in any of those places, local uniformed officers might get there first, but the state police unit assigned to the DA's office was required by law to investigate. In 1988, the unit investigated 213 suspicious or unattended deaths, including 25 homicides. The unit also answered 422 complaints, served more than 70 search warrants, and arrested 13 people on murder charges.

Maryann and Jose knew it was tough on their colleagues when the two of them were taken off the on-call list and were glad they didn't grumble, at least within earshot. Everyone in the unit was working together, trying to get information, trying to solve what they feared might be an unsolvable case. Maryann and Jose, often joined by New Bedford detective Richie Ferreira, cruised the streets four to five nights a week tracking down street people. During the day, they made calls, went to court to find potential witnesses who were there facing criminal charges, and sorted through the tips on a case hotline set up by the district attorney. They knew other troopers and local detectives were doing the same: following up leads, and interviewing people in the county jails, state prisons, and rehab centers. Some people — or teams of people — were assigned a specific person to investigate. Members of the

Bristol County Drug Task Force were quietly asking about the lawyer Kenny Ponte who had moved to Florida and checking with Florida authorities to see what he was up to down there. One detective from Freetown, Alan Alves, inquired about any satanic cult ties to the deaths. Others were checking which fishing boats had come up from the south and when they left to see if a fisherman might be the killer. Still others checked Coast Guard records and the background of a petty officer who had been arrested with a prostitute. Everyone was searching records for known sex offenders, keeping an eye out for cars and trucks matching the descriptions of the vehicles driven by violent or kinky men who picked up prostitutes, and looking through past reports of suspicious activity on the highways.

In any homicide investigation, detectives interview acquaintances, friends, coworkers, and relatives of the victim to try to create a timeline of the person's last days and hours. They try to pinpoint who last saw the person, where the victim had been, and who might want to do the individual harm. If a suspect surfaces, detectives will check the person's alibi and, if there is physical evidence to compare, take fingerprints as well as blood and hair samples. In 1988, DNA samples were just beginning to be taken. In this murder case, there were several people of "interest" to police and different teams of investigators set out to find out as much as possible about them. Some fell quickly by the wayside. Nancy's boyfriend, Frankie Pina, was one of the first eliminated because he was jailed during part of the killing spree. Others needed a harder look.

In the highway killing case, police looked at crewmembers from out-of-state fishing boats, long-distance truck drivers, drug dealers, former and current cops, cop-wannabes, businessmen, construction workers, strike-breaker truck drivers at a nearby business, and military personnel. They looked at men who had been arrested picking up prostitutes, and they looked at the men never arrested who prostitutes said picked them up. They followed up on one tip that a guy in a bar confessed to the killings and another about a Rhode Island–based prostitution ring.

The information coming in was promising — and there was a lot of it. New Bedford detective Gardner Greany talked with a hooker who said a Rhode Island man once gripped her throat tight, saying "I could kill you right here and throw you right out of my truck." Detective Gary Baron brought up the name of a Freetown man who picked up prostitutes and was known to be violent. Trooper Deborah Bruce and New Bedford detective Richard Ferreira talked with another woman about a john who foamed at the mouth and spoke in "tongues." Trooper Kevin Butler interviewed a prostitute who got two black eyes when she was knocked out with a punch to the face then raped for nearly an hour. Trooper Kenneth Martin was keeping track of evidence and helping to interview people. And there were more, so many more, doing whatever they could to include — or exclude — suspects. For every suspect crossed off the list, two more were added. They needed to narrow the focus and broaden the investigation simultaneously.

Finding information in the late 1980s was laborious. There were few surveillance cameras. There were no smartphones. Narcotics detectives used the chirping Nextel push-to-talk radios to communicate; most of the other cops still used a handheld radio or one in the cruiser, transmitting information the public could hear on a police scanner. The daily lexicon did not include Google. There was no Twitter, no Facebook, no MySpace. People had passbook savings accounts, and canceled checks came back in the mail. Record searches were done by hand. There were major gaps in the statewide database for people wanted on warrants or reported missing. Files were sent by mail, not e-mail. Office computer systems were clunky, often slow, and unreliable. People still wrote things on yellow legal pads.

Police investigations centered on people, not technology, and that face-to-face interaction came with a price. In the six weeks since the remains of Dawn Mendes were found by the search dog in November, state police investigators worked more than a thousand overtime hours on the case, depleting the state police unit's $170,000 budget. The Bristol County District Attorney's Office added another $25,000 to the pot, but as January was coming to a close, that money was also running out.

Maryann and Jose were working, on average, about ninety hours a week. Three others in the unit were averaging about forty-five hours a week, juggling the highway killing case with other cases. Under the union contract, state police were forbidden to work overtime without getting paid. However, many of the investigators were working even longer than they were putting in for, just to get the work done. Maryanne and Jose were hoping if they worked longer, the case would be solved quicker. The payoff wouldn't be in the paycheck; it would be with justice.

With a brown bag filled with junk food, Maryann and Jose slipped into their unmarked cruiser and began the hunt anew each night.

They circled the North End, the South End, and Weld Square. They criss-crossed the narrow city limits. When they saw someone they recognized, they stopped, talked, and moved on. Sometimes they stopped people on the street they didn't recognize, hoping this new face had new information. By now the working girls knew the troopers — and just about all of the cops — by sight, if not by name. The girls no longer turned to run or walk briskly away. They now waved the cruisers over, offering tidbits from the street. They were all listening and watching and hoping. They were afraid.

One woman told them she was choked then raped months earlier by a man in a truck; another shared a similar story; yet another woman said a friend was taken to a local cemetery, then choked and raped. Women gave the names of friends who had been attacked and those friends, some now in the women's state prison, named others. Sometimes the man claimed to be a boxer and sometimes the women assumed he was. He appeared well built and had a flattened nose, the kind so many boxers sport after years of fighting. In each case, the attacks came without warning: a hand to the throat, some-times a punch, then the rape. A few of the women said the grip was so tight they blacked out. One said she thought she was going to die. One kicked her way out of the truck and ran to an apartment at a nearby housing project for help and called a friend. Another woman told friends about her attack when the man brought her back to Weld Square. No one reported the attacks to police at the time. One woman said she feared cops would arrest her instead for walking the streets. Another thought she had outstanding warrants. Yet another said she tried to tell a cop what happened and he shrugged her off.

Maryann and Jose took note of the man's description. Other troopers and city detectives on the street were hearing similar stories. Who was this man? Was he *the* man?

THE MANDATE, as expected, came down fast mid-January: No one in the state police unit assigned to the Bristol County District Attorney's Office would be allowed to work more than eight hours a day. The overtime account was dry, and the union contract forbade working without getting paid. "They are now only putting in a minimum of half of the amount of time," the district attorney's spokesman, Jim Martin, said at the time. "It is now slowing the investigation down. Until now, they have been moving full-steam ahead. Now it's taking them that much longer to get to the next step."[6]

The district attorney wanted the troopers in the unit to work different shifts to save money, a violation of the contract. Until more overtime was available, the rule was in by eight in the morning, out by four-thirty in the afternoon. Get done what you can in that time.

Jose and Maryann, as well as others, knew about the mandate. However, they couldn't just stop; the families were counting on them; the girls on the street were looking to talk with them. There was a stack of potential leads to be checked out. They would pull one thread and unravel complex stories in interview after interview. Not everything happened during daytime working hours, Monday through Friday, especially in this investigation. They still worked into the evening, trimming their hours a bit but not much. Time, they knew, was not on their side in this case.

They continued to check the streets at night, talking with the prostitutes, the drug addicts, the drug dealers, hoping to find that one thread that would solve the case.

Jose and Maryann wove the cruiser through the side streets of the city to Weld Square, just to check who was there. They weren't officially working this night, but they wanted to stay in contact with the people on the street, to stay on top of what was going on.

Jose recognized the figure walking along the sidewalk and pulled over. Jose knew the person's backstory well by now: the man took the first steps of a sex-change operation, a procedure funded by a wealthy boyfriend. When the relationship ended, so did money for the surgery. Prostitution was the quickest way to make money to finish things up, he once told Jose. Both Jose and Maryann talked many times with the man about his past and what he was seeing on the street. He was perceptive, funny, and from what they could tell, he wasn't an addict. He could make a good witness, if needed.

Jose swung the cruiser to the curb and waved the man over. Jose could see the broad smile of recognition on the man's face. Jose thought the man looked a bit different, a bit more "shapely," this night.

"Things are looking good," the man told him. "Really good. I got new boobs. Want to see them?"

Jose shook his head. "No, that's okay," he answered.[7]

The man lifted his shirt. "Look. Look. Don't they look good?"

Jose averted his eyes and kept shaking his head. "That's okay. I don't need to see them, really."

The man lowered his shirt, smiling brightly. Nothing else new on the street, he told Jose.

Jose shifted the cruiser into drive and the troopers moved on. Anything can happen on these streets. Anything at all.

WITH A RADIO STATION TAPE RECORDER at his feet, Bristol County district attorney Ronald A. Pina stood before the microphone stand with the governor at his side. Two months earlier, Governor Michael S. Dukakis lost a chance at the presidency to Republican George H. Bush and with it the Washington-bound dreams of dozens of Massachusetts politicians. Some predicted a Dukakis win would send the district attorney, always larger than the New Bedford political stage, to the nation's capital. Jobs like U.S. attorney and state attorney general were bandied about by the political gossips.

Instead of standing outside the White House, the two, hands stuffed in winter overcoat pockets, were standing outside the downtown New Bedford Free Public Library before five microphones stuck on a stand with gaffer's tape. The state was bailing out the financially depleted murder investigation.

"I can assure you we will provide the resources necessary in this investigation and that we will move forward," the governor told reporters on January 26, 1989.[8]

The state would be adding roughly $100,000 into the overtime account, money the governor said would be well spent. "We're not pouring money down any rat hole."

The money, the district attorney added, would keep the investigation moving "full speed."

A few blocks away that same day, Trooper Kevin Butler and New Bedford detective Gardner Greany were in the DA's office interviewing a woman named Violet about snuff films.

IT WAS THE THIRD TIME Violet F. Farland, who had a record for drug offenses, had been at Kenny Ponte's Chestnut Street house, and she knew what to expect. Kenny would want to shoot coke; would get paranoid and think someone was hiding behind the couch; and she would be there a really long time. Kenny didn't like the girls to leave his house, she knew. Sometimes he would bolt the doors to make sure they didn't. He would always ask the girls to shoot him up with the coke, usually in the neck. He liked the girls to strip, and sometimes he would wander around the house in his underwear. Violet once worried there was too much cocaine in the needle and syringe. "I'm not going to shoot you up with all that," she told him. "You're going to die on me."[9] He chased her around a table in the house a couple of times until she did it. He didn't seem interested in sex, just coke and company.[10] Kenny was weird and seemed a little bit lonely. Other than that, he appeared harmless.

This time, after they did the coke, Kenny wanted to watch a movie. Violet wasn't interested. She was too busy getting high. He slipped the videotape into the VCR. On the screen was a naked man who appeared to be strangling a woman with a belt.

"Kenny, will you shut that goddamn thing off," she told him.[11]

"Oh, I want you to see this," he answered.

"I don't want to see shit like that," she said.

Kenny turned it off.

It wasn't the first, or the last, time Kenny would play a porn tape depicting what appeared to be a murder, police knew.

Another woman named Jeannie Kaloshis, before she eventually kicked her drug habit, spent days on end with Kenny during the summer of 1988, doing drugs, talking, and watching movies. The movies were usually porn films brought to the house by one of his friends. Most of the films were S and M films. When she saw the film showing a man strangling a woman, she noticed the woman's eyes. It looked like the woman was dead.

THERE WAS A STACK OF VHS TAPES on Jose's desk. It was going to be a long night, he knew. He needed to watch this latest stack of porn videos as part of the highway killing investigation and try to get the tapes back to the store by morning. The videos, he knew, would be grainy and the audio scratchy. Most would be in black and white.

Watching the films was needed to prove or disprove yet another theory in the murder case. Police kept hearing vague stories about snuff films being made in the area. They were also hearing stories that area women were appearing in locally produced pornographic films. Was any of this true? And if so, were any of the victims in these films? Did Kenny know about any of these tapes? That was what police needed to know.

For months, investigators had followed rumors about "snuff films" being made in the area as well as reports that local women were appearing in pornographic movies. They wondered: Could the films — if they existed — be tied to the killings? There was one report someone was making movies with women and a pig in a local motel room; another alleged someone was making movies in his home. One prostitute said the owner of a shady Weld Square magazine store frequented by addicts gave the girls money to dance naked while he videotaped them. Another prostitute claimed someone stole a sex tape and tried to blackmail a man; the tape never surfaced, and the claims were never substantiated. As part of the homicide investigation into possible ties with the creation of porn films, the owner of a Dartmouth video business had appeared before the grand jury and handed over his business records, and several video-store owners voluntarily gave police the porn tapes from their shelves so authorities could check to see any of the victims appeared in them.

It wasn't the first time police had investigated the possibility of locally made porn tapes in the county. U.S. Customs agents helped investigate allegations in 1987 and in early 1988 that a Dartmouth business was producing child pornography. Adult videos were found, including one involving sex with animals. So were bootleg copies of popular films. But no movies involving children, one of the investigators said. No tapes involving people being killed were found either.

The stack of videos Jose now had was from the owner of a business on Bakerville Road in Dartmouth; some other videos were borrowed from a store in Fall River. Investigators would borrow roughly twenty at a time, give the owner a receipt and promise to get them back as soon as possible. Jose, Maryann, and other investigators had been reviewing the tapes for days, looking for familiar faces or places. Sometimes they fast-forwarded to the next scene to see the face. They never saw anyone being killed. There was no plot in any of the videos, just a lot of naked bodies. The films were barely watchable. Some were even boring.[12]

Jose took his stack home that night and, after dinner when the kids went to bed, plunked down on the couch in the den. He searched through one tape. Then a second. Then a third. Then a fourth. After a few hours, his wife peered into the room. He was sound asleep, remote in his hand. She woke him gently to say it was time to go to bed.

If snuff films were being made and if the murder victims were in any of them, investigators still couldn't find them.

6 IN THE CROSSHAIRS

BOB ST. JEAN strode into the waiting room of the Bristol County District Attorney's Office and motioned to the heavyset man rising from the chair. It had been decades since he had been in the same room with Kenny Ponte, the last time was probably when the now attorney was arrested in his twenties on drug charges. Bob gave him a quick scan. Kenny had put on some pounds over the years but he still had that same cumbersome look.

Let's go into the conference room, Bob suggested.

There, for a few minutes, the two talked and sized each other up before moving on to Bob's office at the other end of the building. Kenny didn't want anyone to see him there. He didn't want to talk with anyone else. Only Bob St. Jean, nicknamed "the Saint." The conversation in January 1988 in the office, like the ones on the phone, went in circles. Kenny wasn't being unhelpful, but he wasn't being helpful either. He seemed to want to mitigate his ties to the women and the drug scenes, Bob would later say. "He was looking to see what we knew, looking to cover his tracks."[1] This January meeting, the first face-to-face meeting, had a different tone though from the phone conversations. While Bob detected arrogance in Kenny's voice in the telephone calls from Florida, he thought he could hear fear and a rising anger now. Over the phone, friends in New Bedford had read Kenny the newspaper stories suggesting he was tied to the victims — or killings. One newspaper report said a search dog had taken an interest in a rug in the office. Why did police search his old office, Kenny demanded. What was this about the dog and the rug? What were they trying to do to him? Why were they doing this?[2]

Bob sat back and listened. Kenny, we think you can help us. What can you tell us about Rochelle?

Bob knew the attorney was close to Rochelle Clifford Dopierala. The Cape Cod woman had stayed with Kenny for a while, and Kenny had driven her several times from New Bedford to Cape Cod. He had waited outside a mobile home one day in April while she met with a man inside. People saw her with him.

Bob knew Kenny didn't come back to New Bedford from Florida just to talk with him. The real reason was a court case with ties to Rochelle. Nine months earlier, on April 3, 1988, Kenny was accused of pulling a gun on a guy Rochelle claimed had raped her that spring. Kenny wound up charged in district court — the court where most shoplifting, drug, and assault cases were tried — on charges of assault with a dangerous weapon. Rochelle, who had allegedly recanted the rape allegation, was supposed to be a witness. But by late April and early May, no one could find her. The case was set for trial February 27 and Kenny was back early for a pretrial court hearing — where attorneys can file additional motions and deal with other matters — in his case.

The conversation in the office continued to seesaw. Bob eased up when Kenny's voice rose. He hit hard with questions when Kenny calmed down. Up and down. Down and up. Bob wanted to know what Kenny knew. He had the feeling Kenny was there to find out what the police knew.

Kenny circled back to the search of his Dartmouth law office. Why? And why tell the press, he demanded.

Bob denied the information — credited to "sources" in the media — came from his office. The interview was not going well.

Less than a half hour after it started, the meeting was over. Bob escorted the attorney out to the back elevator.

It would be the last friendly face-to-face meeting the two would have.

The next time Kenny called, he had a simple question: Am I a suspect?

Bob had a simple answer: Yes, one of several.

Kenny hung up.

Days after the meeting in the district attorney's office, Kenny was standing in the same courthouse where Lizzie Borden had stood trial back in 1893, and a cadre of reporters were watching. A Bristol County grand jury had indicted him on the old gun case from April of 1988, a legal process which moved the case from district to superior court, and he was now being arraigned on those charges. "Not guilty, Mr. Clerk," Kenny said when the clerk read off the charges.

Moving the case to a higher court where more serious cases are tried meant, if convicted, Kenny could face a longer sentence. It also gave the district attorney a chance to ask a judge to get hair and saliva samples from Kenny.

Kenny was cooperative at first: he let a state trooper pluck hair — including the root — from his head. He allowed saliva samples to be taken. He had no problem with the fingerprints or the palm prints. But when it came to taking off his jacket and rolling up his sleeve, supposedly so police could take a photo of a tattoo, he balked. His lawyer convinced a judge to impound all of the samples — at least for now.

Bristol County district attorney Ronald A. Pina didn't give all those details when he stood on the steps of the courthouse after Kenny was arraigned on gun charges on January 18, 1989. What he did instead was intensify the media spotlight on Kenny. He said the attorney knew several of the murder victims and, when asked to assist, wouldn't cooperate in the homicide investigation.

"He refused to help us," Pina told reporters. "He had nothing to say. . . . We were hopeful we would be talking to him today."[3]

Pina claimed to reporters that Kenny originally agreed to provide samples of his hair, saliva, and fingerprints — then backed off. Investigators wanted pubic, head hair, saliva, finger, and palm prints and full-body photographs as part of the "identification" process, the district attorney insisted. Court papers filed by the prosecution would note that Kenny knew at least three of the women found dead. The prosecutor stopped short of calling him a murder suspect.

There was no DNA evidence needed in the gun case, and Kenny's attorney, Joseph Harrington, knew that. He noted, in opposing the request, that what the prosecution wanted was "far reaching." A judge later that month would agree. The saliva and hair samples would stay impounded; the prosecution could have mug shots as well as finger and palm prints. In a nine-page ruling, superior court judge George Jacobs made it clear to the prosecution: just because someone knows a person who was killed doesn't automatically make that person a suspect. "The information supplied to the court does not even amount to the articulation of a suspicion or hunch. There has been no demonstration of a need to search."[4] A layman's translation: the prosecution was on a fishing expedition.

JOSE GONSALVES was now getting worried. The district attorney was coyly tossing the name of an attorney from the city to reporters along with bits of information: Kenny Ponte may know the victims. Kenny Ponte wasn't cooperating. Kenny Ponte left the area in November. Kenny Ponte had a history of drug use. The individual bits were tossed like bread crumbs. Follow them. Wink. Where does it lead? Wink. What does he know? Wink.

This was not how Jose, or any of the investigators, liked to work. To him, it seemed like the DA developed that "tunnel vision" Jose always guarded against. Put on investigative blinders and you may miss evidence. Keep an open mind, Jose would always say. Things aren't always what you think. Jose wasn't sure why the DA was so focused on Kenny Ponte. There were other suspects, potentially better suspects, out there, men who had beaten and raped prostitutes, violent men with records, sex offenders. They were still looking at these other people. There could even be other suspects they haven't come across yet. Kenny was odd and Kenny was arrogant and he wasn't a person Jose would want to spend a lot of time with. But that didn't make him a killer. You needed proof to show that.

Jose knew that the New Bedford detective who had planted those first seeds of the investigation, John Dextradeur, considered Kenny an intriguing character who might have some type of role in the case. John, though, initially was focused on Nancy's boyfriend. Dextradeur was also out of the investigation before it really took off, and for all intents and purposes off the job — out on a job-related medical leave and headed for a disability retirement. Things can shift from the start of a case, Jose knew. A good suspect today could turn out to be an unfortunate boob with just the wrong friends or someone who was in the wrong place. Was that Kenny? There was political pressure, Jose suspected, to solve this case quickly. He hoped no one would break under it. The case against Kenny Ponte was just one part of the investigation. They couldn't get sidetracked. They couldn't get tunnel vision.

In the meantime, there were more people to interview, more information to follow up with, more forensic evidence results to come in. It would now be even harder to do than before. By February 20, 1989, Maryann and Jose were back on the on-call rotation, which meant they would also be investigating other homicides in the county. After roughly two months working the case full-time, their time would now be split between newer murders and the biggest serial-killing case in the state since the Boston Strangler in the early 1960s.

IN THE LOCAL LEGAL COMMUNITY, the focus on Kenny Ponte was troubling. Some defense attorneys thought Kenny was the victim of trial by media and innuendo. Some found it unethical and unfair. The lawyers talked about it in the courthouse hallways, over lunch, over after-work drinks. What was going on? Why was the district attorney taking this approach? What would it mean for other cases?

Only one attorney, other than Kenny's lawyer, would speak out publically at first. "I am disappointed that a man who has not been indicted and not been charged . . . in a series of heinous crimes, could have his personal life depicted in your newspaper," Thomas R. Hunt, the attorney, told the *Standard-Times*. Kenny was surprised by the allegations, he said. "He's disappointed, surprised; he's outraged. He can't understand it and frankly neither can I."[5]

Thomas R. Hunt was a local attorney who worked quietly in the city. His general-law practice focused on the usual cases average people went to court for: personal injury and probate matters. His cases didn't garner headlines and neither did his personal life. His speaking out illustrated how troubling the criminal-defense community was finding the case.

At the state police unit in the district attorney's office, people were also concerned. There was a long list of suspects they were still looking at. Why was Kenny's name out there?

Staff Sgt. Gale P. Stevens, commander of the state police unit in the DA's office, tried to downplay speculation that Kenny was a suspect, saying troopers didn't view the lawyer as "one of the key hitters" in the investigation.[6] He also downplayed the reaction of the state police search dog at Kenny's office, saying it could have been prompted by human scents. The dog may have just made a mistake.

INVESTIGATORS WORKING out of the district attorney's office were puzzled. How did word of the search of Kenny's office get out to the media, particularly the Boston press? Who was the leak? Did it come from the office or someone who saw them there? Things spread quickly in the community, they knew. Likely, the information did not come from anyone on the case, they agreed. However, the district attorney demanded answers — and demanded action regarding the leak.

Freetown detective sgt. Alan Alves was not part of the inner circle at the DA's office but had always worked well with the state police members assigned there. He was eager to work on the task force — particularly since one of the victims turned out to be one of his informants. He thought he was doing a good job: coming up with suggested leads and angles. He knew some people scoffed at his suggestions of a link to Satanism, but he had found signs of what he believed was a cult in the Freetown State Forest over the years and felt it was something they needed to at least examine. He was also one of the first cops at the scene when the first body, that of Debra Medeiros of Fall River, was found in his town. With the work he had put in, Alan was stunned when he got the word he was off the task force. Why, he asked. The official answer was silence. He would later be told the district attorney's office thought he was the leak.

He was off the task force but he suspected he wouldn't be off the case for long. There were a lot of places along Route 140 in Freetown where bodies might be and, as the town's detective, he would be there first.

THE PHONE CALLS from Kenny kept coming, even after Bob told him he was a possible suspect in the murder case, even after Kenny was arraigned in superior court on the gun charge. In the months that followed, sometimes Kenny would call Bob's office in the morning, sometimes in the afternoon. Sometimes he would call several times a week, sometimes a couple of weeks would go by without a call. The calls all had a familiar pattern: Kenny, who had been allowed to return to Florida after his arraignment, would start somewhat calmly then something, usually a question, would agitate him. Kenny would hang up abruptly. Bob didn't worry. Kenny always called back. Bob still wasn't sure why. Did he think something would slip? Was he hunting to see what they knew? Did he have something to hide? It was becoming an odd, long-distance game. Bob was patient. He could wait it out.

BRINGING IN "OUTSIDE" EXPERTS to the case was the next step for the district attorney's office. Ron wasn't shy about asking federal agencies or nationally known forensic experts, such as Douglas Ubelaker, for help in the past and if there was ever a case where extra help was needed, this was it. Others in the office suggested one of the FBI's units could offer needed insights into the case.

Jose wasn't sure what to expect as he and Maryann sat down with the three FBI criminal profilers on January 11, 1989. The agents had met with a few members of the district attorney's staff earlier that day and now they wanted to talk with the investigators in the field. Jose had read about the work the Behavioral Science Unit at the National Center for the Analysis of Violent Crime in Quantico, Virginia, was doing and he was intrigued. In theory, the unit could develop a criminal profile of a suspect by evaluating the crime, the crime scene, the victim, and the range of autopsy and police reports. The profilers could also give them suggestions on how to interview potential suspects. Details about the highway killing case had already been sent to FBI's Violent Criminal Apprehension Program (VICAP), a database created in 1985 to compare and contrast murder and other violent-crime cases. The VICAP computer system would generate a computer printout ranking the top ten matches in the database that would then be given to a crime analyst.[7] In theory, if the killer from Bristol County moved on, analysts would be able to identify similarities in the slayings and hopefully identify him or her.

The FBI's Behavioral Science Unit had a long history in profiling work. It began profiling criminals informally in the early 1970s using crime-scene information and eventually expanded the work. The FBI profilers discovered they could see patterns in an offender's personality by examining the crime-scene evidence, patterns that might help identify a suspect[8] As part of a four-year study by the unit, thirty-six convicted killers in sex-related homicides were interviewed and provided insight into how investigators could talk with the suspects. The study found nearly 70 percent of the killers' families had alcohol issues and a third had drug-abuse problems; half of the families had histories of psychiatric disorders and there was a history of physical abuse in 42 percent of the cases.

It was cutting-edge social science in law enforcement, but Jose at first wasn't sure how effective it would be. Earlier, the FBI unit had provided a verbal profile of the possible killer of a twenty-seven-year-old New Bedford woman named Dawn Copeland who was found stabbed and clubbed to death on a beach off Rogers Street in Dartmouth on June 26, 1988, after leaving a city bar. They still didn't have a suspect under arrest. Jose had hoped that profile would have been much more precise and would have pointed directly to the killer.

Jose personally found the profiles he had read in the Copeland and other cases he researched too general; just about any killer, once caught, could fit the descriptions. However, he also knew the criminal-profiling work couldn't be discounted, and if there was a chance it would help the case, he was all in. Jose knew the FBI profilers interviewed dozens of offenders, including serial killers, and gained insight into how the individuals thought, how they acted, and, most importantly, how to catch them. These researchers could see the big picture. He kept that in mind as he went over the evidence with the three profilers and showed them where the women were found dead. For three days, the profilers gathered information about the case, talked with the investigators, and viewed the crime scenes. The sessions reinforced some of Jose's thoughts and also broadened his perspective.

In the months that followed, Jose and others in the office checked back with the unit and flew to Washington, D.C., to review the case yet again. What they learned was the killer most likely was what was classified as an "organized" killer. Robert K. Ressler, Ann W. Burgess, and John E. Douglas, in their book *Sexual Homicide: Patterns and Motives,* note that the "organized" offender generally has an average or better than average intelligence with an uneven work history at skilled jobs. He usually lives with a partner, has a good car, often is angry when committing the crime but relaxed while doing it and may be drinking alcohol.[9] He often looks average, may plan the crime even if the victim is a stranger, and transports the body from the crime scene. Those considered "disorganized" may know the victim, but the scene is random and sloppy, the body is left where the killing occurs, and the person likely lives alone with a poor work history, among other things.

The profile could be considered general to some, but it was designed to help those in the field understand the type of offender committing crimes — and to catch them.

Everyone investigating the highway killings case was hoping science could hold the answer to the case if investigative shoe-leather methods couldn't.

ORGANIZING THOUSANDS OF PAGES of interviews and evidence in the case was becoming a daunting process. State police and local investigators met regularly to swap information, but there was always a fear some shred would get lost in a report. Was there a tiny detail that could lead to an "aha!" moment? The massive amount of collected information needed to be put in some type of order. How to do that in the late 1980s was not easy. Computer systems — when they didn't crash — were clunky at the time, and few police officers used them to write reports. While creating a database of information was foreign to most cops, by the summer of 1989 the head of the Bristol County Drug Task Force, Louis J. Pacheco, decided that's what was needed in the case and began hiring interns for the work.

The interns at the district attorney's office sat in front of the four Wang computer terminals normally used by narcotics detectives to listen to the wiretapped phones of drug dealers. For hours, these interns would input the typed and handwritten police reports, about missing women, drug crimes, attacks on women, interviews with potential witnesses, and possible suspects. The computer hard drives were purchased with confiscated drug funds and had capacities topping out at 150 to 250 megabytes — the equivalent of a third of a single CD today. Only text was entered; there was no capability for photos, and none of the computers initially "talked" to one another. Police captain Louis J. Pacheco, and two civilians, Julian Paul and intern Dan McCabe, learned to write a software program that would allow someone to search the database using keywords because nothing existed like that for the system they were using. They jerry-rigged the computers so they would share information. When they were done with the project, investigators in theory would be able to search reports for similarities in different cases to identify a possible suspect in the killings. One of the first things they needed to do, though, was upgrade the Wang computers in the office because they wouldn't run Microsoft Word. "They were 98 percent Microsoft compatible but they didn't tell you it was in 2 percent of every Microsoft program you would use," Louis Pacheco said. "We changed cards in all those, we did it all ourselves, and then we bought two or three stand-alone PCs with drug-forfeiture money.[10]

In this pre-Google era, it was cutting-edge computer work in local law enforcement.

The system was the brainchild of Lou, considered the computer genius in the district attorney's office. He was a police captain in Raynham, a bedroom community about forty minutes north of New Bedford, on loan to the Bristol County Drug Task Force. The DA's office reimbursed the town for his salary while he was working full-time on the task force, an arrangement the prosecutor also made with other communities. The captain understood the power of computers in law enforcement in the then non-digital world and looked for ways to utilize them whenever possible. He and Julian Paul, another computer buff who ran a database for a Fall River charity, originally developed a database for the Drug Task Force to track drug investigations, initially using a $3,000 Radio Shack Tandy TRS80 with a 5-megabyte external hard drive, roughly enough memory to store two photos — or a single mp3 song — on an iPhone in 2017. "The guy told me it would be good for the rest of my life," Lou recalled. Within 129 days, the task force needed a hard drive with more memory for the drug cases.

The first database developed by the Bristol County Task Force was used to organize information, such as telephone numbers, for investigations where wiretaps were used. The database, the detectives believed, would help identify patterns in phone calls to specific parties and help identify larger drug-dealing operations. Police would look at who was calling a drug-dealing suspect then try to identify those individuals. Were those people, and the numbers they were calling from, involved in earlier cases? It wasn't always easy to figure out who was calling, though. "We would have telephone numbers and we would have to try to figure out how many times they called this person," Dan McCabe, who was fresh out of high school at the time and is now a Taunton, Massachusetts, police captain, recalled. "If you did know who the person was, that was a bonus."[11]

The trio took what they learned in organizing wiretap information and expanded it to develop a database to help in the murder probe. In the first months of the highway killing investigation, massive amounts of information were being collected, and it all needed to be organized in a way investigators could use. As Lou Pacheco noted, "A lot of the reports and other information were spread out all over the place," he recalled. "It was in all different forms. We computerized the information in a searchable database. It seems so simple now, but it really didn't exist for us back then."

Data entry, however, was slow, and the captain worried that not enough information from enough law-enforcement agencies was in the system. Ideally, he wanted a wide range of reports that could be cross-referenced, such as towed trucks or descriptions of people. He would start small and build on the data. "As each case came up, they would have something to go through on the computer rather than go through it by hand," he explained. "Let's say if a victim was seen getting into a green car with a dented fender or something like that, then the guys could go through and search the other cases very quickly for green cars. It seems so simple now but then it was like magic."

Lou researched what other departments in the country were doing with databases and how they handled complex cases, such as serial killings. With the blessing of the district attorney, he and Julian Paul flew to Seattle in August of 1989 to see how detectives in Washington State handling the then unsolved Green River–killer case compiled information and coordinated investigative agencies. There, the two talked with an investigator, looked at some of the crime scenes and examined how the Green River Task Force organized and cross-referenced files. "That was still an open case at the time," Lou said. (The Green River Killer, Gary Leon Ridgway, was finally caught in 2001, confessed to killing seventy-one women and was convicted of forty-nine slayings between 1982 and 1998.)

By the time the two flew back to Massachusetts, they were feeling upbeat.

"I thought we were on the right track," Lou recalled. "The stuff was coming together."[12]

The information going into that database was coming from more than a dozen local and state police investigators. However, in early 1989, in the months leading up to the creation of that database, it was a much more basic investigation. The human end of the investigation, where detectives were delving into the lives of those on the edge and trying to prod the hazy memories of addicts was more difficult. Some of what they learned could not be boiled down into a cold computer entry. Sometimes the stories the investigators heard were heartbreaking, like when one of the women they had interviewed several times discovered she was HIV positive. Sometimes it was uplifting, like when one of the women noted she had been clean for six months. Sometimes it was just unexplainable to anyone except those "on the job." Sometimes things were just plain weird.

THE DOOR WAS OPEN to Trooper Kevin Butler's office at the district attorney's office in New Bedford. In the days, weeks, and months since he saw Andy Rebmann's dog find the remains of Dawn Mendes on Interstate 195 in Dartmouth, the trooper found himself — like many of the investigators — bouncing across the region to find witnesses and evidence. Now, the trooper, who grew up in Brockton about forty-five minutes north of New Bedford, was staying late yet again to interview another potential witness in the murder case. Each person he talked to yielded another piece of information. Sometimes what they said was irrelevant, other times it appeared to cut to the heart of the case.

This night, he was in the office with a female colleague interviewing a New Bedford prostitute. The woman sitting in the office knew the drug scene, she knew Kenny Ponte, and she knew the women who had been assaulted by johns in the past year or so. She appeared to be a credible witness who remembered details and sometime rough dates, despite years of drug use.

Jose could hear the troopers talking as he walked down the hall, toward his own office. He could hear snippets of the questions and the answers. Curious, he stopped at the open door and noticed Kevin was deliberately looking away from the woman. The female trooper looked bemused.

Jose glanced at the witness as she nervously crossed her legs once, twice, three times. Then he noticed: she wasn't wearing panties. He hurried back to his office. Years later, he was reminded of that scene while watching the 1992 film *Basic Instinct*, where actress Sharon Stone, dressed in a skimpy white dress, seductively, during an interrogation, crosses her legs to reveal she wasn't wearing underwear. For now, though, this wasn't a movie scene. It was just another night in the investigation.

For the state and local police detectives on the case, it still remained a nearly around-the-clock job in early 1989. Each daytime tip meant a night-time trip through the city searching for potential witnesses and sources. Sometimes a state trooper paired up with a city detective, sometimes with a fellow trooper. Sometimes they went alone.

Jose and Maryann usually searched the streets and interviewed people together; sometimes New Bedford detective Richard Ferreira joined them. Richie worked check and fraud cases, the type of crime many addicts — particularly women — were drawn to. There were several reasons: some businesses at the time were more likely to cash a check from a woman, and it was a nonviolent crime often drawing fines, not jail terms.

After years in New Bedford's detective division, Richie knew quite a bit about the city's heroin and cocaine addicts. He knew where they lived, where they hung out, what they looked like, and who their friends were. Richie, like nearly all of the detectives working the case, was juggling a full caseload with this new, top-priority investigation. There was no one, anywhere, to pick up the slack. Often Richie would be in the New Bedford station, typing out reports on the case — he typed the fastest of the three — when the phone would ring and he either rushed to the DA's office or Maryann and Jose would pick him up. They would head to MCI Framingham, the state prison for women, or someone's house, or to any of a handful of lockups in the state to interview possible witnesses. Sometimes they would circle the city streets, searching for the people who might know something. With his broad smile, easy laugh, and earnest talk, Richie could get just about anyone to talk. He came across as the good friend there to help. Richie was a good addition to the team, Jose knew.

One thing nagged the trio as well as others working the case: the district attorney's continuing fascination with Kenny Ponte, who had already been indicted in January 1989 in a gun case. There were other people who looked better and needed to be examined closer. Technically, the district attorney wasn't naming Kenny as a suspect. The prosecutor would always note investigators were looking for the "person or persons" responsible for the killings. However, Kenny's name somehow made its way onto newspaper pages and onto the television and radio airwaves as a person tied to the dead women. It wasn't helping the investigation. Putting Kenny's name out in the media wasn't forcing him to cooperate. It was having the opposite effect. He wouldn't talk with anyone in the office now. It also wasn't fair to suggest, even in broad terms, that he was a suspect. Kenny wasn't charged in the murders. From what police had so far, there wasn't any evidence linking him to murder. None of the girls who went to Kenny's house said he tried to kill them. Most of the girls said he wouldn't even have sex with them. Kenny knew the murder victims, but so did a lot of other people.

In December and early January of 1989, Jose flipped through the Boston and New Bedford newspapers each morning and afternoon, scanning the headlines: "Lawyer Was Pardoned on Two Drug Convictions," read one. "Lawyer Was Seen with 3 Highway Killing Victims, Witness Says," read another. "Lawyer Was Seen with Victim," read yet another. As January came to a close, Kenny remained in the headlines and, it appeared, the focus of the investigation in the district attorney's mind.

Tunnel vision, Jose said to himself yet again. *I hope the* DA *doesn't have tunnel vision.*

THE FILE FOLDERS were brimming with reports. Some were typed, some handwritten. There were interviews with drug addicts, with store owners, with psychics, with families of the victims, with friends of the victims, with employers, with social service workers. There were neatly typed official reports from medical examiners, from laboratories, from technicians. There were motor-vehicle reports, criminal-background reports, and photographs. There was information from the tip lines. The information gathered was detailed and massive. There was a problem, and it was a serious one, Bristol County district attorney Ronald A. Pina knew. Many of the witnesses were drug dependent, some were infected with the AIDS virus, and could be gone, or dead, before the case — if they could even press one — went to trial. He wanted these people on the record, under oath. He also wanted to make sure they were telling police everything they knew.

We are going to launch a grand jury investigation into the case, Pina told his chief investigator, Robert St. Jean, the state police staff sergeant, Gale "Pat" Stevens, as well as Maryann and Jose. Get everyone under oath. Get the stories — all the stories — on the record. We can sort it all out later. Bob St. Jean knew it made sense to do it that way. Drugs and alcohol can fade the memory quickly. They needed to lock in the evidence, whatever it may be, and the testimony. A special grand jury, just to hear this case, seemed sensible. Hopefully, Bob thought, it will go smoothly.

Word spread quickly through the office in February of 1989 that the murder investigation — the district attorney was still reluctant to call it a serial kill-ing — was taking a different turn. The district attorney would launch a special grand jury investigation into the deaths, and he would handle it personally. He would question the witnesses. He would present the evidence. Some worried it would be a disaster. Others predicted it would turn into a media circus. Ron Pina was bright, personable, and a good politician but district attorneys generally hired the prosecutors to do the boots-on-the-ground work. Rarely did they try a case or present cases to a grand jury. The staff could count on one hand the number of cases the DA personally prosecuted while in office. They weren't shining courtroom moments. So, why was he doing it now?

Jose saw the upside of the plan in theory: get people under oath while memories are still fresh. But doing that took more than just issuing a sub-poena. It took manpower to find these people and manpower was already stretched thin in the county. More than a dozen state and local detectives were still tracking leads, interviewing witnesses, scouring motor-vehicle, financial, prison, and arrest records. The teams were already regularly logging an average of fifteen hours daily in the case. Overtime money already ran out once, and there was the fear it would yet again.

Generally, a prosecutor in Massachusetts will present concise evidence and testimony to a grand jury then ask the panel to hand up an indictment charging the suspect with a crime. Grand juries sit fairly regularly, often once a month; and there are usually up to twenty-three people on the panel. Unlike a trial jury, grand jurors do not have to unanimously agree to indict; only a dozen or more must agree. For a case to move to superior court in Massachusetts, a person must be indicted by a grand jury; as a result, a typ-ical grand jury may hear testimony in cases ranging from armed robbery to rape to murder. However, a special grand jury can be used as an investigative tool by prosecutors to subpoena records, witnesses, and other evidence with the plan to eventually charge someone. The main difference: prosecutors presenting to a "regular" grand jury have the evidence to hook a suspect;

prosecutors presenting to a special grand jury are still fishing. The question now was whom was the district attorney trying to bait?

The district attorney, through his spokesman, stressed the panel wasn't targeting any one person. "We are not seeking an indictment at this time," the district attorney's spokesman, James Martin, said at the time. "We are using the grand jury investigative powers to compel witnesses to testify."[13]

This new, special session of the grand jury was originally set for March 1, 1989, but it was already being put off for a day. The district attorney was testifying before a State House committee on a state forfeiture plan that day. The extra twenty-four hours would come in handy for the police on the case. The investigators had had only two weeks to serve subpoenas, track witnesses, reinterview them, and figure out how to get them all to court.

Meanwhile, new tips were still coming in.

IT WAS VISITING HOURS at the Bristol County House of Correction in New Bedford, a century-old walled-off, two-story red-brick building a few blocks just outside the city center, and Jeannie Kaloshis was there to visit her husband. She was also there to slip him a little something extra, some heroin. The two had a history of drug arrests and heroin addiction. Going through withdrawal in jail, cold turkey, was not pretty. One's body shakes and sweats. There are stomach cramps, vomiting, nervousness. Some people get diarrhea. Nearly everyone says it feels like death. This "gift" to him would keep that pain away.

Bristol County House of Correction was the oldest working jail in the country, and it wasn't air-conditioned. Even for this June 1988 visiting day, it was hot. Visitors were corralled in the center-caged rotunda of the jail and, separated by wire, would visit for up to sixty minutes. The correction officers would try to keep watch inside the rotunda with the visitors and outside the caging with the inmates. They didn't see everything.

On the day Jeannie Kaloshis visited her husband, only one person saw her slip heroin through the caging. She discovered this when a man approached her as she was leaving. He saw what she had done; she could get in trouble for that, he said. By the way, he added, when would she be coming back?[14]

The man was a lawyer. His name was Kenneth Ponte.

The next day, she met him again outside the jail at the corner of Ash and

Union Streets. He liked to party, he told her. Want to get some coke and heroin?

She hopped into his Datsun 280Z, and they drove to his Chestnut Street home. He handed her lingerie. Put it on, he told her. Then they did the drugs.

The first time, she injected cocaine into Kenny's neck because he didn't like to do it himself. He began to foam at the mouth and sweat. Then paranoia set in. *The police were outside,* he told her. *They're raiding the house.* He was frantic and tossed a quarter ounce of cocaine down the sink.[15]

She would later tell Trooper Kevin Butler and New Bedford detective Gardner Greany that she stayed with Kenny often that summer of 1988 doing drugs. When she wanted to get away for a bit, she would introduce him to a friend who wanted to get high. One of those friends was Rochelle Clifford Dopierala, the woman later found dead in the Dartmouth sandpit.

There was a steady stream of women at Kenny's house between the spring and fall of 1988. He always supplied the drugs or gave money to the women to buy him the drugs so no one would see him. He was using so much cocaine at the time, even the hardcore addicts were nervous. "I would have to keep hitting him with cocaine. I was afraid I would kill him," one woman told police.[16] Another woman said he was injecting coke every fifteen to twenty minutes when she was with him.[17]

When Kenny talked, he bragged. He claimed he got high with the district attorney's girlfriend, although there was never any evidence of that; that he knew important people; that he was important. He was, he reminded them again and again, a lawyer. He was also, as one woman told police, kinky and paranoid.[18] Another woman called him a "real freak" who ran around in his underwear.[19]

One woman with a fifteen bag a day habit — roughly $300 at the time — remembered walking along Franklin Street in the city in May of 1988, desperately needing a fix. A Datsun 280Z pulled up.

"Looks like you need what I got," the driver told her.[20]

She hopped in. They first drove to Hazard Street to buy three bags of heroin, then to Rivet and South Street in the South End to buy a sixteenth of coke. Kenny flashed a $16,000 check and drove to a bank across from the district courthouse. While inside, the woman searched the glove box and found a letter addressed to Attorney Kenneth Ponte.

At his home, she injected him in the neck with coke and she did a "speed ball," a combination of heroin and cocaine. Then he ordered her to strip. He locked the doors. *Give me another shot,* he told her. Paranoia set in. Kenny began crawling through the house on his hands and knees, checking the door locks. He wouldn't let her leave for two days. The next time it happened, two months later, she escaped by telling him they needed more drugs.

More women began to stay at Kenny's house for longer stretches, burning through his cash and coke. "He would do coke, then walk around the house on all fours and bark like a dog and sometimes foam at the mouth," yet another woman told police.[21]

Things started to get stranger.

While a pornographic movie played on his widescreen television, he crawled naked on the floor peering out the windows. One prostitute said he used to throw her around while trying to get aroused. He pulled a gun on another woman who tried to leave his house. "You're not going nowhere. Just stay here," he told her.[22] He accused people of ripping him off. One woman claimed he would dress up in women's clothes.[23] Yet another claimed he locked her inside a house in the nearby town of Fairhaven where there were handcuffs and women's clothing in a room. He took two Polaroid photos of her: one holding a two-headed dildo against her buttocks, the other holding a bottle against her vagina, she claimed. All of the girls would tell police Kenny was odd. None would say he tried to kill them.

Kenny told a guy who used to sell him drugs he would kill him if he or anyone he knew testified against him.[24]

With each interview, the detectives learned one more secret in Kenny's life.

They also discovered he had known a growing number of the missing or dead women.

Rochelle Dopierala seemed to spend the most time with Kenny. She was pretty, personable and struggled with drug addiction for years. The Falmouth mother of two had been in a detox center in Quincy for three or four days before bolting. She had bounced between Cape Cod, where her family still lived, and New Bedford, where her drug connections were. Like many others, she was rootless, crashing with drug friends on floors or couches or with men enchanted with her beauty, hoping to help her get clean. She stayed with an aging dentist who lived not far from the county jail; then with Nancy Paiva for a few days. When she stole a VCR from the dentist's home, it was Nancy's boyfriend who helped sell it on the street. She gave her family the names and phone numbers of the people she stayed with. She told her mother about the dentist and, prosecutors later said, about a lawyer — Kenneth Ponte — who she was now staying with. Kenny would drive her to the Cape and back when she needed to deal with a welfare check or other issue. She would also drive around with him to buy cocaine. "He used to have her bring coke dealers to the car; and he would stick 'em up," Nancy's boyfriend would later tell authorities.[25] When she moved out, she took his VCR and other things. Kenny wasn't pleased. "She was afraid of him," Frankie Pina said.

Debra Medeiros, the first woman found dead, also stayed with Kenny for a while, part of the group of girls rotating in the apartment. Mary Rose Santos, who disappeared in late July, once hired Kenny as an attorney. Nancy Paiva hired Kenny for a bankruptcy case, and he used to call her apartment. Dawn Mendes was seen outside his house. Robbin Rhodes told people about the lawyer she knew, later identified as Kenny. But knowing someone was not evidence of murder. There were other suspects on the list, suspects with a knack for violence. There were men who raped the girls, men who beat them, at least one who choked several into unconsciousness. Kenny, the girls were telling investigators, was just a weirdo who wanted company, who was afraid to be seen buying drugs.

Maryann and Jose knew all these stories about Kenny. New Bedford police, the Bristol County Drug Task Force, and the state police amassed what would be boxes filled with reports detailing his drug use, his acquaintances, and his times sharing cocaine with prostitutes at his house. One guy claimed Kenny was growing marijuana in the basement and had blocked the basement windows of his Chestnut Street home. Months after Kenny moved to Florida, police searched Kenny's basement. It had been cleared out.[26] There was no evidence of drugs. Police knew about Kenny's paranoia; about how the life he fought to get was now gone again in a storm of drugs. What they did not know was if Kenny was a killer.

JUDY DESANTOS tried to focus on typing the file cards. Name. Address. Party affiliation. She filled the information for each new voter. A routine task on a routine workday in the city's election commission in March 1989. She kept her eyes down and avoided the friendly, idle chatter of the office. She was afraid she would cry if anyone asked her that simple, offhand, everyday, well-meaning question: How are you doing? She was afraid if they did, if she answered, it would all come streaming down her face, leaving her coworkers' mouths agape, fumbling for the right words when there were none. She was afraid of screaming: I'm afraid, I'm angry, I'm confused. How did this all happen? Why did it happen? It was better to stay quiet, head down, and type. No questions, no answers.

Up the street, just outside downtown center, a gaggle of television, radio, and newspaper reporters were watching witnesses parade into the courthouse as the special grand jury convened to find her sister's killer. Judy wondered, as her fingers danced across the typewriter keyboard, if she would recognize any of the faces going into the courthouse if she was there. If she did, what would she say? Would she say anything? As she sat at work, her heart raced as she mentally flipped through the scenarios: yelling at Kenny Ponte to tell the prosecutor everything; screaming and slapping Frankie Pina for dragging her sister into a drug life; pleading with the line of addicted women waiting to testify to get help before it was too late. What if the killer was there, calmly waiting on a courthouse bench, to testify before the panel? Would her heart instinctively point to him? Would he look average? Would he be scared? She felt as if she were watching a made-for-TV movie from across a crowded room, waiting for a calming commercial break. This was not something that happened to average families like hers. This was not something that happened in a small city like New Bedford. This is not something that should happen to her sister.

People were always talking about the investigation, about what was going on at the courthouse, about the reporters gathered on the front lawn and steps. Judy could hear waves of the conversations then waited as the words receded like the tide. She looked up at the clock. Just a few more hours left at work. Just a few more hours before she could turn on the evening news to learn what happened a few blocks away. She slid another file card into the typewriter and hit the keys.

THE TELEVISION STATION VIDEOGRAPHERS outside New Bedford Superior Court slung the nearly fifty-pound video cameras on their shoulders and gave chase. Attorney Kenneth Ponte tried to duck through the back of the courthouse to avoid the scrum of reporters on the front steps and lawn. It didn't work. There was a fence. He veered to the side of the building. He stopped and scowled. Reporters were waiting.

It was a wretched end to a miserable day. Kenny had spent most of March 2, 1989, the first day of a special grand jury session, in a second-floor courthouse waiting area, trying to avoid reporters. Kenny was agitated as he waited. He knew several of the people called to appear before the grand jury, including his friend the cab driver Arthur "Goldie" Goldblatt. Goldie knew all of the girls on the street and often drove them in his cab to Kenny's house. Goldie had told reporters he would appear before the grand jury but he wouldn't testify. "There's no sense," he said.[27]

Reporters milled through the courthouse hallway that day, watching as witnesses strode into the grand jury room. Inside that first-floor room, where a few grand jurors smoked cigarettes, the district attorney questioned the witnesses one by one. There was Donald Santos, the husband of Mary Rose Santos, one of the women still missing, who later told reporters he couldn't understand why he was called because he was cooperating with police. There was former Freetown police chief Wayne Snell, who once owned the North End restaurant called Pal's, who said Kenny once bounced a sixty-five-dollar check at his place. The only reason he even let him cash it was because someone said Kenny was a lawyer, he told reporters. There was a woman who simply told reporters this about Kenny: "He's no killer."

Kenny couldn't be sure what people were really saying in the grand jury room; it was a closed door, secret session. He was convinced of one thing, though. The district attorney was asking questions about him, likely about his drug use and the girls who came to his New Bedford home. He was very sure he was the target of this investigation, and he didn't know what to do about it. He was only partially correct about what was being said in that grand jury room. He didn't know three prostitutes told the grand jurors about kinky johns and about attacks by a guy in a truck. He didn't know the names and photographs of other men were presented to the grand jury, including a Tiverton, Rhode Island, man who gave hookers roses, a couple of New Bedford drug dealers, a fisherman, a cab driver, and a Freetown man who prostitutes said choked them. He didn't know on this first day that the district attorney was trying to pin down the last time anyone saw the dead and missing women. He didn't know one person testified a shaken prostitute said two cops chased her around a parking lot at the mills on North Front Street, wanting sex. Or how people talked about another cop selling drugs. He didn't hear the story about the prostitute who suffered a broken kneecap trying to escape the guy with "very, very big hands" and "psychotic eyes" who tried to choke her. Stories about Kenny were woven in the testimony — "he was scared and paranoid when he got high"[28] — but he wasn't the only character. When he saw the reporters camped outside the courthouse or when he recognized a witness being called, his only thought was he had a legal target on his back.

"Just get away from me. Just get away from me," he told reporters when they swarmed him as he arrived at court or when he briefly emerged to get coffee.

At the end of the day, after waiting hours without being called to testify, he left the courthouse and was again surrounded by the media scrum. He shoved his way through, an image shown repeatedly on the nightly news for months to come. "Get away from me," he screamed.

The next day, Kenny would do it all again, but this time court officers would escort him in and out of the building.

It was a different scene when District Attorney Ronald A. Pina would come and go. The prosecutor would smile as he passed reporters, often saying hello to one or two by name. Before leaving the courthouse that first day of the grand jury, he had a simple comment. "I think the information is coming a little more fluidly now," he said.

The jurors were getting a hint of at least six possible suspects and a glimpse into the hardened streets of drug addiction. The jurors, originally scheduled to temporarily adjourn the next day, were also told they would be back the next week.

After two and a half days of waiting, Kenny finally strode into the grand jury room. Earlier, the district attorney coyly told reporters that if a witness cited his or her right against self-incrimination, he would ask a judge to step in. Minutes after Kenny stepped into the grand jury room, the district attorney and Ponte's lawyer, Joseph Harrington, met with a judge. Reporters were left to draw their own conclusions.

When the special grand jury recessed that week, Kenny was on a plane back to his single-level duplex in Port Richey, Florida. He never testified before the grand jury. He was hoping this would be the end of his involvement in the case.

BY THE TIME Kenny's plane touched down in Florida, investigators were already talking with more women who spent time in his Chestnut Street house. New Bedford detectives had amassed a wealth of information about the life of the once-recovered addict turned lawyer. One man doing time in the Massachusetts Correctional Institute in Bridgewater told Troopers Kevin Butler and Kenneth Martin that the lawyer knew at least two of the highway-killing victims, used coke, and even more women talked about getting locked inside his house. The incidents dated back years and the files on them were beginning to fill a box.

HER HEART was thumping so loudly Judy DeSantos worried people could hear it as she walked into the courthouse where the special grand jury was meeting. She had been there twice: once when she divorced her first husband, and once to be sworn in as a notary. The building was a small by modern standards: a courtroom on the first floor and a courtroom on the second with a series of offices off a long hallway by the entrance. It was easy to navigate, and there was always someone to answer questions. She even recognized some of the employees from around town. None of that mattered, though. She was still a little intimidated by the formality of the courtroom and the uniforms of the court officers. Now, after passing the cluster of reporters outside, she could feel herself shaking as she walked to the district attorney's small courthouse office across from the grand jury room. She wasn't sure what she would do once she got there. She wasn't sure if she could do anything. She only knew she had to be here rather than at work, to bear witness and watch the parade of witnesses into the grand jury room.

Her sister's children were too young to comprehend the intricacies of this grand jury investigation, Judy knew. She had a hard time figuring it out herself. Maryann and Jose insisted she didn't have to be at the courthouse; there was nothing for her to do there; there was no reason to be there. She couldn't hear what the witnesses were saying in the grand jury room. She would be sitting there, in a hallway, doing nothing. Judy didn't see it that way. There would be answers at some point at that courthouse. If she was there, if the witnesses saw her sitting and watching, maybe they would talk more, maybe they would remember more. To her, the grand jury would lead to the holy grail of the case. This grand jury and this district attorney would give her — and all of the families — answers.

Judy liked Ronald A. Pina, the district attorney. He was smart, he was cool under pressure, and he seemed committed to finding her sister's killer. He was on the news a lot, talking about the case, keeping the investigation alive, providing the families confidence that something would be done. He seemed sincere and caring and dedicated and smart. She believed him when he said they would do everything possible to find the killer. She believed he would find justice for Nancy.

Judy's boss at the election office understood the situation. When the woman noticed how nervous Judy seemed, then realized it was the second day of the special grand jury, she told her to head up to the courthouse. Work could wait; schedules could be adjusted. This was important. So Judy grabbed her pocketbook, left the office and walked three blocks up to the courthouse.

Judy was uncertain when she opened the door to the district attorney's office at the courthouse. She was afraid her voice would crack when she introduced herself to the person behind the counter. A victim/witness advocate hurried from a back room to greet her. The woman told Judy what she had been told before: she didn't have to be there, there wasn't anything she could do there. Judy smiled. I need to be here, she told the woman.

Judy turned back into the hallway and waited. She paced the corridor as witnesses walked into the grand jury room to testify. She flipped through her memory, trying to recognize the faces. She wondered what these people were saying, what they knew, what answers they had.

Nancy the brave one, the adventurous one, risk-taker, was gone. Judy the timid, quiet one, the sister who watched from a distance, who was too often afraid, was here in her place.

Judy tried to calm herself by silently repeating the mantra: *I need to do this for Nancy.* Judy slowly paced the hallway for the rest of the day, imagining her sister watching from above.

At the end of the day, as Judy walked home alone, she thought about the other missing women and their families. She wondered if knowing someone was dead was better than that grief-limbo, that shadow between hope and despair. She wondered if the search dog, when and if it came back, would help answer that.

7 "CATCH THIS GUY"

IT WAS THREE MONTHS into the new year, and Andy Rebmann was back in Massachusetts, giving a stretch of Route 140 in Freetown another look. Massachusetts trooper Kathleen Barrett and her dog had already checked it four months earlier, back in November of 1988, but it wasn't unusual to "double cover" a search area. He also knew Kathy's dog was fairly new and still learning the finer skills of looking for the dead. This search, both for her and her dog, was good field training, but he felt better doing a second sweep — just in case.

So far, two bodies had been found in 1988 along this highway in Freetown: one by a passing motorist in July and a second in December by his own dog.

This time he was here with troopers and their dogs from four different New England states. It took a little longer to get back here: he had to coordinate everyone's schedules, and he was waiting for a break in the weather. He didn't want the dogs searching in the ice, snow, and freezing temperatures. He also needed to make sure his schedule was clear in Connecticut before returning to help in what was now one of the biggest and most intriguing murder cases in New England.

Shortly before two in the afternoon on March 28, 1989, he was walking along the side of Route 140 with Josie trotting nearby. The number of tires discarded on the side of the road was striking.

The Chase Road exit sign was just ahead when Josie let him know she found something. There, about twenty-eight feet inside the tree line, were the remains of what appeared to be a woman with long brown hair. She appeared to be about five feet one or so. Her teeth were intact.

Neighbors in homes near the highway would later say they smelled something foul in the area the previous year. No one could pinpoint the location. No one could pinpoint the smell.

Maryann got to the scene quickly and was rounding her cruiser as her colleague, Trooper Kathy Barrett, passed. She knew Kathy pretty well. There were more women on the state police now than in decades past, but it was still a small, and often tight, group. Kathy was very intense and focused. She was a single mom, raising a young son, and determined to show nothing would keep her back. Maryann worked with her — and her dog — several times and knew not to try to pet the animal. Maryann strode toward the scene as the leashed dog passed her side.

Snap.

She felt the dog grab the elbow of her wool coat. *Great,* she thought, walking ahead. *Just great. Even the dog is working against me.*[1]

Within minutes, more cruisers pulled up. More troopers arrived. More reporters lined the road. Everyone knew what to do. They had done it all before.

Chris Dextradeur was driving down Route 140 with his dad after a light round of golf and saw the line of state police cruisers along the side of the road.

"Christ, they found another body," John Dextradeur, the former New Bedford detective, told his son. "Pull over, Chris."[2]

Chris slowed down and began to merge toward the breakdown lane. "Never mind, let's just keep going," John told him. "Never mind."

The man who convinced others that the disappearances of the New Bedford women were linked knew it was no longer his case.

As the two drove off, Maryann and Jose were watching as Trooper Kenneth Martin went to work, meticulously searching the ground for evidence. He would be there for hours. As darkness fell, he kept working as a fellow trooper, Kevin Butler, held a light close to the ground.

One day later, body number seven would be positively identified as Robbin Rhodes, a twenty-nine-year-old woman who had disappeared in April of 1988.

"I was hoping it was somebody else," her mother, Jean Arsenault, said at the time. "I was hoping to hear from her. Now I'll never see her again."[3]

THREE DAYS AFTER THE BODY was found in Freetown, a twelve-year-old boy named Robert Bauer was walking with his best friend, fourteen-year-old Paul Keyes, in the woods by their homes in the Kirby Street neighborhood in Westport, a waterfront town peppered with sprawling farms. Paul's dog got off its chain and the two were trying to find it as they followed a stream paralleling Route 88, the road leading to the popular Horseneck Beach, a state park known for rolling waves and pristine beaches.[4] It was a bit chilly on this afternoon of March 31, 1989, as the boys searched along the stream, keeping on the grassy edge. The boys often played in the woods but this was a new spot they were exploring as they called for the dog. Then they stopped cold. They spotted what appeared to be a skull. They turned and ran toward home. *Did they really see a skull?* the boys wondered. They went back to double-check. It *was* a skull. It took five minutes for Robert and his friend to get to his house and tell his mother what they had found.

When the call came into the Westport police station, Officer Michael O'Connor swung by the boys' homes and brought them back to the scene. The boys were right. There in the woods were what appeared to be the remains of a woman, propped up a bit on what looked like a slight hill. Dogs had searched just north of Route 88 that week and the handlers had wrapped up efforts about an hour earlier, planning to finish that road sometime after the weekend. The remains were found about ten miles from the Interstate 195 exit in Dartmouth where the bodies of three other women had been found a year earlier.

Reporters were already starting to gather along Route 88 by the time Jose and New Bedford detective Richie Ferreira pulled up in separate cruisers.

How did they get here so fast? Richie remembers thinking.

When Bob St. Jean, the chief investigator for the district attorney's office, arrived, he first thought the scene looked different somehow from the others. He couldn't quite put his finger on what it was. The position of the body? The type of road? The breakdown lane on Route 88 at the time was narrow, too narrow he thought for a car or truck to stop without being noticed. However, he knew it had been done before, in a different case. In that earlier case, the body of a Fall River woman was found dismembered on the side of Route 88 in Westport. One suspect was indicted but the charges were later dropped because potential alibi evidence wasn't introduced as evidence to the grand jury. Charges in that case were never refiled. That death, however, was not tied to the highway killings, Bob knew. Police had already checked.

When Bristol County district attorney Ronald A. Pina arrived, he looked at the scene and strode to the bevy of cameras and reporters waiting in the road. He talked a little about the scene and then made a startling proclamation to reporters: someone sent him a "personal and confidential" two-page, typed letter on March 16 saying if a body was ever found on Route 88, he or she had information to share. The letter would be in a Bible.

"They said if there was a body found on 88, they would feel comfortable and come forward. We now have a body found on 88. We want them to come forward," he told reporters.[5]

The remains were identified three days later, on April 3, 1989, as Mary Rose Santos, the woman who went missing after a night of dancing at the Quarterdeck bar on July 15, 1988. "I knew she was going to be one of them," her mother, Mary Jeronymo, said after the identification was made.

The death toll was now at eight.

ABOUT THREE FEET from the brush line, the state-highway-cleanup worker picking up litter along Interstate 195 in Marion the morning of April 24, 1989, spotted something odd. He walked closer and saw what appeared to be human remains. The person was slumped in a fetal position. The person was face up, feet toward the highway. "It was like someone was in a hurry," Frederick Gomes, the foreman of the crew, said at the time.

Things like this didn't happen in the quiet town of Marion, and troopers called to help control curious drivers slowing with traffic could see how unsettled the highway crew that made the discovery was. When a pickup truck driver yelled out his window "Is that another one?" a trooper quickly pulled him over to get his name

The town of Marion is twelve miles and a world away from New Bedford. The waterfront community of roughly four thousand residents in 1989 boasted a median household income of $46,189 and was home to Tabor Academy, an elite private school. It was considered a wealthy community, where more than two hundred of the fifteen hundred households earned more than $100,000 a year.[6] Actor James Spader's family were considered townies; television personality Geraldo Rivera had a house there; and there were stories that Jackie O. once stopped at the local pharmacy to replace a pair of sunglasses that fell overboard. It was a community where it was impolite to point out the rich, the powerful, or the famous. It was also relatively crime free. There hadn't been a homicide in the town for close to forty years, and that was when a lumberman killed his wife with an axe then killed himself. "That was a really bloody one," the town's eighty-eight year-old historian, Edmund Tripp, recalled in 1989.[7] In addition to being a quiet town, Marion was also in Plymouth County, where another district attorney had jurisdiction and a different group of state troopers worked the homicide cases. Some of those troopers were not big fans of Bristol County district attorney Ronald A. Pina. One of those in the Plymouth unit was state police corporal Nelson Ostiguy, who was one of the state troopers booted out of the Bristol County office when Pina won reelection in 1982. Nelson wasn't a big fan of the district attorney.

Jose and Maryann weren't thinking about politics, though, when the remains were found in Marion. The investigation workload was now overwhelming the Bristol County unit, where other, unrelated cases continued to come in. To the pair, as well as others in the unit, assistance from a neighboring district meant more hands to help and a fresh perspective.

The remains found in Marion were identified a few days later through dental records. They belonged to Sandra Botelho, age twenty-five, who disappeared after heading to a neighbor's apartment to get "bread."

"How can a man live like that and sleep nights, knowing he killed all those girls?" her father, Joseph Botelho, said at the time.[8]

The body count was now at nine. Two women still were missing: Marilyn Roberts and Christina Monteiro. Both were related to cops.

NELSON OSTIGUY was gearing up the investigation into the murder of Sandra Botelho on the Plymouth County end. He was making plans to send troopers from his unit and Marion's sole detective to New Bedford to get up to speed on the case and share whatever information they gathered. Everyone in the Bristol unit seemed excited and eager to work with his guys. Now, he was just waiting for the phone call to set up a time to meet the next day. The call never came.

He called the commander when two days passed. "Hey, what's up? How come you didn't get back to me?"[9]

The Bristol County district attorney didn't want them involved, Nelson would later learn. Political rancor ran deep and long. Troopers in Plymouth County would complain the district attorney indirectly ordered everyone not to give information to them — an order those in the Bristol County state police unit ignored and a claim the district attorney, through a spokesman, would later deny.

It was tense for a month as Ostiguy persisted in working the case, with troopers in the Plymouth unit conducting a parallel murder probe focusing on the single slaying in Marion. Police dredged a murky drainage pond off the highway in Marion; metal detectors were used to look for jewelry, and Massachusetts state police dogs searched the stretch of highway for other bodies and evidence. The Plymouth County investigators were now looking at eleven suspects, all from the area. They expected to look at even more.

In Bristol County, the suspect list was also long, but it now appeared the district attorney had his eye on two people. One was Kenny Ponte; the other was a man with a flattened nose the prostitutes claimed attacked them. The name of a third suspect, Neil Anderson, also accused of attacking prostitutes, had come up in the grand jury earlier but interest in him appeared to wane as the sessions continued. The special grand jury met for a third session in April; teams of searchers with dogs from throughout New England earlier examined a twenty-five-mile sweep of roads in Bristol County; and money was yet again becoming an issue as overtime hours mounted.

More than a month after Sandy Botelho's body was found in April 1989, the state police in two counties were now looking at a wide range of suspects and conducting rival investigations. The situation was getting tense.

The Plymouth County district attorney, William O'Malley, was an even-handed prosecutor with a good reputation among cops. He was accessible to the press but was not a grandstander, only appearing before TV cameras when necessary. The cases were important to him. While his was an elected office, he set a clear line between politics and prosecutions. What was now going on in the highway killing case bothered him. It was not how things should work.

He was at his Brockton home, recuperating from a leg injury, and hearing the complaints from the field. Something had to be done.

He called his colleague in Bristol County and set up a meeting at his home.

For an hour, the two met in Brockton. A compromise was reached. Plymouth County investigators could go to the task-force meetings. Ronald Pina's office would still control the overall investigation.

It looked good on paper, Nelson thought. In practice, the case was now firmly in the hands of Ronald Pina's office, and his people in Plymouth County — several who had served under Pina years back — were shut out yet again when it came to the nuts and bolts of the investigation. They went to a few of the meetings but little of substance would be shared with them, and the Plymouth County investigators eventually stopped going, he would later say.

MARYANN SLIT OPEN the large manila envelope, pulled the audiocassette tape out and sighed. It was yet another tip from yet another psychic who claimed to have "seen" what happened using her psychic abilities. Most of the psychic tips came in the form of letters. This was the first tape. Maryann knew she had to listen to it. She knew she would take note of what was said. She also knew it would go nowhere. She would add it to the list of tips from beyond. One psychic claimed to "see" water. Another said the killer didn't like prostitutes. Most of the information seemed to have been taken from news reports. Some of the information was sheer nonsense. Some could be plausible. None of the information panned out — yet. There was always that caveat: yet. They couldn't discount anything, and there was always the possibility someone with solid information could be claiming to have gotten it via psychic abilities just to protect him or herself.

She slipped the tape into the cassette machine and listened. It was interesting but it wasn't helpful, she thought. That's how most of the psychic "tips" turned out.

One psychic told New Bedford detective Richie Ferreira there were five more bodies out there, including one not far from where Sandy Botelho was discovered along Interstate 195. There was still another off the highway heading toward the Cape, another near a marshy edge off a highway, and yet another in a sandpit-like area.[10] The psychic said the information came from a psychic "communication" with the slain woman Sandy. The psychic said the killer bragged about the killings and told two people he "cracked the life out" of them.

Yet another psychic from San Francisco sent a typed letter to New Bedford police claiming to have had a recurring dream about battered bodies pushed from a car then rolling down an embankment. The psychic wrote following this scene in the dream that a man, between the ages of twenty-eight and thirty-four, is then seen. The man has a name badge with four letters.

The information from the psychics, just like the dozens of anonymous letter writers purporting to know who the killer was, was unsolicited, and formal interviews in the office with the psychics weren't done. "Nobody came down to meet with us," Jose later said.[11]

While police weren't finding usable answers from the psychics, some relatives of the missing and the dead weren't discounting it. Christina Monteiro's desperate mother had gone to one psychic, hoping to find something, anything, that could lead to what happened to the nineteen-year-old. She later told Jose the psychic reported her daughter was near water. Another psychic, years later, told Debra Greenlaw DeMello's daughter her mother was killed in a warehouse-like building by a group of men. If investigators couldn't find the answers, a few of the desperate families believed a higher power could.

8 NEW SUSPECT

FOR MORE THAN A YEAR, before the eleven women went missing, before the words "serial killer" and New Bedford were linked in local news reports, the girls on the street were talking to each other about the weird guys, the really weird guys, the ones who would rape them, the ones who would choke them, the ones who scared them. There was one who stood out, the one who often circled the city blocks usually in a pickup truck. He seemed normal when he first picked them up. Sometimes he was a bit quiet. Then he would park and lunge at their throats, he would choke them, he would rape them. Some of the women mentioned this strange guy to the police officers that they knew. And they all shared a warning among themselves. Stay away from the guy with the pushed in nose, the guy who looks like a boxer.

By early 1989, police had put a name to that description.

Anthony R. DeGrazia, a man in his twenties, lived in semirural Freetown, a community bordering New Bedford and home to the sprawling five-thousand-plus-acre state forest where Satanists were once rumored to worship. He grew up in nearby Lakeville, another rural town, and was, from all descriptions, a likeable-enough young man but with deep, personal family problems. In recent years, he was a regular at the St. John Neumann Catholic Church, a modern building overlooking the clear waters of Long Pond in Freetown. When he was still in high school, he left home and bounced from one home to another, often crashing on couches, sometimes camping in the woods. A family in town who felt for this sad-eyed young man opened their tiny home to him. There, for several years, he lived with the couple and their two daughters, and, from all accounts, he seemed to flourish. In a series of photographs taken during that time, Tony sported a childlike, almost elfish grin as he posed in pictures. A few years after moving in, Tony began dating the couple's teenaged daughter who was reeling from the drowning death of her high school boyfriend. Tony worked hard and was polite. He was described as gentle and sweet. He liked beer, sometimes smoked a little weed and, like many young men in wooded towns, knew how to shoot a gun. He had a small circle of friends and adored his girlfriend like a "china doll." He had the look of a fighter in the ring, the flattened nose of a young man having gone too many rounds. Eventually, he worked construction-related jobs, everything from masonry to hanging Sheetrock.

But there was pain in his eyes. His parents' nineteen-year marriage had ended in a bitter divorce in 1980, a proceeding peppered with complaints of cheating, spousal abuse, child abuse, and mental cruelty. Tony once told police his mother hit him in the face with a baseball bat as a child; there were allegations he would be beaten and humiliated when he wet the bed; another claim that his mother once hit him with a belt and beat him in front of his third-grade class when, during a school visit, she saw him misbehave. His brother would allege their mother beat them when they were young — a claim she vigorously denied to state police. (A psychiatrist hired by Tony's mother during the divorce proceedings to evaluate the other DeGrazia children, but not Tony, saw no signs of systematic abuse.) His father would allege in the divorce proceedings that his soon-to-be ex-wife abused Tony. Tony's mother alleged her husband abused her. It was the type of divorce with cross-allegations that are common in court when some marriages break down. The divorce judge gave the mother custody of the couple's four minor children.[1] Nearly a decade later, Tony told a court psychiatrist, Dr. Patricia Ryan Recupero, that he experienced flashbacks of abuse and sometimes "the bad person comes out."[2] Sometimes, he told the psychiatrist, he could smell strange odors or heard people call him when no one was there.

By age eighteen, he had moved out of the home of his girlfriend's parents and was living on his own in nearby Lakeville. He had been arrested on fairly minor charges such as trespassing, disturbing the peace, resisting arrest, assault and battery, and threats in two separate cases. Eventually, all of those charges would be dismissed. By age nineteen, now back in Freetown and still living on his own, he faced more serious charges. He was accused of indecent assault on a girl from Maine, but that charge was also later dismissed. By age twenty, he was accused of picking up two teenaged Dartmouth girls hitchhiking in New Bedford after their car broke down on July 7, 1982 and later sexually assaulting them.

The girls told police the man was playing a tape of *Some Girls* by the Rolling Stones in the blue Mustang. There was a dried flower on the dashboard, and the passenger side door couldn't open from the inside. They asked for a ride home to Dartmouth, but instead he drove to the Freetown State Forest, where just four years earlier a fifteen-year-old high school freshman abducted while riding her bike in Raynham was found tied to a tree and dead. One girl said she was sure she was going to die that night. The girls told police they were sexually assaulted.[3]

When that rape case went to court, the mother of one of the girls bolted across the foyer in the Fall River courthouse during a break in the trial and punched the handcuffed Tony in the side of the head.[4] Tony's girlfriend testified in the case, insisting he was with her the night of the attack, Freetown detective Alan Alves, who investigated the case, said. The jury deliberated roughly three hours before finding him not guilty.

This is what investigators in the murder case would eventually learn once they identified Tony as the man suspected of assaulting prostitutes in the city. In 1987 and 1988, most of the girls on the street just knew to stay away from the guy who looked like a boxer. But caution and sometimes memories fade when the body shakes and craves heroin. And it all blurs when the drug kicks in.

One woman told Trooper Kevin Butler, Trooper Lorraine Forrest, and New Bedford detective Gardner Greany that a man driving a pickup truck took her to a Fairhaven park where he pulled out a switchblade before beating, raping, and robbing her in 1987. "I'm going to kill you, you bitch," he said as he kept hitting her in the face.[5] The man, who told her he initially wanted to drive to Lakeville, had brown hair, "heavy hands, and was likely five feet eight or shorter." She told police she could tell he was a beer drinker — there were empty Budweiser bottles in the truck. She said his nose reminded her of a dog: "Ya know, the dogs with their noses pushed in."[6]

Another woman who, the previous day, had been stabbed in the leg and arm and robbed of twenty dollars by a john, was hobbling down the street to the pay phone by a fence at a gas station near Coggeshall Street. She saw a car go by with three men in it. One jumped out and ran toward her. They talked briefly. He knew she was a prostitute. They agreed on a price: twenty dollars for oral sex. The other men in the car had taken off. "Well, let's just go around the fence," he told her.

"No, it's all muddy and stuff. I don't want to go around there. I don't want to go there."[7]

The man pulled her; they fought; the stitches in her arm pulled out. He put her in headlock. She was gasping, trying to breathe. He threw her on the ground, one hand on her neck. "And he was growling like or making funny noises like, urrr, he was going to punch me, like he was going to punch me out. He's got a big fist."[8]

She would later say she went along with it, afraid he would kill her. Then it was over. "And then he got up, zipped up his pants, and ran toward Coggeshall."[9] Her shirt was covered with mud and prickers. She remembered his nose. It was flat, as if someone had punched him, like the nose of a boxer. A few nights later, a black truck pulled up to her on Purchase Street. As she went to get in, she caught a look at the driver. It was the same man. "You gotta be kidding me," she would recall saying later before turning away. A month later, she saw him again. "I never did that to you," he told her. She looked at him, answering: "Bullshit. I'll never forget your face."[10]

A dark-haired woman whose pale Irish skin would be ravaged by drugs within a year on the streets told the story of a guy in a truck with a "pushed in" nose who took her to a cemetery on January 11, 1989, flashed a fifty-dollar bill then put her in a headlock. "You know, I mean, he had me in a headlock so I couldn't breathe. And I was fightin' him. And I could hardly breathe."[11] She said she was sexually assaulted and, as she jumped out of the car, the man drove off. She was able to grab her pants. Her shoes were still in the car.

Another prostitute told of a john who picked her up three times. "He took me up towards the airport first time I went out with him. And I've been out with him I think twice. And the third time, he was drinking. And he just started going crazy on me. And he told me that if I didn't fight him, he wouldn't hurt me. And so he tried. He started to take my pants off. And I reached in my back pocket, and I pulled a knife. And I told him if he didn't let me go, I was going to stab him. And he let me go. And I got away from him," she recalled.[12]

The man, who looked like "he's been punched in his nose a couple of times," tried to pick her up again. She didn't go. Other girls did, she said, like Dawn Mendes, who was found dead on Interstate 195 in November of 1988.

Another woman suggested to Trooper Kevin Butler and Detective Gardner Greany during an interview on January 23, 1989, that police investigate an ex-boxer with a flat nose who may work construction and drives a truck. He raped several of the girls on the street, she told police.

Yet another woman told Detectives Gary Baron and Richard Ferreira a man who called himself "Tony" or "David" attacked her. She later identified her attacker from a photo array. "That's him," she told Trooper Kevin Butler,[13] pointing to a photo of Anthony DeGrazia.

The attacks chronicled by New Bedford police and state troopers dated back to July of 1987. As the special grand jury met, these stories would be intermingled with others as witnesses appeared before the grand jury. While the headlines in January of 1989 publically screamed the name of Kenneth C. Ponte, the testimony before closed doors two months later told the stories of other men, like Tony, and the broader story of addiction, life on the streets, and how women in the late 1980s struggled to pay for heroin.

By mid-April, police were ready to bring Tony in for a chat.

TONY DEGRAZIA was at his rented Freetown cottage when the unmarked state police cruiser pulled up on April 19, 1989. We would like you to talk with you, the two troopers told him. Some women in Weld Square said you attacked them. Can you come with us to the office to so we can clear some things up? He didn't want to go at first. He called his parish priest saying he was afraid he was going to be arrested. He was afraid someone would try to pin the murders on him. Father George Harrison tried to assure Tony: if he didn't have anything to hide, if he was innocent, there was nothing to fear. Go with the police.

So Tony left the small cottage near the shores of Long Pond. He got in the back of the Ford Crown Victoria and began to talk with Troopers Kevin Butler and Lorraine Forrest as they began to drive south toward New Bedford. He never picked up a prostitute, he insisted. And he never raped anyone. He appreciated the opportunity to clear it all up, he told the troopers.

As the three drove to New Bedford down Route 140, the highway where three bodies had already been found, a team of state police and New Bedford detectives were pulling up to Tony's house with a search warrant. Troopers Jose Gonsalves, Maryann Dill, Kenneth Martin, and New Bedford detective Richard Ferreira strode into the house and looked through the drawers, the closets, under the bed, and through Tony's personal papers. They looked through Tony's 1987 black Ford pickup truck and took a cigarette lighter, a drywall cutting knife, a four-inch butcher's knife, a steak knife, a sock, a bottle cap, and mail. They found a human fingernail on the passenger side of the floor. They swabbed the black interior air vent of the truck and found blood. There were signs of blood on the driver's seat. There were footprints on the passenger side ceiling, on the center strip of the ceiling and hairs under the floor liner.

They stayed at the house for hours, looking for evidence in the rape and beatings of at least seventeen prostitutes. Tony lived alone in the cottage, and it was not the cleanest of houses. There was quite a bit to go through. If there was anything there, they planned to find it.

Roughly twenty miles away at the district attorney's office in New Bedford, Tony was read his Miranda rights then was interviewed by the two troopers who for months were meticulously following stories by prostitutes that an ex-boxer with a pushed in nose had attacked them. Kevin Butler and Lorraine Forrest had culled similar information from the files of New Bedford detectives and fellow members of the state police and then had reinterviewed many of the victims. They discovered Freetown detective sgt. Alan Alves, who had been bounced off the highway killing investigative team, had arrested a man matching Tony's description years earlier in two other rape cases.

Lorraine and Kevin were troopers who liked to delve deeply into a single project, drawing out the meticulous and obscure details to cement a case. They liked all of the i's dotted in their investigations. The t's were crossed perfectly. They believed that attention to even the tiniest of details helped solve cases. They also believed the man sitting in the back of their cruiser was the one who was attacking prostitutes in the city. Was he also the man who committed the murders?

Lorraine Forrest was a head-turning blonde who had been a trooper for a little more than a year and a half before joining the investigative unit. She would be the first to admit she was the least experienced in the office, but she was determined to learn and pull her weight. She embraced the challenge of the work and this investigation in particular.

Kevin Butler was an intense investigator with a wry sense of humor who had grown up in Brockton. He was detail oriented and approached investigations unfettered by hometown ties and with a laser-focused, out-of-town eye that some mistook for aloofness.

When Tony agreed to talk without an attorney present, the troopers got right to the point. Did he pick up prostitutes? Once, a long time ago, he told them. He didn't need to go out with prostitutes. He had a beautiful girlfriend for nine years until they broke up in October of 1988.

The troopers told him that at least seventeen prostitutes had identified him as the person who attacked them. Tony then admitted he did pick up some girls in the past but that was more than a year ago, and he never assaulted any of them. Some did tell him that he looked familiar and that he looked like someone who assaulted them, Tony said. People often mistook him for someone else.

Then the troopers detailed the allegations and showed him photographs of the women who were attacked. They also showed him photographs of the highway killing victims. Some of the faces looked familiar, he said. Most did not.

"Usually when I deal with people like this, I try to forget them right away," he told the investigators. "I don't want to be seen with them. I don't know why I even stop for them."[14]

The trooper pressed him about the allegations. Why would the women identify him? Why would they say this? Look at the photos again. Are you sure you don't recognize them? No. Maybe. I don't know. Tony's answers fluctuated with each question. "She looks like a girl I picked up but I can't really tell," he said when shown one photo. "I don't look at their faces."

Does he black out? How about when he drinks?

"I don't usually black out, and I don't think I ever hurt anyone," Tony said. "I hate going with these girls because it's degrading. These girls only want money so they can buy drugs. They're dirty. I couldn't take a chance of bringing something home to my girl. I'd be riddled with guilt. She would know right away. The few times I did, it was probably after I broke up with my girl last fall."

Tony's answers swung from insisting he never went to Weld Square and never picked up prostitutes to saying he just couldn't remember the faces of the women he went with. "I could have picked them up, but I don't remember them," he told the troopers. "I have picked up girls that I don't remember. These girls are such scumbags that I don't want anything to do with them. I've been approached a hundred times. I just don't want anything to do with it."

He was never violent. Sometimes he pushed girls out of the truck, he admitted. Sometimes he did lose control if he was drinking. "Sometimes I get out of control and I just want to get away from them. I don't know why I pick them up. Then I just want to get rid of them. I have to get them away from me."

Yes, he did choke girls in the past but they weren't unconscious, he said. "Sometimes I get screwed up and make a mistake," Tony told them.

He didn't kill anyone, he insisted.

"If I killed one person, the next person would be me," he said. "My guilt feelings would kill me."

Five hours into the interview, Lorraine left the room. The search of Tony's house in Freetown had wrapped up and Jose — now back at the office — joined the interview.

Jose quietly asked Tony about when he went to Weld Square and how many times. Did he remember if he was there on Labor Day? How about Memorial Day weekend? Tony believed he went to Weld Square about fifty times, often on the alternating weekends his girlfriend worked. Sometimes he went there late at night after she went back to her own home.

Tony was shown the photo again of Sandra Botelho, the mother of two found dead in April in Marion. Yes, he now said, she did look familiar.

We know you wrote a personal check to her, he was told.

Tony admitted he did write a check to a girl for oral sex. She was crying about her kids. The check was for thirty or forty dollars. He never wrote checks to other prostitutes, he insisted.

He answered a series of questions. No, there wouldn't be any blood in his car, he answered the troopers. No, he never brought prostitutes back to his house. No, he didn't kill anyone. He would never go back to Weld Square again, he promised. Never, ever, ever. Just give me another chance. Just let me go.

"I fucked up and got out of hand before, but I didn't kill anyone."

Tony looked at Jose and paused. You remind me of my father, he told the soft-spoken trooper.[15]

Jose paused and changed the subject. He would later wonder if it was a missed opportunity. What if he had followed that line, what if he had told Tony his father would want him to tell him everything? What would the young man have told him? Would it have been anything?

It was now getting late — it was quarter to one in the morning — and Tony was getting tired. He had to work in the morning. He said he would like to go home.

As Lorraine and Kevin drove him back to Freetown, they broke the news that police had already searched his home and his truck had been seized.

When they got to the house, the troopers took the clothes Tony was wearing as evidence: leather work boots, blue jeans, and a blue, purple, and tan flannel shirt.

A polygraph test was scheduled for a few days later, Monday, April 24, 1989.

He never showed up. He now had a lawyer, Edward Harrington, the former mayor of New Bedford, an affable but shrewd attorney who was a fixture in all of the city courthouses. He could spout off legal precedent and arguments with such ease some people claimed he made up the cases. Do not talk with my client again, Tony's lawyer now ordered.

The next month, a prostitute by the name of Margaret Medeiros appeared before the special grand jury. She said a man named Tony picked her up, but when she asked for the money upfront, he lunged at her. "He just lunged at my throat; and he tried to — you know, he was twisting my neck He tried snapping my neck."[16] The two struggled, his hands still on her neck, she said.

"And he told me what he was going to do to me like he did to the other bitches," she said.[17]

She said she couldn't lift her arms and felt like she was going to pass out. "So I just gave every strength that I had; and I kicked him. Because that was the only thing I had free was my feet."

She kicked him in the gut and the groin. He grabbed his stomach and called her a bitch. She jumped out of the vehicle — it was either a Bronco or Blazer, she said — and ran home. She didn't get the plate number then. It was a new vehicle, though, "because it still had the smell to it, you know, like a new car smell."

For the next two days, he tried to pick her up again; she didn't get in the vehicle. Then he drove by in a dirty, beat-up hatchback. She didn't recognize him — he was wearing a hat — or the car. She got in. They drove a couple of blocks before she recognized the face. When the car stopped at a red light, she jumped out. He yelled, calling her a bitch as she bolted down the street.

When Margaret left the courthouse after testifying, she told television and newspaper reporters the same story — including the claim that her attacker said he would do to her "what he did to the other bitches."

In May of 1989, one month after state police searched his house, Tony stood before a judge to face four counts of rape, six counts of assault and battery, and one count of assault with intent to rape. All of the charges stemmed from attacks on six prostitutes from April 1988 to April 1989. It included the time span of the murders.

THE BRISTOL COUNTY HOUSE OF CORRECTION and Jail on Ash Street in New Bedford was chilly in the winter and brutally hot in the summer, and the corridors were eerily shadowed. The walls throughout the building were painted in either steel gray, green, or dirty white, colors that covered the walls of nearly all municipal structures at the time. It was a noisy place, difficult to sleep in. Prisoners often stuck their hands through the bars, clutching small mirrors to see down the halls. Sometimes there were so many prisoners the sheriff was forced to double them up in the 287 cells.

The jail held men doing time and men awaiting trial. They were technically separated but the building was small enough and the prisoner network tight enough that everyone, from the guards to the inmates, knew who was coming in. Most of the prisoners were drug addicts, arrested or serving sentences for crimes ranging from drug possession to bank robbery. These were the prisoners with drug-addicted girlfriends or wives still copping heroin and cocaine on the street. These were the prisoners who knew how some of the women earned money to buy drugs. These were the prisoners waiting for Tony DeGrazia.

For seven months, Tony bounced from the jail to Bridgewater State Hospital where he underwent weeks of psychiatric evaluations. When he was at the jail in New Bedford, the staff either kept him segregated or under close watch. His bail was $75,000 cash, too high for anyone to post. His lawyer, Edward Harrington, kept trying to get it lowered and judges kept refusing. Finally, on December 11, 1989, a judge agreed to reduce the bail to $37,500. There was a good chance Tony would now be out by Christmas.

Tony was on the phone in a social worker's office in the jail on December 14, making plans for his release, when the psychiatrist who did work at the prison walked in.

"Hey, I hear you're getting out. Now you can start getting your life back together," the doctor told him.[18]

"I'm not getting my life back together. Why should I? Pina's made my life miserable. Now I'm going to make his life miserable. I'm going to end it," Tony answered.[19]

The doctor, Robert Sisson, paused. That isn't a smart thing to say, he told Tony. Tony didn't answer.

It wasn't unusual at the jail to hear prisoners threaten prosecutors or police officers. Most of the comments were idle "letting off steam" remarks. Neil Anderson of New Bedford, another man once considered — but dropped as the investigation continued — as a suspect in the highway killings had been arrested a year earlier, accused of choking and raping prostitutes. He said similar things to the doctor when he was jailed. He immediately said he was just angry and didn't mean it. But Tony didn't do that, and the doctor was worried; he told jail officials he was afraid Tony was serious.

Officials at the jail had been keeping a close watch on Tony since his arrest in May of 1989 on the rape and assault charges. They knew he was named a suspect by a grand jury witness in the highway killings and was once considered a suicide risk. No one was taking any chances: the threats were reported to the state police after Tony was released on bail. A court complaint was issued from New Bedford District Court charging Tony with attempting to commit a crime by threatening to kill the district attorney.

A retired plumber named Peter Duff, who had once employed Tony, posted the $37,500 bail, using a savings account as collateral, on a Thursday. Tony was arrested five days later as he waited in district court for a routine hearing on earlier, unrelated drunk-driving charges. His lawyer, Edward Harrington, was livid and told the judge the prosecutor's office was overreacting and the remarks, if his client even said them, were taken out of context and couldn't be taken seriously. The judge agreed and released Tony. "It's absurd. I didn't threaten to kill him," Tony said after he was released.[20]

It was the latest court ordeal for Tony. He had been in and out of the public investigative spotlight for months in the murder case. In May of 1989, Tony had been ordered to provide a blood sample to prosecutors, and that sample was later sent to the FBI to compare with the blood found on the seat covers of the passenger and driver sides of Tony's truck and the vent grille near the glove box. The blood sample could be used both in the rape case and other cases.

His lawyer would later insist the tests cleared his client of murder for a simple reason: the police never charged him.

9 LOOKING IN OTHER CORNERS

PAUL BOUDREAU LISTENED to the intercepted telephone call through the headphones. He and other members of the Bristol County Drug Task Force had spent months investigating allegations that large amounts of cocaine were moving out of Whispers Pub in the city's South End, the same bar several highway killing victims used to frequent. One informant told police "he/she" saw sales of cocaine in the bar and heard people on the phone setting up deals. Yet another saw someone carrying cocaine to be sold. It was January 26, 1989, day three of a court-authorized wiretap for the case, and the listening detectives expected to hear more talk that would bring the drug ring down. They were also keeping an ear open in case anyone mentioned any of the dead women.

Whispers Pub was one of several neighborhood bars lining the southern section of County Street, where patrons were often hanging out on the sidewalks. It was a cramped area of the city with apartments above local businesses and tight side streets with tenements.

A number of the dead and missing women hung out at Whispers Pub, and one, Nancy Paiva, was at the bar at one point the night she disappeared. Homicide investigators were curious if there were any links between that bar — or any bar — and the case. This wiretap — even the entire drug investigation — could wind up giving the murder case a major boost. Someone might slip and mention the women — or even dumping a body. Stranger things have happened.

The wiretap on the bar phone was already yielding promising and incriminating information on the cocaine-dealing ring. A day earlier, members of the task force had picked up calls detailing several suspected cocaine sales. New Bedford detective Bruce Machado heard one woman ask to buy cocaine and if she could "get two for fifty, referring to an amount of cocaine."[1] The man on the other end of the phone told her he is at the bar and will bring it by. He also warned her the phone was tapped. That warning apparently didn't stop people from talking on the tapped phone. Raynham detective Mario Bettencourt heard someone say he was going to the North End "to pick up good shit" and yet another caller asked if the person on the other end had "good stuff."

It was now 23:10:55 hours on the third day of what was to be a thirty-day court approved wiretap spanning forty-five days.

"Hello, Ronnie," the caller said.

"Yah," the person on the other end answered.

"I need three."

"Of what?"

"Twenty-eight."

"Ah, yah all right."

"You gonna bring it over here?"

"Where are you?"

"At the bar."

"Oh, wow!"

Paul listened closely, trying to recognize the two voices arranging a meeting at a bank in ten minutes. The next night, he intercepted another call to a beeper number listed to "Ronnie."

"Give me a call at Whispers right now. This is very, very important. Give me a call now as soon as possible. I'll appreciate if you call me right now."

The call, they believed, based on other information gathered, had to do with drug deliveries and sales. Eventually, thanks to the wiretap, informants, and undercover drug purchases, the task force was able to shut down the ring and convict its leaders.

But the narcotics detectives never heard anyone talk about the dead women. They never heard anyone talk about bodies.

"There was nothing, nothing at all," Louis J. Pacheco, who led the task force at the time, would later say.[2]

Once the Whispers Pub drug investigation started to wrap up, the drug task force turned its sights on the dealings of Kenny Ponte and his friends in Florida to see if they could find any ties to drug dealing in Massachusetts — or to the deaths of the women. State police investigators were still also checking on other suspects.

JOSE GLANCED into the rearview mirror at the handcuffed prisoner in the back seat of the cruiser. The prisoner — a man named Ronald Ray Griffith — had been locked up in Missouri until four days previously when he had been flown under guard to Massachusetts. The twenty-eight-year-old Griffith had told a correction officer at the South Franklin County jail in Union, Missouri, where he was locked up on larceny charges, that he killed the women in New Bedford when he was living back East. The guard wasn't sure if the story was true, but he passed it along — just in case. Now, Jose was in the car with this prisoner, tooling around the area in the August heat of 1989, trying to figure out if the story he was telling was yet another yarn. Since the start of the case, investigators followed up on claim after claim that someone confessed to the killings. None, so far, proved true.

Jose and the other investigators had already checked motor vehicle records, arrest records, and interviewed people who knew the guy. His story could be true, Jose thought. The guy had been in the area between April and September of 1988 — the time of the killings — with his then wife. He was only sent back to Missouri, where he was a fugitive from justice, after police in Attleboro arrested him on car theft and disturbing the peace charges. The timeline made sense. This could be the real deal. But he and the other investigators were still cautious. They had teetered several times on identifying the killer before, only to see the cases were built on rumor, innuendo, and outright lies. In some cases, the people with the information were just plain crazy. In some cases, the suspect had an alibi.

The case had extended beyond the homicide unit. Narcotics detectives both in the city and county were looking at possible ties between their cases and the murders. After the Whispers Pub cocaine-trafficking case and its related wiretap failed to reveal ties to the killings, members of the Bristol County Drug Task Force looked in other directions. The New Bedford city narcotics unit raided an apartment the husband of one victim was sharing with a group of people — finding cocaine but no evidence to help the murder probe.

And, earlier, New Bedford and state police investigators had spent weeks checking on a group of dangerous sex offenders who were released on days-long furloughs from a state facility called the Treatment Center for the Sexually Dangerous in Bridgewater, about forty minutes away. Under state law, sex offenders could be civilly committed for life if a judge found they were likely to reoffend and if they were a danger to the community. But being committed didn't mean all of the offenders stayed locked up, thanks to the furlough program at the time. As part of a rehabilitation effort to prepare the offenders for possible release, some of them were allowed to leave the facility to work or attend other programs. At least ten of the convicted rapists who were out on furlough during the summer of 1988 either owned or had access to vehicles, ranging from compact cars such as a blue Pinto to full-sized vehicles and a truck. One rapist on furlough was a man named Kenneth Junier who had been convicted of raping two women and trying to attack a third in the 1970s. In one of the cases he pulled over the victim, claiming to be a cop. In all three cases, he grabbed the women by the neck or throat. In 1988, he had been working and staying with his wife in New Bedford from Mondays to Fridays while on a furlough, returning to the center just for the weekends. (He was eventually moved to a minimum security state prison after he was deemed not "sexually dangerous" in 1991. He was denied parole five times and was still in prison in 2017). Another convict was out for a few hours; yet another for a few days. One of the men, Michael Kelley, was convicted of raping two women in Boston in 1976 and 1977. (He was later charged with the murder of two women months after he was released in 1992.) Yet another man, Ronald Leftwich, who raped and tortured a sixty-seven-year-old Nantucket woman in 1977, was moved out of the furlough program in August of 1988 because of a "pattern of lies and inappropriate behavior."[3] (A year after he was deemed "not sexually dangerous" and released in 1995, he beat a pastor in Brimfield, Massachusetts, to death.) The men at the treatment center were considered the worst of the worst sex offenders: violent pedophiles and serial rapists. The group of men who were now out on furlough topped the list for investigators to check out.

The furlough records, however, were not as detailed as the investigators had hoped. Sloppy was the way one person later described them. There were some cases where police suspected the prisoners weren't supervised properly.

There were other cases where the prisoners weren't supervised at all while out on a furlough. There were reports the men were seen in Weld Square and that some were dealing or using drugs. In some cases, it was difficult to pinpoint the exact times prisoners returned or were let out. The furloughed sex offenders were never "ruled in" as suspects in the murders. Some were never completely ruled out either. They were, like so many others, in that "maybe" pile.

As Jose drove in the cruiser this day, Maryann in the front and Richie, the New Bedford detective, in the back with the prisoner, he wondered if this latest suspect from Missouri would be yet another dead end.

For three days now, they had driven for hours with the prisoner, past the areas where the women's bodies had been found. Sometimes the prisoner would say a spot looked familiar. Sometimes he said nothing as they drove by. The investigators were careful to keep quiet during the ride. In interviews with the troopers and detective, the prisoner talked about the case but never gave specifics. The only information he provided was what anyone reading a newspaper would know: the women had been strangled and left along the highway.

Between his answers, the man kept repeating the same question. Now could he see his estranged wife, who was still living in the area? He asked in the morning when they picked him up. He asked as they drove him around the towns circling New Bedford. He asked when they ate lunch. He asked while they interviewed him at the office. He asked as they returned him to the county jail.

Ronald Ray Griffith had an agenda and it didn't include solving the highway killings, they were convinced.

By the fourth day, the trio was weary of Griffith and weary of his blathering about his wife. They needed to lay a trap to confirm he was lying.

The cruiser passed by a spot off the highway. Richie was smiling in the backseat. "Isn't that where that other body was found?" Richie asked.[4]

Ronald took the bait. He launched into a description about how he killed a woman and left her there. Richie shot a look at his colleagues and grinned. There was no body found there, the investigators knew. The guy was wasting their time.

Finally, we can get this guy out of the car, Jose thought.

Ronald Ray Griffith was on the next available plane back to Missouri with a U.S. marshal. He never got to see his estranged wife.

AS MARYANN AND JOSE CONTINUED to follow what seemed at times unrelated but intriguing leads in the case, the troopers were getting reports the drug task force was taking a keen interest in what Kenny Ponte and his friends were doing in Florida. Questions were being raised about the business dealings of one of Kenny's friends, and they were hearing reports about disturbances at the lawyer's Florida home. It would be interesting what the narcotics detectives came up with, the troopers thought.

PAUL BOUDREAU leaned the Canon SLR on the dashboard to keep it still as he focused on the shoebox-like duplex ahead. The building reminded him of a double-wide trailer in a rundown neighborhood: indistinctive and a bit trashy.

Slowly, his boss in the DA's office, chief investigator Robert St. Jean, inched by the house. Paul, sitting on the passenger side, peered through the camera lens.

Click. Click.

One shot of the car.

One shot of the car and duplex.

The pair had flown down from Massachusetts in October 1989 to scope out Kenneth Ponte's Florida place for a couple of days to see — firsthand — what he was up to. They heard from Florida investigators, Sgt. William Sager and Detective David Buhs, that there had been a few problems at the lawyer's house about two blocks from the Port Richey police department. A rock thrown through a window. Shotgun blasts in front of the house. Arguments. Fights. Lots of people coming and going. The "general arguments and fights."

Port Richey police were keeping a close eye on the house after getting more than a few reports in late December of 1988 and early 1989 about the murder investigation in Massachusetts and Ponte's possible ties to the case. Now, nearly a year after the attorney had moved to Florida, Paul and Bob were at the police station to meet with Port Richey investigators first, getting the not-on-the-report background on the neighborhood, the people coming and going, and the general "cop feel" for what was going on at the house.

Kenny Ponte didn't go out much: an occasional trip to the grocery store or take-out at Hooters. Most of the trouble he got into — or when trouble found him — was at his own duplex.

Now, it was time for the Massachusetts investigators to find out for themselves what was going on at the place. Paul was already looking into the business dealings of one of Kenny's friends, a former corrections officer in Massachusetts by the name of Paul Ryley. The man was a braggart: a few years earlier he stopped into Boudreau's video store in the North End of New Bedford and told him he had invested in fifty movie theaters in Tennessee; bought a two-hundred-unit condominium complex in Texas; had money in an Acapulco hotel and gold company, and had invested in Florida property. He also claimed he was working undercover in Texas. He told the detective he was doing great and making lots of money. *Want to go into business with me? How about a private investigation business in Florida?* At least once a month, Ryley would stop by the movie rental shop to talk about business, his life, and the money he was making. In December of 1988, the visits stopped — around the same time the narcotics detective began a side investigation into Kenny Ponte's drug issues.[5]

Paul Boudreau was intrigued by one of calls from the Port Richey detectives. Did he know a woman named Elsa Johnson from Dartmouth, Massachusetts, who was living in the duplex next door to Kenny? And did he know the woman said her "old man" was a guy named Paul Ryley? And did he know Paul Ryley was "married" to a woman named Sandra Castro? The New Bedford detective was interested — especially since he knew Paul Ryley was not divorced from his wife who was still living in the New Bedford area. What was going on down there, he wondered. For months, the Florida police department had been keeping a daily watch on the duplex, reporting back what they saw to the detective.

For a few hours, Boudreau and St. Jean watched the lawyer's house from a distance in a rented car as people came and went. Then, as the sun set, they hid out back in a swamp-like area about seventy-five feet away to see what went on at night. Paul made sure he wore long pants, even though the night was warm. A couple of years earlier, he was on the east coast of Florida on a drug surveillance and felt something crawling up his leg. He had been bitten by red ants. That wasn't going to happen again.

Through binoculars, they could see shadowy figures moving in the windows and the flicker of the television. Was that a woman's figure? Paul wondered. Who was it? The two kept looking. Was it someone from New Bedford? Was it someone they should know?

Paul slapped a mosquito on his arm. Then another. Then another. He mentally added "hazmat suit" to his list of "must haves" for the next surveillance before packing up for the night.

FOLLOW THE MONEY. Follow the paperwork.

That's what Paul Boudreau tried to do when he returned to New Bedford and tried to untangle Paul Ryley's business dealings to see if anything illegal was being done. It turned out to be fairly easy. Ryley was cocky and he was sloppy. A close look at the man's late mother's estate found a document had been forged to get about $60,000 of a 1970 real-estate trust's assets. There was already a civil case pending, but criminal charges could also be lodged.[6] Paul began putting together his case.

A grand jury handed up an indictment in Bristol County Superior Court on December 12, 1989, charging Kenny's friend with uttering a forged instrument — the charge covering the forgery — and larceny. After a bench warrant for the man's arrest was issued, the detective was on the phone with Port Richey police sgt. William Sager. *Arrest him.*

By three o'clock that afternoon, Kenny Ponte was standing in the doorway of his Sun Glo Avenue duplex, watching police lead his friend away in handcuffs.

Ryley turned to Kenny briefly. "Call Joe. Tell them to be very careful."[7] Police never identified who he was talking about.

Inside the duplex Paul Ryley occasionally shared with his girlfriend from Massachusetts, police found a foot-thick pile of "hard core pornography books." In a dresser drawer were Polaroid photos, including two of his girlfriend partially dressed. In the trunk of Ryley's car, they found a fully loaded 9 mm Smith & Wesson automatic with two extra clips. At the police station, they found he had two Bristol County sheriff's badges along with four deputy-sheriff photo IDs.

Five days later, Ryley called the New Bedford detective. It was the first time they had spoken in four months.

"What's going on?" Ryley wanted to know.

"You don't have to talk with me," Paul Boudreau answered.

"I don't understand why I'm being arrested. Get me back to New Bedford as soon as you can."

Ryley told the detective he knew hanging around with Kenny would be trouble, without elaborating.

"So why do it? "Paul asked.

"Who else can I bum around with?" was the answer.[8]

By the time the detective and Bob St. Jean arrived in Florida on December 27, 1989, to bring Paul Ryley back, it was clear they didn't want to talk about forgeries or estate trusts. Bob read him his Miranda rights against self-incrimination.

You want to ask me about Kenny Ponte, he told the investigators.

He knew Kenny from New Bedford, and the attorney had done some legal work for his mom, Doris Trimble. They socialized a couple of times and went out to eat at a Chinese restaurant in Westport, Massachusetts. In Florida, Elsa the girlfriend needed a place to live, and Kenny had a cheap place to rent next door for $275 a month. His wife Sandra — well, maybe the marriage wasn't quite legal because he never got a divorce — was living in Springhill, Florida, and didn't know about the girlfriend.

Are you aware of the investigation into the murders in the New Bedford area? You know Kenny's name came up, Paul Boudreau told him.

"What do you think? You think I killed the girls or Kenny did it," Ryley answered.[9]

Paul could see the suspect was getting agitated, at times "almost jumping out of his seat."

They took a break and returned to talk to him at the Florida lockup later that day.

"I want to cooperate with you," Ryley said. "Ask me any questions you want and I will answer them truthfully."

Bob St. Jean read the Miranda rights again. Ryley again said he understood.

Two heavy-set sisters used to hang out with Kenny in New Bedford, he told them. The detective nodded. (The detective knew the sisters were still alive; the women had talked with police.) There was a woman named Rochelle from the Cape who was there, too, in 1988. In Florida, he thought a woman named

Linda stayed with Kenny along with a short, very thin blonde woman with no front teeth named Mary. Yet another woman named Amber who spent some time in the Hillsboro County jail was also there in Florida at one time.

Kenny was living off "residual checks" from three New Bedford attorneys who picked up his cases in Massachusetts, and he hadn't worked at all in Florida. Ryley said he suggested that Kenny practice law in Florida. He never did.

By the time Paul Ryley was back in a Massachusetts to enter a not-guilty plea to forgery and larceny charges on January 2, 1990, the district attorney's office was sketching out the witness list for the next special grand jury session.

The lawyer representing him on the larceny charges, Stephen J. Amaral, withdrew from the case after his client was served the subpoena to testify "in the case of John Doe," citing a conflict of interest. His law partner, Joseph Harrington, was representing Kenny Ponte.

"We have reason to think we know who John Doe is," Amaral told a judge on January 16, 1990.[10]

"The whole city of New Bedford knows who John Doe is, if they read the newspapers," Superior Court judge John Sheehan answered.

Nine days later, New Bedford detective Paul Boudreau testified before the special grand jury for one and a half hours.

Ryley appeared later with his new lawyer, Joseph Macy, and stayed in the grand jury room for nearly as long. After testifying, the former prison guard and Bristol County deputy sheriff was escorted back to the Bristol County jail in handcuffs, ordered to return the next day.

To the media, the district attorney, Ronald Pina, called the session "very productive" and said that his office would be following up on the testimony. "We'll have a full day of work," the prosecutor told the growing group of reporters outside the courthouse.

Ryley would indeed be back before the grand jury, testifying for roughly two more hours.

Some people in the city were speculating Kenny Ponte was now the target of the grand jury. In the grand jury room, the prosecutor, however, was also presenting testimony about other people. On the streets, police were still tracking new leads, different suspects, and a wide range of scenarios.

Publically, the district attorney was telling reporters the case could be coming to a close. "I think we're very close," Ron Pina said during a radio

show on WHTB in Fall River on February 15, 1990. "I think we're really focusing down to a possible suspect — not three, four, five, or six but a possible
suspect. And where we're at is looking for that last piece of evidence or those
last pieces of evidence."

He had said similar things before in this roller coaster of an investigation.
Six months earlier, in June 1989, he told reporters there could be an indictment within a month if some information provided to the grand jury was
borne out. There was no indictment, and by July of that year Pina would
admit the information couldn't be corroborated.

That "information" centered on claims someone stole a sex tape from
Kenny's house featuring local women and then tried to blackmail the lawyer.
The tape was never found, and the woman who purportedly stole it insisted
it was all a lie.

In Florida, Kenneth C. Ponte was likely seeing hopes for a new life in Port
Richey slip away.

10 THE CIRCLE TIGHTENS

AT AGE THIRTY-SEVEN, Kevin Reddington was a lawyer's lawyer: no-nonsense, respectful, and schooled in the law. He grew up in Stoughton, Massachusetts, a midsized middle-class town between Boston and Brockton, with childhood dreams of becoming an attorney. As a child, he had even signed a note to his mother "Esq.," foretelling of his future career. He graduated from Boston College, got married, graduated Suffolk University School of Law cum laude in 1975, eventually set up his law office in Brockton and was raising four children in the suburban town of Easton, Massachusetts, less than twenty minutes from his parents' home. He was, everyone agreed, one of those grounded, down-to-earth individuals who remembered the names of secretaries and clerks, who never forgot his roots. He was tenacious in the courtroom but didn't hold the petty, post-trial grudges some other attorneys harbored. His job was to defend his client; it was the jury's job to render a verdict. And he did that job well. From drunk-driving cases to the first murder acquittal using a battered woman's defense in Massachusetts, he was one of the busiest lawyers in the state. He worked long hours, crisscrossing the county and eventually the state, honing his skills and drawing more clients. He was always learning new skills in the courtroom, even more than a decade after passing the bar. He would watch the top attorneys of the time quiz witnesses, listen to opening statements and closing arguments, always paying close attention to what worked and what failed. He prepared for the unexpected and took the trial adage "never ask a question you don't know the answer to" seriously.

Kevin was in his second floor office on Route 123 in Brockton, waiting for his newest client to show up. His wooden desk faced the doorway, giving him an easy view of visitors. A few days earlier, an attorney he never met by the name of Kenneth C. Ponte had called asking if he would represent him. Kenny was in a bit of a mess in New Bedford and was afraid things would get even worse. Come in and we'll talk, is what Kevin Reddington told him on the phone. Before the meeting, Kevin did some cursory research on what his potential client was facing and was troubled by what he found. A lot of innuendo, a lot of headlines. Trial by media, he thought. To him, it appeared the prosecution was tainting a potential jury pool before charges were even brought. He thought it appeared unethical, and it would be an interesting case to defend.

When Kenny walked through the door, the defense attorney was struck by the man's awkward appearance. Kenny was a big guy who didn't wear suits well. He was agitated but not obnoxious. He wasn't what Kevin expected, based on what he had read in the papers and seen on TV. "I expected him to be scratching to make the bugs go away," he recalled. "He was just a regular guy who got caught in a bad situation through no fault of his own."[1]

Kenny was upset about his treatment by the district attorney; angered by suggestions he could be a killer. He was complaining the prosecutor was looking to ruin him. He didn't do anything wrong. He didn't hurt anyone. It was a witch hunt.

Kenny couldn't understand why moving to Florida in late 1988 was such a big deal to the district attorney. He had been telling people for a while he wanted to move south, start fresh, and get away from New Bedford. Yes, he moved a month after the disappearances ended; but that was because the move was delayed. It was a coincidence, he said.

Looking over the desk as Kenny's voice rose, the defense attorney knew what the first step would be if he took this case. Kenny had taken to calling television, radio, and newspaper reporters, complaining "off the record" to anyone who would listen. The district attorney was out to get him, Kenny would rant. Occasionally, he would end up on the local radio call-in show, railing against the district attorney. He was angry and he let everyone know it.

By the end of the meeting in the Brockton office, Kevin Reddington agreed to represent Kenny — with some provisions. Here are the rules: Keep your mouth shut, let me do the talking, listen to what I tell you to do, and, please, stop calling the media.

Kevin didn't realize how hard that last request would be to enforce.

THE LEGAL COMMUNITY in New Bedford in 1990 was a tight political circle. Personal ties went back, in some cases, to elementary school; alliances were woven through families, through jobs, through church, through sports, through children. Most people in New Bedford hired New Bedford lawyers, just as those in Fall River twenty minutes to the west hired Fall River lawyers. Occasionally, a public defender would come down from Brockton or Boston to represent an indigent defendant accused of murder, but, generally, law and justice were decidedly local.

Then Kevin Reddington drove up to the New Bedford Superior Courthouse in his red Porsche convertible, sporting the Massachusetts license plate NG — the abbreviation for not guilty. He was jovial as he chatted with court officers and clerks. He smiled, as he always did, at the lawyers he knew. Sometimes before the start of a court session he would make small talk or joke around, breaking the tension in the emotionally taut room. Judges called him a gentleman; fellow attorneys called him a worthy and fair trial opponent; defendants called him their savior. That year, the Office of Public Counsel named him Massachusetts Attorney of the Year, and in the following decades he would top the lists as one of the best lawyers in the state and country. He would represent Red Sox baseball ball player Mo Vaughn on drunk-driving charges, Catherine Greig, the girlfriend of Boston mobster James "Whitey" Bulger, a host of average joes on average charges, and a growing number of people accused of murder. There would come a time when young lawyers would sit in court to watch his closing arguments to learn new skills, and when people in a jam called him first and prayed he would take their case. This wasn't that time. He considered himself still a young attorney with a wry sense of humor with a young family, working hard and trying to learn from defense attorneys he admired.

He also disliked two things: pedophile cases and snitches. While he sometimes represented pedophiles, he vowed to never represent an informant. He hated those cases so much he eventually had the Latin slogan *Nunquam redo an intentor* tattooed on his right forearm — "Never represent an informant." If a defendant wanted to cut a deal and testify for the prosecution, he would recommend another attorney to handle the case. Otherwise, he would fight hard at trial for an acquittal or negotiate the best deal for the obviously guilty. He was a realist. He knew everyone was presumed innocent in a court of law; not everyone was.

In his first days as Kenny's attorney, Kevin Reddington hit hard against the district attorney's office in the way he knew best: in court. First, he asked Superior Court judge Chris Byron to order the DA not to discuss the murder case. He claimed the district attorney "labeled by innuendo" his client as a suspect in the killings. Look, he told the judge, look at the news articles quoting Ronald Pina saying his client was uncooperative. Look at this statement by the DA to reporters saying if he leaves the grand jury room to see a judge, it means a witness refused to testify. The district attorney was forced to answer the allegations in an affidavit, saying he never divulged grand jury testimony: "My answers to these questions were of a general, informational nature on matters of law and procedure and at no time did I, either explicitly or implicitly, make reference to any particular individual or case scenario."

The judge ruled the district attorney didn't divulge grand jury testimony but cautioned the extensive media coverage could hinder a fair trial.

Kevin lost that first fight. He didn't plan to lose again.

PAUL BOUDREAU immediately recognized the typed return address on the envelope sent to his North End video rental store, Movies To Go: "5848 Sun Glo Ave., Port Richey, FL" It was Kenny Ponte's address.

"Dear Mr. Boudreau: I am sincerely puzzled as to why you and Mr. St. Jean failed to come over and knock on my door during December of 1989. Instead you chose to look in my windows (you were seen by myself and others) and run around my backyard like the undercover idiot [*sic*] you both are. Next surveilance [*sic*] mission to my house you should make it easy on yourself. Stop by and have a coffee. Surely you must have gotten numerous mesquito [*sic*] bites hiding around the nursing home like you were," read the typed letter from Ponte, postmarked March 1, 1990, from Tampa, Florida.

Amused, Paul kept reading. It had been months since he and Bob St. Jean were at Kenny's house back in October of 1989, battling mosquitos. They swung by the house again after talking with Paul Ryley two months after that but weren't doing much surveillance when that arrest was made. Port Richey police were already keeping tabs on the house. Paul held the letter in his hands, chuckling. Why did it take so long for Kenny to write? If Kenny saw them, why didn't he invite them in?

When the letter arrived, Paul and the members of the Bristol County Drug Task Force were wrapping up loose and not particularly nice ends in the two-year cocaine-dealing operation centered at Whispers Pub in the South End. Thanks to a wiretap, the task force was able to get enough evidence to shut the operation down. Or so they thought. Paul later learned from an informant that the dealer was out on bail and back in business. Armed with information from the informant, Paul obtained a search warrant to raid the dealer's home where, he was told, there was a cache of cocaine and lots of cash. There was just one problem — a big problem — with this second case. Paul's informant in the case had swiped money from the suspect's home about a half hour before police raided the house in September of 1989. Now, the dealer's attorney was using that information to try to get all the charges dropped, suggesting the drugs were planted before the raid and that there was police misconduct. Paul was pissed. He was pissed at the informant for screwing up what he considered an airtight case, and he was pissed that what this informant did was tarnishing his law-enforcement reputation. Paul knew the defense attorney would use this to try to get his client off. But this was a good drug case, a damn good case, and Paul was angry at how it was turning out. He was certain Ponte was now needling him about the Whisper's Pub case in this letter.

"Next time you are observed around my home I'll have you arrested before you can frame me like you've obviously done to others," Kenny wrote. "It does not surprise me that you would accuse me of being a murderer without any evidence at all. It is your style apparently to simply plant the evidence that you need to convict. Luckily the system weeds out corrupt cops like you before they can do any further damage."

Paul later slipped the letter and envelop into an evidence bag for safe-keeping.

Kenny is losing it, he thought.

Reporters gather on the courthouse steps to interview
Kenneth Ponte on August 19, 1990 (author on the far
right) (*Standard-Times* photo by Hank Seaman)

Home of Kenneth C. Ponte in Port Richey, Florida
(photo by Paul Boudreau)

Franklin Pina, the boyfriend of Nancy Paiva, is led from New Bedford Superior Court after testifying before the special grand jury on July 30, 1990 (*Standard-Times* photo by Ron Rolo)

Anthony DeGrazia, accused of attacking prostitutes, with his first attorney, Edward Harrington, in New Bedford Superior Court on May 11, 1989 (*Standard-Times* photo by Hank Seaman)

Neil Anderson, accused and later convicted of raping prostitutes, in district court to face charges on December 14, 1988. He was one of the early suspects in the case. (*Standard-Times* photo by Jack Iddon)

Kenneth Ponte confers with his lawyer, Kevin Reddington, before his arraignment on a single count of murder in New Bedford Superior Court in August 1990 (*Standard-Times* photo by Hank Seaman)

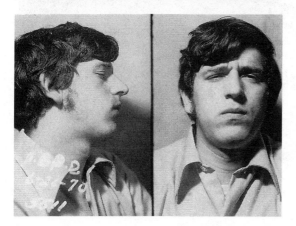

Kenneth C. Ponte mugshot from New Bedford police department, 1970

Funeral of Mary Rose Santos on May 2, 1989. Her mother, Mary Jeronymo is *left*, son Joseph is *front*, and husband Donald is *far right*. The family is waiting at St. Joseph Church in Fairhaven as her coffin is loaded into a hearse. (*Standard-Times* photo by Mike Valeri)

New Bedford detective sgt. John Dextradeur in 1984 photo pointing out burglary locations in New Bedford (*Standard-Times* photo by Ron Rolo)

TOP LEFT Richard Ferreira, retired New Bedford detective, in 2015 (photo by Maureen Boyle)

BOTTOM LEFT Robert St. Jean, former chief investigator for the Bristol County District Attorney's Office, in 2015 (photo by Maureen Boyle)

Maryann Dill and Jose Gonsalves outside the old Massachusetts state police barracks on Route 6 in Dartmouth in undated photo (photo courtesy of Maryann Dill)

Photo of Dawn Mendes circulated to the media in 1988

Wedding photo of Debra Greenlaw DeMello provided to media by her family. The photo hung on her mother's wall for years.

Photo of Nancy Paiva supplied to media and police by the family

Photo of Debra Medeiros supplied to the media by the Bristol County District Attorney's Office

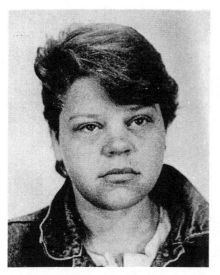

Photo of Debroh Lynn McConnell supplied to the media by the Bristol County District Attorney's Office

Photo of Mary Rose Santos supplied by family to the media and to the Bristol County District Attorney's Office

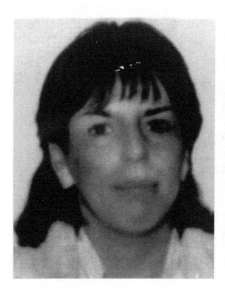

Marilyn Cardoza Roberts, missing, photo supplied to the media by the Bristol County District Attorney's Office

Christina Monteiro, missing, photo supplied to the media by the Bristol County District Attorney's Office

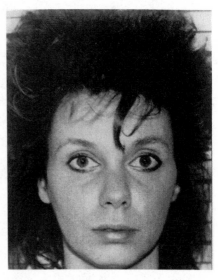

Photo of Robbin Rhodes supplied
to the media by the Bristol County
District Attorney's Office

Photo of Rochelle Dopierala supplied
to the media by the Bristol County
District Attorney's Office

Photo of Sandra Botelho supplied to
the media by the family and by the Bristol
County District Attorney's Office

THE CALLS came into newsrooms in Massachusetts from Florida at least once a week even after Kenny Ponte's attorney warned him to stop talking.

This is Kenny Ponte, the caller would start. You have to agree this call is all off the record.

Some reporters agreed. Others did not.

It is off the record unless you confess to a crime, one reporter told him. Sometimes Kenny would hang up immediately; sometimes he would snort and agree. When Kenny did stay on the line he would rant: the district attorney was out to get him, he was corrupt, he was using the case to get reelected, to get a job in Washington, D.C. He would make allegations about the DA's second wife, question the validity of her widely questioned reported abduction two years earlier and her struggles with sobriety. He even created bumper stickers asking "Who put Sheila in the trunk?" Kenny would ramble in those phone calls, his voice rising in frustration or anger. And then he would abruptly hang up. Sometimes the click would come with a question asked. Sometimes it would come if the listener failed to agree with him. Sometimes there was no reason. He called newspapers, he called television stations, he called radio stations. Kenny liked to talk.

He sent a letter to the editor of the *New Bedford Standard-Times* titled "THE EMPEROR HAS NO CLOTHES," comparing his case to the fable of the same name. "The time as arrived to state the obvious to the people of Bristol County — YOUR EMPEROR HAS NO CLOTHES. Despite his many press conferences and television appearances in which he has cutely portrayed four (4) different persons as being guilty of this horrendous crime, the obvious truth is niether [sic] I nor anyone else has been shown to have any involement [sic] in this crime," Kenny wrote in the April 1, 1990 letter.

"The general public is apparently afraid to criticize you Mr. Pina but I am not. You can bring all the phony charges you like against me but just remember that when the smoke clears you will be left standing alone as a court defendant answering my charges that your intentional abuse of your power has violated my civil rights," he continued in the three-page letter.

Even when there were no articles about him, Kenny called reporters or wrote to complain about Ronald A. Pina.

Kenny was seeing his life and his career slip away, and he was angry. "It was really a travesty what was happening to him," Kevin Reddington recalled in an interview years later.

FROM AFAR in this pre-Internet world, Kenny learned what was going on in New Bedford through phone calls and newspaper clippings sent to his Florida house from the few friends he had left in the city. The secret he tried desperately to keep hidden — his relapse into drugs a couple of years earlier — was now fodder for headlines and television news teasers in Massachusetts and Rhode Island. In Port Richey, police were keeping watch on his single-story duplex. An anonymous, scrawled printed note on lined paper mailed from Groton, Connecticut, to the Florida town's police chief a year earlier simply said "Keep an eye on this guy." The cops in Florida took it to heart. His closest buddy Ryley was locked up in a New Bedford jail overseen by a sheriff both he and Kenny campaigned for and served under as part-time deputies. It was likely he would stay there, too. The bail was set at $25,000, and Kenny figured it would stay that high until the guy testified before a grand jury. Where would it all end? Kenny had already flown back to New Bedford once to meet with his new attorney, Kevin Reddington, and now he was in a sort of limbo in Florida, not sure what would happen next.

At the district attorney's office in Massachusetts, prosecutors and members of the Bristol County Drug Task Force were deciding what to do with Kenny. By February 9, 1990, a report by the prosecutor's office entitled "Factual Report of the Indictable Offenses of Kenneth C. Ponte" had been written to outline the evidence against Kenny in a drug case. It detailed Kenny's cocaine purchases and use; how he bounced checks; how he had two handguns; the girls who came to his house; the girls who claimed he wouldn't let them leave. It quoted a man who told police and the grand jury that Kenny said he would kill him or his friends if they ever testified against him. By the end of March, that evidence was presented to a grand jury separate from the highway killings.

That grand jury handed up a three-count indictment in the case of "K. P. Doe," charging Kenny with conspiracy to possess cocaine in 1988. A cab driver, Arthur "Goldie" Goldblatt, was also indicted on charges of conspiring to violate drug laws. The attorney for Goldblatt, Paul Walsh Jr., questioned why the charges were lodged now, two years later. "I wonder if there are any motivations other than solid investigative work here," the attorney said.[2]

When the indictment was handed up, Kenny booked a flight back to Boston.

KENNY BOWED HIS HEAD, lips tight, as his lawyer whispered in his ear.

Kevin Reddington always told his clients the same thing at arraignment: don't show emotion, don't shake your head, don't glare, stay dignified. Say two words: "Not guilty."

Kenny did all of that during his arraignment in New Bedford Superior Court on drug charges on April 13, 1990, two weeks after the indictment on drug charges was handed up. His attorney stayed close as Kenny carefully entered a not guilty plea before Superior Court judge Gerald O'Neil and was released on personal recognizance — his personal promise to come back to court without posting bail — and ordered to return to court in six days.

Ten minutes later, Kenny was handed a subpoena to appear before the grand jury investigating the highway killings.

This time, Kenny did not try to duck reporters as he left the courthouse. He stood next to his attorney on the courthouse steps, the same spot the district attorney often stood to chat with reporters. Kenny's attorney called the subpoena "another indication of harassment" of his client, a move he would fight. He also called on Bristol County district attorney Ronald A. Pina to hand the murder case over to someone else. "After all of the passage of time, the investigation is really breaking down and I think it's time for Mr. Pina to step aside and an independent prosecutor to take over, and it's time to appoint a special prosecutor," Kevin Reddington told the reporters.[3] He said the foreman of the grand jury, talk-show host Henry R. Carreiro, disliked his client because of another, unrelated case. (Carreiro denied those allegations, saying he tried as hard as he could to avoid sitting on the grand jury. "I said my rosary every night so I wouldn't get a celebrated case."[4])

Then, with the cameras trained on the pair, Kenny spoke. "I feel completely victimized by the system," he said, adding he had written an unpublished book called "Presumed Guilty."

After a few minutes, client and attorney walked calmly away, camera crews trailing.

The stage was set. Kevin Reddington thought it went pretty well as he drove out of New Bedford back to his office.

KENNY WAS PACKED and ready to leave New Bedford right after the arraignment. His friend, Daniel Branco, would drive him to Logan Airport, he
would hop on a plane and go home to Port Richey, Florida. As they hit the
road, they could see what appeared to be an unmarked police cruiser behind
them. The blue lights went on; they pulled over. His friend was arrested on
an outstanding warrant for motor-vehicle violations. Kenny pulled his lug-
gage out the trunk and started walking down the street, looking for a pay
phone. Police followed him as he walked along the street. "Are you having a
bad day, counselor? The bag looks very heavy, counselor," Kevin Reddington
later quoted a trooper as saying.[5] When he found a pay phone, Kenny called
his lawyer. Then he called his brother, asking for a ride to the Brockton law
office. Unmarked cruisers followed them as they drove up Route 140 and
onto Route 24. The cruisers followed the car as it took the exit for Route 123
toward Easton and as it pulled into an office-complex parking lot.

Kevin Reddington gave explicit instructions to his client. Pull in and go
to the end of the lot at my office. He asked his secretary to get in her car and
block the exit when Kenny's vehicle and cruisers pulled in. He had already
called a photographer to come over to take pictures.

Kenny's brother pulled in; Kevin was outside the building, waving them to
the rear of the lot; the cruisers pulled in; his secretary blocked the only exit
from the lot; a photographer for the *Brockton Enterprise* stood near Kevin
with his camera. *Click. Click. Click.*

A trooper looked at Kevin. "She said something like, 'Oh, my God,'" he
recalled.

Later that day, the defense attorney described the incident to reporters as
"Gestapo tactics" and said it showed the district attorney was harassing his
client. "How many cops working for how many hours following Ken Ponte
around does he have?" he asked.

The defense attorney had now fired a verbal and public round at the prosecution. He figured he could now steer this case in the right direction without
any surprises.

PAUL F. WALSH JR. was a newcomer with a local political pedigree when he
decided to run for district attorney against twelve-year Democratic incumbent Ronald A. Pina. His father, known warmly as "Doc," was on the local

school committee, active in Republican Party politics, and close friends with two of the most powerful Democratic leaders in Greater New Bedford. As a child, young Paul grew up in the shadows of politicking. He watched his father go door-to-door asking for each vote, saw how aligning with different camps was important, and how a tight campaign organization made it all work. He saw how a campaign coffer could illustrate the strength, or weakness, of a candidate. People didn't put their money on a loser, even if it was five bucks.

Paul, who, unlike his father, was a Democrat, toyed with running for the Bristol County prosecutor's seat for a couple of years in the predominately Democratic county. He was just waiting for the incumbent to move on and up. Every so often, Bristol County district attorney Ronald A. Pina's name would surface as a possible candidate for a higher state or federal office, such as governor, or even Congress. When Governor Michael Dukakis's run for president was strong, Ron Pina was mentioned for a high-level Washington post. At the state Democratic Convention, Walsh had heard the DA's name floated for two offices: lieutenant governor and state attorney general. If the DA left New Bedford, Paul wanted to be ready to run.

The younger Walsh began his careful planning in 1987, after leaving the Suffolk County District Attorney's Office in Boston where he worked as a prosecutor after law school. It was a great job, but he was looking to do more. "There is an old Russian proverb: 'It is a poor soldier who doesn't want to be a general,'" Paul said. "I loved working as an assistant district attorney, it was the greatest job I had, but I thought, I would like to be general. That was always in the back of my mind."[6]

He quit the Boston job and moved to Portugal where he enrolled in a language-history program at the University of Lisbon. For nearly a year, he was immersed in Portuguese culture and language, preparing to run for district attorney in the largely Portuguese Bristol County. When he came home, Paul quietly made inquiries: If I ran, could I win? If I ran, would you support me? If I ran, what type of political organization would I need? If I ran, how much money would I need?

He learned the importance of planning and teamwork early in life on two fronts: his father's campaign work and his own experience on the basketball court. As the captain of the Holy Family High School basketball team in 1972, he watched who was in the best position and learned to look for the strongest players to throw to. "I was probably the third best of the starting five," he said. "But I knew who the ball should go to. . . . It's not all about you, it's about your team." His high school team won the state championship.

The same skills Walsh used on the basketball court and in the courtroom — planning and observation — were now turned to politics and a possible run for Bristol County district attorney when he returned home from Portugal. He opened a small law office in New Bedford, became active in Democratic politics, and kept his ears open. "I wanted to have my ducks all in a row," he said.

To find out how much money he would need to run, Paul needed to see how much his opponent had. He drove to the state campaign-finance office in Boston where candidates were required to file financial reports. As he flipped through the file for Ronald Pina, he expected to see a campaign chest of at least $100,000. What he saw was a tally under $5,000. "I remember thinking he is having a tough go with this. He has no money in the bank," Paul said.

On the drive home, he stopped at the Howard Johnson's at the Route 24 rest area in Bridgewater to call his older brother. Forget about waiting for Ron to leave office. This is it. "Billy, he has no money in the bank, I'm in, I'm going," Paul told him excitedly.[7]

Just come home and we'll talk with Dad, his brother calmly answered.

Six months before the Democratic primary, in early March of 1990, Paul F. Walsh Jr. stood in Weld Square and formally announced his candidacy for Bristol County district attorney. "I chose that site because it represents what has gone wrong with the criminal justice system," he wrote at the time in his campaign's "drug policy for the 1990s." "Weld Square, which not too many years ago was a vibrant, safe neighborhood, is today dominated by criminal elements who prey on the innocent. And, at the root of that area's problems is the illegal drug trade."

Before he even announced, Walsh had quietly set up a campaign organization throughout the county, tapping into the expertise of his father and other seasoned politicians in the area. "We were in and we ran hard," Paul recalled.

At age thirty-five, he was viewed as "the kid" trying to topple the seasoned prosecutor with a dozen years in office.

Ron Pina was once in the same position as Walsh. He was just twenty-six when he first ran for state representative in 1970, part of the "new breed" of politicians. He was young, handsome, and touting change. In 1979, at age thirty-three, he won in a five-way race for district attorney with 29 percent of the vote. He was aggressive, took on tough cases, started new programs, created a child-abuse unit, and was touched by the pain of victims and their families. He was also, after years in office, becoming politically complacent. Some said he stopped returning phone calls and lost touch with political allies. Others said he took the job for granted as he looked for higher offices. Still others said he was struggling to deal with the highly public alcohol problems of his second wife.

Once Walsh jumped into the campaign, Pina discovered the political base he took for granted had eroded. Some of his strongest past supporters were working for his opponent or sitting out the election. The New Bedford Police Union endorsed Walsh; so did the Metropolitan Police Patrolman's Union, even though it was out of Boston. Pina tried to hit back, issuing campaign press releases saying "integrity is the issue" and claiming his opponent had little experience to run the office. He kept referring to his opponent as the "fresh-faced rookie." Pina touted the endorsement of the Massachusetts District Attorney's Association, a group for which he served as president three times. In radio spots and newspaper political ads, Pina was highlighting old cases involving marijuana smuggling. One ad featured a comic strip illustrating the case. Voters were looking forward, though, not back. Then the district attorney made a crucial error. In what political observers at the time called a turning point of the campaign, Pina issued a press release claiming his opponent's campaign manager, Joaquim "Jack" Nobrega, took the job only after his son was given a lifetime court job by the candidate's father. "Being part of machine politics seriously questions Paul Walsh Jr.'s ability to make decisions on his own," Pina said in a campaign press release.

Jack Nobrega was livid. He and the elder Walsh served together on the school committee, were close friends and shrewd political insiders. They were considered among the most politically powerful men in the city. The two friends shot back that there was no "deal" for the job — the younger Nobrega had been a probation officer who was qualified for the job, and three judges approved the appointment.

Friends of the elder Walsh and Nobrega stepped up efforts to unseat Pina. One of the most powerful politicians in the area, state senator William Q.

"Biff" MacLean, was a close friend of the elder Walsh and Nobrega. He had said he was staying on the sidelines, at least publically. However, political insiders at the time said he was quietly working behind the scenes to help Paul Walsh win without publically endorsing him. The incumbent's political misstep of criticizing Nobrega was seen by some as the beginning of the end for Ron Pina.

Walsh slammed Pina on spending, including paying a press secretary $50,000, which was much more than what an assistant district attorney was earning in 1990. In a July 16, 1990, campaign press release, Walsh hammered the incumbent on his public handling of the highway killings murder investigation. Walsh insisted the intense pretrial publicity in the investigation, and the incumbent's statements to reporters, might jeopardize the case. He said it was turning into a media circus, tarnishing the city's image just as the intense publicity in the earlier Big Dan's rape case had. It highlighted the community perception of a prosecutor more concerned with image than justice — and it struck a chord with voters.

Pina was upbeat throughout the campaign. His opponent was a "kid" without the experience needed to run the office. His inner circle and supporters were loyal and determined. They would win. What was important to his campaign was identifying and charging the person or persons responsible for killing nine women, and hoping the police would find the bodies of the two who were missing. The case was increasingly becoming part of the campaign, with a growing number of people criticizing Pina's press conferences and the focus on Kenneth Ponte. Jaded voters wondered aloud whether an indictment would be handed up just before the election. Pina's media-darling image was turning into a political problem.

The case would pose a more concrete problem for Pina as primary day neared. His hands-on approach was keeping him off the campaign trail. While Walsh courted votes at the senior centers, the incumbent was in the grand jury room questioning witnesses. While Walsh was making phone calls to potential voters at night, Pina was at home reading grand jury transcripts and police reports. While Walsh was on the streets with new people, Pina appeared to tighten his circle of confidantes. Walsh was young, fresh-faced, and single, while the incumbent was dogged by questions about his second wife's alcohol problems: in addition to the time Sheila Martines-Pina was found locked in her car trunk, there had been several reports of drunk-driving cover-ups and one instance where she rear-ended a local newspaper delivery truck.

Ron's daughter from his first marriage, Kari,[8] was proud of his work and saw his dedication to the murder case firsthand at home. She also saw the growing number of Walsh campaign signs on the front lawns in the city and suburban towns. As the campaign progressed, the sixteen-year-old girl thought for the first time there was a chance her father might lose the election.

11 FLORIDA FOLLIES

MORE THAN A YEAR BEFORE the primary for Bristol County district attorney, a woman named Diane Doherty entered the murder investigation and the case started to take an odd turn.

Diane Doherty was living in the apartment in the house next door to Charles Dana Kuhn on Conomo Avenue in Lynn, Massachusetts, and would rattle off her troubles whenever she saw him. She suffered from narcolepsy, had contracted some other type of disease, and was about to be evicted. Diane told him she worried that she and her teenaged daughter would wind up on the streets of Lynn, the nondescript mill city in northern Massachusetts where they lived. She needed some help fighting the eviction. She couldn't get to court because she was sick. Could he go for her as a friend? She kept pressing her neighbor for help. Dana, who was a private investigator, felt sorry for her. He finally agreed to assist. Armed with a power-of-attorney document, he went to court on October 26, 1989, and got her a few days' reprieve. But that wasn't the end of it, or his involvement in her life. She had found a new apartment but couldn't move in yet, she told him. She had to get out of her current apartment by November 1, she told him, but she couldn't get into her new one right away. Could she stay in his house with him until then? It wouldn't be long. Sure, he finally answered and let Diane and her daughter move in for what he thought would be a few days.

But when November 1 came around, she and her daughter were still in the house and didn't show any signs of leaving. There was a problem with the new apartment she found, she told him. She needed to stay with him a little bit longer. It was then that things got a bit odd, he later told investigators.

As the three were watching television in November, a few weeks after she moved into Dana's home "temporarily," a news report about the highway killings came on. "Gee, Kenny looks very good," Diane said.[1]

Dana was taken aback. He remembered that she casually mentioned earlier that she knew a man named Kenny Ponte. He didn't remember the context of the conversation, and he didn't ask her at the time for more information. This time, however, he decided to press the issue a bit.

"What do you mean?" he asked when she brought up the name.

She shrugged it off but later told him she had dated Kenny. She couldn't say exactly when. Maybe it was the summer. Maybe it was 1987. Maybe it was 1988. At another time, she told him she and her daughter were in New Bedford, in the kitchen of Leslie Mello, a woman she had shared a cell with in the women's state prison. Kenny Ponte was there, too, and he was depressed. Then Diane dropped the bombshell: Kenny told them he killed six of the women found along the highways.

He was stunned. "Well, what have you done about this?" Dana asked her.

"I like Kenny. I like Kenny," she answered, he later recalled.[2]

She told him she was worried about her daughter's safety and couldn't say any more. "Kenny Ponte has powerful friends," she told him. She planned to send her daughter to Arizona. Once that happened, she would tell him more.

The conversation nagged at the private investigator, and he repeated it to a colleague, Andy Tuney, who was a former state police lieutenant. His friend talked with Diane, heard the same story and then notified the lieutenant colonel of the state police, John O'Donovan. Eventually, the two private investigators met with Bristol County district attorney Pina and his chief investigator, Robert St. Jean, at the Tara Hotel in Randolph, Massachusetts, on November 21, 1989, to go over in detail what Diane had said and formulate a plan to verify her tale.

Dana and his colleague, in a written agreement, promised to work for free for a month for the district attorney's office to get more information from Diane. By the day before Thanksgiving, Dana had learned three important things: Diane was on probation, that she claimed to have a diary detailing Kenny's admission, and it was really hard to keep her on topic. "She'd go back and forth to different stories and constantly change her approach to things," he later told the district attorney. "Probably the most difficult person I've ever tried to interview in my life."[3]

The apartment elsewhere in the city that Diane was to move into never materialized in November, and in early December she and her daughter were still living in a spare room in Dana's house with him. The district attorney's office extended the agreement with the private investigators for another thirty days, hoping the extra time would yield something, anything. Dana tried hard to get more information from Diane but it was difficult. She kept repeating the story about being in Leslie's kitchen with Kenny. One time she thought it was June of 1987 — before any of the women went missing. Another time she thought it was 1988. She wasn't quite sure about the dates. He asked her to show him the house in New Bedford where Leslie lived. She never did. She claimed Kenny said he had sex with the dead women and it involved Satanism but she wasn't specific, Dana would later recount.[4] One time she told him the diary where she documented the admission went missing when her car was stolen; another time she said it was at her mother's house. She repeatedly told him that her daughter wasn't living with her and was in a safe place out of Massachusetts but she didn't say where.

Diane would provide minute details about Leslie Stanton Mello, her former cellmate, though. Leslie grew up in South Dartmouth, her parents were well off and she had long been addicted to heroin. She talked about Leslie's sister, about how Leslie had demanded money from her father on the day her mother had died years back, about her brief bouts with sobriety — usually while locked up — before plunging back into heroin use. What Diane didn't say was that all of this information was in a newspaper clipping Leslie kept with her, a feature story about Leslie's life. Leslie would show the article to people, often cops, to let them know where she came from, who she was. Providing background about Leslie's life might on the surface give initial credence to the confession tale but not for long. Leslie knew Kenny Ponte from her earliest days of using heroin, and at the women's prison she, like others from New Bedford, would talk about the lawyer. However, Leslie never considered him a killer. He was just someone she used to "run" with on the street.

However, Dana didn't know the full, detailed background of Leslie or Leslie's early history with Kenny Ponte. He was just trying to figure out what, if anything Diane knew about a murder case. He also wanted Diane to get out of his place. He got his wish in mid-December, when Diane and her daughter finally moved. He was relieved. Close to six months later he got a phone call from her. Diane said she and her daughter were planning to become paralegals, and they were filling out a questionnaire, and there was a question asking about "death by snapping of the neck." What did that mean, she wanted to know. Dana described what asphyxiation was, how someone dies when the air passages are cut off. "Is that a painful death?" he remembers her asking.[5]

Then she abruptly changed the subject. She and her daughter were appointed to a Tercentenary Salem Witch Commission. She also had a book for him to read, *The Devil in the Form of a Woman*. "Who wrote it? You?" he asked her.

Months later, Diane would insist to authorities in Massachusetts and Florida that she never told anyone Kenny confessed to murder. She said she never met Kenny and was being pressured to testify before a grand jury investigating the highway killings. She eventually called Kenny's lawyer and told him his client was being framed. Kevin Reddington met with her to learn more; he listened to her tale and knew within minutes his client needed to stay away from this woman — far away.[6]

Leslie Stanton Mello, who knew Kenny since they were both in their late teens, provided a blunter description of Diane's claims. "That's bullshit," she said.[7]

KENNY PONTE'S ATTEMPT to keep a low profile in Florida wasn't going very well. He was fielding phone calls from a couple of people in Massachusetts, telling him the latest in the murder investigation. He was indicted on drug charges in Massachusetts. His friend, Paul Ryley, had been hauled back to Massachusetts on charges of uttering a forged instrument and larceny and was subpoenaed to appear before the special grand jury in the murder case. Paul's girlfriend, Elsa Johnson, who lived next door to Kenny in Florida, was back in Massachusetts. The Port Richey police were swinging by his house constantly, and Kenny was convinced he was being watched around the clock. He did have his cats for company, though. Kenny loved cats. Everyone knew that. He brought his cats down to Florida with him from New Bedford, and he would feed strays that wandered by.

He wasn't sure how things would shake out back in his hometown of New Bedford, but he was trying to stay upbeat nonetheless. He had a new lawyer, one of the best, or so everyone told him. He kept telling reporters he was innocent. He wrote letters to newspapers saying just that and insisting the district attorney was trying to frame him. Now, a woman who claimed she was being pressured to say he confessed to the killings was coming down to Florida to visit him for about a week in June of 1990. He didn't mention the upcoming visit to his lawyer.

As he drove to the airport to pick up Diane Doherty, Kenny wasn't sure what to expect. She contacted him out of the blue in a letter and they wound up talking quite a bit on the phone. She seemed sincere and nice. There wasn't anything to change that opinion when he finally met her and drove her back to his house. She was petite and blonde and kind of cute. Maybe life would finally get better for him in Florida.

Once they were back at the house, Kenny finally told his lawyer about his visitor.

"You're out of your mind," his lawyer, Kevin Reddington, told him. "Stay away from her."[8]

Kenny didn't listen.

Then things got bad, really bad, in Florida. A thirty-year-old Port Richey woman told police Kenny tried to run her down in his driveway after they argued about a fifty-dollar deposit she put down on the duplex he was renting next door. When he heard about the allegations, Kenny turned himself in at the police station to face charges of careless driving and leaving the scene of an accident with injuries. Diane was with him — and things got even worse.

Diane, wanted in Massachusetts for a probation violation on a larceny charge in Essex County, was also taken into custody. After her arrest, she told Port Richey police a horrifying tale of how Kenny choked her and threatened her at gunpoint during her visit. She said she had gone to Florida to marry Kenny, a man she said she had known for at least four months. Kenny was hit with new charges: aggravated battery, aggravated assault, false imprisonment, use of a firearm during the commission of a felony.

A few days later, Diane recanted.

Then, a few days later she recanted the recantation.[9]

Then Kenny's lawyer in Florida quit because he believed he could be a witness to Diane Doherty's now conflicting statements.

Kenny's bail was hiked from $15,000 to $207,500 after the Florida state attorney said Kenny was tied to slayings in Massachusetts. "The state attorney's office has learned that the Bristol County grand jury in the state of Massachusetts has received testimony which would implicate the defendant in homicide," read a motion to the Florida judge at the time.

Port Richey police searched his two duplexes and a shed on his property at the request of the Bristol County District Attorney's Office. Massachusetts state trooper Kenneth Martin was there to help.

And the search dogs were back on the highways in Massachusetts looking for bodies. Kenny's name was included in nearly all of those news stories.

Things were looking pretty grim for Kenny in Florida.

MARYANN AND JOSE sat in the air-conditioned office at the Pasco County Detention Center in Florida, waiting for the deputies to bring in the prisoner. The troopers had flown from Boston to bring back a Lynn woman wanted on a relatively minor probation violation and they wanted to talk with her about Kenny Ponte while the legal rendition process moved forward. The troopers heard the *swish-swish* of slippered feet enter the room.

Escorted by deputies, the fair-haired Diane Doherty, dressed in prison garb and jail-issued slippers, plunked down in the chair in front of the troopers. Then she began to talk. The monologue bounced from stories about her daughter, to her time with Kenny to flying to Florida to her fears about her safety. Her train of thought weaved through tunnels of subjects and over bridges of people. She seemed jumpy to the troopers as she yammered. They asked her about Kenny, about her stay at the house, about the assault allegations she made against him. She repeated what she had told Florida authorities: she wrote Kenny a letter, talked with him on the phone, then later flew down to Florida on June 3 to marry him. She claimed Kenny at one point tried to choke her and threatened to kill her daughter.

Five minutes into the hour-long interview, the troopers looked at each other and knew these stories wouldn't hold up in court: they were wasting their time. A few days later, they were flying back to Massachusetts with Diane.

KENNY WAS PREPARED to argue before the Florida court why his bail should be lowered, not increased as prosecutors wanted. It was a fairly routine argument, one made daily in courtrooms across the country. He made those arguments regularly when arguing bail for clients as an attorney in Massachusetts. He always reminded people, particularly cops, what his professional occupation was. He wasn't practicing law in Florida—he hadn't taken the bar exam—but he was a lawyer in good standing in his home state. He knew court procedure and, as he stood in the Florida courtroom, he wanted the judge to know it. He didn't have a lawyer to help him—he was planning to meet with a private attorney that day—but he would give it his best. Ties to the community, no record of violence, and a property owner: those were all the things that showed a defendant wasn't a flight risk. Bail was a legal mechanism to guarantee someone would return to court. It was not supposed to be punitive. After all, everyone is presumed innocent. In Massachusetts, all of the judges had set his bail at personal recognizance—his personal promise to return to court. That should count as something, he was likely thinking as he waited for his case to be called.

The Florida state attorney was asking the judge to increase Kenny's bail on the charges from $15,000 to $200,000 because he was a murder suspect in Massachusetts. It was the first time Kenny was officially linked by a court to the killings. Kenny had been locked up since his arrest four days earlier on Monday. He couldn't even come up with the fifteen grand.

Kenny read paragraph five in the state's motion for higher bail. He asked if he could be heard on the issue.

"Your honor, there have been five people besides me who have been dragged through the mud concerning this matter," Kenny told the judge.[10] "Your honor, the facts of this case is, three of my former clients were unfortunately the victims, and the police questioned me on that and I fully cooperated with them. I have an attorney up there.

"Your honor, I'm certainly—I don't pose any threat to anyone, I never have. I have absolutely no record of any violence towards anyone, ever, and I challenge the State Attorney to show that I have. And simply because I'm a suspect, your honor—and I have an attorney up there that is fighting this. I'm approaching it in a responsible way, and again, I just urge the Court to check with the Bar Association to see that I'm a licensed attorney in good standing. Your honor, I've done nothing. All I ask is a chance to get out so I can prepare for any defense, Your Honor," Kenny told the judge.

His bail was increased.

"Your Honor, may I ask a question?"

"Yes."

"Why is my bond so high?"

"Because of the Massachusetts situation."

Kenny asked the judge to check with the Massachusetts courts about the case and allegations about his involvement. One judge had said the evidence "did not even amount to a hunch," Kenny said.

"I beg you to check that, Your Honor."

"I will be checking that today."

"Will you?"

"Yes, I will."

"Thank you, Your Honor."

Kenny was led off again to the lockup to wait. He would stay there four more weeks, until he was released on July 13, 1990. He was now back home in his Florida duplex, free without bail. The charges eventually were dropped.

KENNY WAS OUT OF JAIL just one day on July 14, 1990, and was planning to fly back to New Bedford shortly to stay with his mother. Then there was a new twist in his case. His buddy's girlfriend, the Dartmouth woman named Elsa M. Johnson, who rented his duplex next door in Florida, told the grand jury in Massachusetts that Kenny threatened to shoot the prosecutor and harm both his daughter and second wife. "If he had to wait on Rockdale Avenue until you came out of the house, he'd blow your brains out there. Because his life was over with anyway. And if you didn't come out of the house, he'd just shoot through the window. 'And I don't care if I harm Sheila or the kid,'" Johnson quoted him as saying.

The prosecutor's house was put under twenty-four-hour watch throughout the weekend. His daughter stayed at a friend's house. At the request of First Assistant District Attorney Raymond P. Veary Jr., a judge approved a restraining order that Saturday ordering Kenny to stay one thousand feet from the district attorney, his family, or his employees.

Threats by suspects in the case were not new. Neil Anderson, an early

suspect in the investigation, made a threat in jail against the DA then immediately thought better of it. Tony DeGrazia, accused of choking and raping
prostitutes, was charged in a threat he made shortly before being released
on bail, a charge later dropped. Neither of those threats led to a round-the-
clock watch. Until now.

The small city of New Bedford also just got smaller. Kenny's mother lived
next door to Ron Pina, and the houses were twenty-five feet apart. Kenny
decided to stay put in Florida for now.

AS KENNY FELT HIS LIFE UNRAVEL in Florida, investigators in Massachusetts were slowly piecing together the last days of Rochelle Dopierala's life.

She was in a car on April 3, 1988, when Kenny allegedly threatened a New
Bedford man with a gun. She went into detox in Quincy but left a few days
later. Two days after she left the detox, a dentist who befriended Rochelle
called her mother to say she ripped him off. Rochelle was seen in Falmouth by
a police officer on April 21. She was due to go to Barnstable District Court. At
some point, a man matching Kenny's description had driven her to the Cape
in April to deal with some court issues. Detective John Dextradeur saw her
walking down the street with Nancy Paiva and Nancy's boyfriend on April
27, 1988, and pulled her aside to make sure she would testify against Kenny.
She said she was staying with Nancy and Frankie and told him she was afraid
of Kenny. A man matching Kenny's description had driven Rochelle to a
mobile home in Acushnet sometime in April, waited outside until she came
out, and then the two left. Police believe that was in late April of 1988, likely
after she told the New Bedford detective she would testify against Kenny.

Rochelle had a meeting at the welfare office in Falmouth on May 19, 1988,
to review her benefits and case file. Her mother was to meet her there. Rochelle never showed up.

And then there was the troubling story from the drug dealer about the
threats.

A FALL RIVER WOMAN named Linda Robitaille, dealing drugs on Purchase
Street, heard and saw a lot. She heard the stories about this weird guy who
got the girls to buy him coke; how he had a gun; how the girls used to shoot

the cocaine into his neck; how some girls would stay at his house for hours or days. A friend of hers went with him twice. The first time her friend stayed out all night, doing coke with him. The second time, the dealer tracked her down to the guy's house and lay on the car horn. When her friend came out, the dealer pulled her into the car and they left. "I took her from the house. Because I was tired of her being in there all night shootin' cocaine or whatever they was doin'," the dealer later testified to a grand jury.[11]

It was sometime in April of 1988 when she saw Rochelle Dopierala driving a big brown car on Purchase Street. Rochelle stopped and got out. Then a man came running toward the car, yelling.

"He said, 'Get over here you fuckin' bitch, because I'm gonna kill you,'" the dealer later recalled.[12]

Rochelle bolted up a nearby street. The man, later identified as Kenny, jumped in the car and took off.

The dealer turned her attention to another car pulling up. It was a customer looking to buy drugs. She didn't see where Kenny went. She never saw Rochelle again.

IT WAS HARD TO MISS JOSE GONSALVES, even from a distance. He always stood straight, so he always looked taller than his six-foot-plus frame. Judy DeSantos spotted him first as he walked up the path to New Bedford Superior Court. Then she saw the woman in handcuffs he was escorting. Who is that? This was a new face. Judy had recognized a few of the witnesses appearing before the grand jury in the past year and a half. A few were cops involved in the investigation, some were businessmen and women, some were drug addicts or street people. She knew a few through their families; others were acquainted with acquaintances. There were even a couple she recognized because they passed through city hall to pay a tax bill or register to vote or pick up a birth certificate.

Judy heard someone talking as Jose and the woman passed inside.

"That's the woman from Florida. That's Kenny Ponte's girlfriend."

Judy wondered what this woman — who she would later learn was Diane Doherty — would tell the grand jury. Whatever it was, Judy hoped it would be a story to solve the case.

RON PINA STARED INTO THE DISTANCE, a book on his lap. His teenaged daughter, Kari, knew the look. He was thinking. Deeply. She knew he was involved in a big case, an important case. She knew a little bit about it: someone was killing women and leaving their bodies along the highways. The women had families that loved them. She saw firsthand how much the families missed them. One woman found dead was the mother of her junior high schoolmate, Jolene. She saw from a distance at that time what Jolene had to go through as some people, even children, tried to downplay the murders because the victims had drug problems. Kari could see how the words had stung her when people referred to the victims as prostitutes and junkies. People could be mean.[13]

Her father was different. He saw stolen lives and the need to find a killer. He wanted justice for those without a voice. She could tell he was haunted by this case, by the grief of the families. She saw his quietness at home, how he would sit and read and think. He was always reading something legal-like and important. To relax in the summer, he would sail on his Tartan 30 named *Cyrano*, after Cyrano de Bergerac, the central character in the play by Edmond Rostand. On most days, though, especially during the school year, he would be sitting in the den area of the house reading as Kari did homework on the dining room table. The first floor was an open floor plan, and she could see him when she looked up from the table or was anywhere else in the house. There was always that sense of quiet urgency in his work when he was at home.

In the office, Ron's staff also felt they were doing something for the greater good — and the highway killing case was part of that. "There is no question he genuinely wanted to find out who the highway killer was," recalled Raymond P. Veary, Jr., the first assistant district attorney at the time. "He clearly wanted to identify the murderer or murderers, and he wanted the investigation to be successful."[14]

But Ron was also a political lightning rod for criticism this election year and everyone knew it. He was handsome, smart, well spoken, and shined on camera. When he entered a room, his presence rippled through the crowd. He laughed hard, smiled a lot, and could, at times, unleash searing comments. The word had always been he was headed to Washington, D.C., maybe the

Senate, maybe a high-level presidential appointment. He was going places. He was a brilliant star.

"Ron has always been a big personality," Ray recalled. "That has always been his strength and, in some cases, considered a fault by others."

The investigators knew the district attorney was the public "face" of the case and never doubted his commitment to both the victims' families and solving the murders. With the primary election coming up in September, they also knew he was heading into one of his toughest political battles. His challenge would be in balancing the two.

12 THE INDICTMENT

JUDY DESANTOS COULD TELL something was different when the grand jury session continued in August of 1990. There was an air of anticipation tinged with uneasiness. The district attorney seemed on edge. The moment he stepped outside the court, reporters were pressing him. *Are you close? Will there be an indictment?*

It was clear to her — and everyone in the city — that Kenny Ponte was the main target in the killings probe. In the more recent sessions of the grand jury, it appeared all the witnesses were tied somehow to the lawyer. Kenny was again making radio and television appearances, saying he was being railroaded. His lawyer, Kevin Reddington, was slamming the prosecutor publically. And there was the steady drumbeat of news stories about Kenny's ties to the dead women. Judy knew that her sister knew Kenny from when she worked at a video store and that he handled her bankruptcy case. Judy's nieces swore the lawyer used to call and come by the apartment, particularly when Frankie wasn't around. One time, Judy was told, Kenny offered her sister a job in his office. There were too many coincidences. If he wasn't the killer, he knew who was. She was sure of it.

Judy also trusted the prosecutors and the police. Maryann and Jose didn't talk about the suspects or Kenny Ponte or about how the grand jury was being handled. They didn't disparage the district attorney. They didn't criticize anyone. When she spoke with them, they would just tell her everyone was working hard and trying to find the person who did it.

In meetings with Ron Pina, she was impressed by the prosecutor's kindness and nonjudgmental nature. He was smart, he was sharp. He was their legal knight charging ahead for justice.

The special grand jury had been meeting sporadically for a year and a half, drawing both state and national media attention. Judy had used her vacation, sick, and personal time from work to wait outside the grand jury room whenever the panel met to keep watch. During that time, she had felt both encouraged and discouraged by its progress. Sometimes she was convinced the end was near and she would quietly celebrate in her mind. Other times, it appeared the killings were unsolvable, and she would try not to drown in despair. She could tell there had been different suspects in the case based on whom she saw going into the grand jury and what the media was reporting. She wasn't sure, though, what type of evidence police had — if any. All she could do was pray they had something.

Judy shared her concerns with the mother of Debra Greenlaw DeMello. Deb's children were young — just like Nancy's — and her mother, Madeline, was easy to talk with during the long grand jury waits. They were both angry and sad and overwhelmed by the case and the media attention. They both also had faith in the district attorney and developed a strong distaste for Kenny Ponte. Madeline lived nearly an hour's drive away in Brockton and wasn't at the grand jury sessions as often as Judy. Madeline wanted to keep home life as normal as possible for her daughter's kids. It wasn't always easy. Sometimes the grief was overwhelming, but Madeline was determined to shield the children from her own pain. She needed to be stronger than ever.

The two women also felt a pull from beyond the grave when they were together. They couldn't shake the feeling that Nancy and Debra were friends, their lives and deaths intertwined. Nancy's clothes were found across the highway near Debra's body. It had to mean something. They just weren't sure what it was. Was the clothing planted by the killer to throw them off? Or was there a simpler explanation? Could the killer have just tossed Nancy's clothes out while rounding the highway ramp to return to New Bedford after dumping her body less than two miles away on Interstate 195 westbound? Could Debra have borrowed Nancy's clothes while staying at her apartment and been wearing them at the time she was killed?

In July, Judy had watched from a discreet distance as Diane Doherty was escorted into the courthouse. Now, on this August day, Judy felt certain the case was coming to a close when she saw Diane Doherty escorted yet again into the courthouse. She found herself trembling slightly.

Is this what justice feels like? she wondered.

THE GRAND JURY ROOM in New Bedford Superior Court was on the left side of the hallway, across from a pay phone and the district attorney's satellite office. Inches from the grand jury door, Court Officer Valerie Fletcher sat guard at a tiny wooden desk, checking in witnesses and keeping the media at bay. Reporters sat on the wooden benches lining the wall, smoking and watching people go in and out. On one side of the grand jury room, there was a line of windows looking into the courthouse hallway, blinds shielding the view to the inside. Reporters tried to peer through the slats on occasion, squinting to catch a glimpse of a witness talking or the prosecutor gesturing. No one could hear what was being said.

It was hot during the summer in the courthouse and the grand jury room was no exception. Smokers huddled occasionally by an open window to catch a cigarette, trying to keep the smoke away from the others. It had been a long seventeen months for the twenty-three grand jurors. They were trying to balance their lives with the biggest case in Bristol County, if not the state. They were average people: secretaries, factory workers, teachers, retirees, office workers. When they were called to the grand jury, most figured it would be a three- or four-day event. Instead, they were spending three and four days every few months listening to testimony about a street world of drugs foreign to them. "It was a difficult year and a half," one of the grand jurors, Charles January, recalled. "The whole thing went on . . . forever."[1]

Some jurors would leave the session and go straight to work in the evening or night, the testimony lingering in their minds of the women from the streets who had been beaten, choked, or robbed. "They weren't easy to forget, the lives they lived," recalled another grand juror, Beverly Powell. "When I came home, I was just glad I had a normal life."[2]

By August of 1990, the grand jurors had listened to testimony from a wide range of people, including prostitutes, drug dealers, drug users, cops, a grieving mother, a grieving husband, a john who knew the dead women and had passed a polygraph test in the case. They heard about Kenny Ponte,

Tony DeGrazia, Neil Anderson, and a host of other people who knew or may have known the dead women. They heard about porn tapes, about drug use, about threats, about rapes, about beatings.

Then Diane Doherty came into the grand jury room in July and August.

She first appeared in July, after she alleged Kenny attacked her in Florida then recanted the allegation then recanted the recantation. Now, she was back, retelling part of that story and talking more about a mysterious film that was made in New Bedford.

Bob St. Jean was familiar with Diane and her stories. As part of the investigation, he knew that Diane had alleged months earlier to someone that Kenny showed her a video depicting someone being killed. She never directly said he was involved in making the video, he recalled. The details she gave, however, were still enough to interest investigators.

In her second appearance before the grand jury, Diane claimed the video production involved people tied to one of the bars in the city's South End — the same bar investigators knew some of the victims went to. It was also the same bar members of the Bristol County Drug Task Force targeted in a cocaine-dealing investigation. But the wiretap obtained as part of the probe failed to turn up anything linking the bar or any of the suspects to the killings or any type of porn tape, Bob St. Jean and the task force members knew. It was not something the detectives listening to the tapped calls would have missed.

Bob knew Diane was questioned about the video several times. She talked about it once in July to the grand jury and would be asked about it yet again when she appeared for a second time. He wondered what the grand jury members would think about her. He still wasn't sure how much of her story he believed.

When Diane was brought before the grand jury in August for another appearance, she insisted she had never met Kenny before she had flown to Florida to visit him in June of 1990. She said she wrote to him first, then sent him a mass card in May. Catholic mass cards are usually sent to indicate someone has made a church donation asking that a mass — and prayers — be said for someone facing a difficult situation, illness, or for someone who has died. Eventually they began talking on the phone, she said. She thought he was being railroaded and told him that. He proclaimed his innocence. She denied that she told anyone she had met him months earlier or that he confessed to murder in her former prison cellmate's kitchen. She said the private investigator in Lynn was harassing her and was trying to force her to sign an affidavit claiming Kenny confessed to murder. That's why she contacted Kenny, she told the grand jury. That's why she also contacted Kenny's lawyer months before going to Florida: she wanted to let people know he was being unfairly treated.

In the month before she flew to Florida, she said they talked about how innocent he was.

After her first night in Florida, she said she got nervous. She claimed he tried to choke her in bed. She claimed he threatened her with a gun. Then, the night before she was set to fly back home, she claimed he talked about a locally produced porn film funded by the owner of a South End bar, about murder, and about the death of Rochelle Dopierala. She claimed Kenny had cats named Rochelle, Robin, and Nancy—the names of three of the dead women. She said it was all very upsetting. She also said she loved Kenny and planned to marry him.

She claimed while he was choking her at his Florida home, he alluded to Rochelle's death. Kenny claimed he "offed" Rochelle, Diane alleged.[3]

"And I was crying and talking to him and everything," Diane testified. "And he told me if I, you know, didn't stop crying and everything, that I would be like that—he used a swear word; it begins with a *c*—and then he called me—like that Rochelle."[4]

Diane claimed Kenny told her Rochelle died because she was going to testify against him and was also trying to blackmail him about the film.

"All those girls, I guess, were, you know, talking too much before when they shouldn't have been. And they all owed money for drugs, too. Like he did," Diane testified. "A few of them went down into his law practice office and were really harassing him."

The film was supposed to go to Mexico and Canada but it never left the United States, she said. The girls just wanted their money for appearing in the film and "kept bugging him," she said.[5]

Diane said she wasn't sure if Rochelle was in the movie, though.

She was asked about what Kenny told her about the other dead women; did he talk about how they died?

"Part of it was to do with a cult-type stuff, like satanic-type things. And he did it three or four times a year. They do like offerings and stuff. And now I'm real, real Catholic. I don't like to keep talking about it. You know. It goes against our religion. And they owed money. He owed money too," she said.[6]

The district attorney and the grand jurors tried to press her for specific information. One grand juror asked her to describe in detail the film she claimed showed women being killed.

She refused. "Mr. Pina," she told the prosecutor. "I don't want to do that. I don't want to do that. I don't want to go through that again."

One grand juror told her she seemed to have "selective memory."[7] Another grand juror called Diane a "fruit loop."[8] The foreman told her there was a "huge credibility gap" dating to before the trip to Florida. Even the district attorney told Diane people were having a hard time believing her.[9]

This was one of the star witnesses in the case against Kenneth C. Ponte.

AS THE GRAND JURY INVESTIGATION FOCUSED on Kenny, he took to the airwaves and went on the offensive. He was calling into radio stations from his Florida home, insisting he was being framed. He was writing letters to the editor. He was even interviewed for a Rhode Island television station in his Florida backyard.

"If I'm indicted, I absolutely know I will be acquitted, and if I'm indicted, it will be for Ron Pina's purely selfish political reasons," he told freelance radio reporter Aubrey Haznar in one interview aired on WHJJ in Providence in August.

Kenny claimed the case had turned into a political sham used by the district attorney to win the upcoming primary. Just wait, he said. Just wait and see.

ASSISTANT DISTRICT ATTORNEY CAROL STARKEY and District Attorney Ronald A. Pina outlined the case of *Commonwealth v. Kenneth C. Ponte* to the group of city and state police investigators gathered in the conference room at the DA's office. It was August 8, 1990 and the grand jury would be meeting again. It was now clear to the investigators that the prosecutor would ask the panel to indict Kenny in at least one of the murders.

For about three hours each day for the next few days, the two prosecutors went over Kenny's ties to Rochelle, the Falmouth woman who once stayed at his Chestnut Street house. The prosecutors noted Kenny appeared to be the last person to see her alive, that a witness said Kenny feared Rochelle would testify against him, and that he reportedly threatened her.

These were the facts:

Rochelle was living with Kenny.

Rochelle was set to testify against Kenny in an upcoming gun case. She was a witness to an April 3, 1988, gunpoint confrontation on North Front Street between Kenny and a man she accused of raping her.

Rochelle was seen two weeks later walking down the street with the boyfriend of another highway killing victim.

Kenny drove Rochelle to the Cape and back sometime in April.

Kenny drove Rochelle to a mobile home where she visited an older man in April. He waited outside until she came out and the two drove off.

A woman who used to sell drugs in Weld Square heard Kenny threaten Rochelle in April of 1988.

Rochelle was not seen alive by anyone else after April 1988.

Diane Doherty alleged Kenny confessed and claimed the attorney possessed a snuff film.

To bolster the presentation, there were charts showing links to other victims, links that might show motive, links that tied Kenny to other victims. Grand jury testimony was reviewed. Ron was wrapping the case up in a neat package.

New Bedford detective Richard Ferreira quietly listened to the presentation. *Yikes, the* DA *doesn't have anything,* Richie thought.[10]

Jose and Maryann listened and questioned why other suspects weren't being considered for indictment. Jose told them he didn't agree with the direction the prosecutors were moving in. "I thought a better case could be made against other suspects," Jose said.[11]

Bob St. Jean thought an indictment might bring more — and stronger — witnesses forward. He also knew a lot more work was needed to get a conviction.

KEVIN REDDINGTON was in his Brockton office, waiting to pick up his thirteen-year-old daughter at soccer camp in nearby Easton. He was hoping on this hot, sunny mid-August Friday to beat the heavy Cape Cod traffic and get to the family's summer house early.

Then the phone rang. Kenny was getting indicted today, a tipster told him.

Kevin called his client. Meet me at the Dunkin' Donuts at the end of Route 140. And wear a suit. You're being indicted.

Then he sped to the soccer field to pick up his daughter.

In less than an hour, on August 17, 1990, Kevin was sitting in a Dunkin' Donuts in New Bedford, his daughter next to him, and a man who would soon be charged with murder sitting across the way. Kenny was wearing a clean, dark suit. Kevin could tell his client was nervous. He had told Kenny to fly back to Massachusetts earlier in the week suspecting this would happen. It was best to be here, to face the charge voluntarily, rather than be arrested in Florida and be returned in handcuffs. Image was important, Kevin knew.[12]

Kevin outlined the plan: they would leave Dunkin' Donuts, drive together to New Bedford Superior Court and walk calmly inside, through the line of media. No smart-ass comments, no scowling, no shielding his face from the cameras. When the grand jury handed up the indictment, they would be there, waiting to be arraigned immediately. This showed Kenny was not a flight risk, that he wanted to clear his name, that he was not a danger to the community.

The three then hopped into Kevin's red Porsche and drove to the courthouse five minutes away. When they pulled into the tiny side lot reserved for court personnel, the reporters, still photographers, and videographers surged forward. Some chuckled at the defense attorney's NG license plate. Kevin smiled warmly. His client stayed calm. They strode into the courthouse together and to the first-floor courtroom and waited outside the wooden swinging doors.

Kevin peered through a small window on the door, watching as twenty-one members of the original twenty-three-member grand jury entered the courtroom shortly after four in the afternoon. He and his client slipped inside and stood not far from a court officer as the foreman handed up the indictment to Judge George Hurd. Reporters filled the courtroom as the district attorney began to speak.

"I'd request that the paper be impounded and the grand jury not be discharged from further duty," Bristol County district attorney Ronald A. Pina asked the judge.

Kevin Reddington saw the district attorney glance toward the door. He swore the prosecutor flinched in surprise.

The judge impounded the indictment. Reporters for the *Standard-Times* and the *Boston Globe* objected to the impoundment. The judge rejected the media request and left the bench.

Kevin was annoyed. So was the judge when he discovered the defendant was in the courthouse and could have been arraigned immediately.

The judge later ordered prosecutors to appear in court on the upcoming Monday to explain why the indictment should be sealed — especially, people would later say, since the defendant was there when it was handed up. "The judge was not pleased," Kevin recalled.[13]

Kevin asked to speak with the prosecutor. A court officer told him the DA would talk with him later. The DA told reporters he needed to talk with the families of the victims first.

JUDY DESANTOS AND GRACE BOTELHO, the mother of Sandra Botelho, the last victim to be found, and Sandra's sister had been waiting in the court hallway all day, expecting something would happen. Other relatives of other victims had also stopped in throughout the week, looking for slivers of information. Everyone at the courthouse was tense. Everyone could feel the anticipation rising with the August heat as more reporters arrived each day.

Judy had been at the courthouse all week while the grand jury met — just as she had since the second day it convened a year and a half earlier. She was now used to passing through the line of media out front and the boredom of waiting inside. She knew it only took a minute to walk up and down the main hallway. She knew the defendants were locked up on the second floor, behind the amphitheater-like courtroom there. She knew the names of most of the court officers, including Ralph Tavares, who gained fame in the 1970s as one of the original members of Tavares, the rhythm-and-blues group of Cape Verdean brothers. She knew how he quit the group to return home to a steady job, where he was home every night with his family rather than on the road. She knew the clerks and the secretaries. She recognized the probation officers' faces. She even knew the reporters.

By late afternoon, word was spreading quickly in the small building. The grand jury might have an indictment. Judy was scared but she didn't know why. She could feel cold, almost paralyzing, fear creep through her body. What, if anything, did she need to do? What would happen when the indictment was handed up to the judge? She wasn't a lawyer. She didn't know the finer mechanisms of the criminal justice system.

Judy slipped into the courtroom, watching as the grand jury entered single file. She would have her answer finally, more than two years after her sister was killed. She would have a name. She would have justice.

She looked around the courtroom, at the reporters, at the lawyers, at the court officers. She took a deep breath, trying to calm herself. The name. She needed the name. She focused on the DA. She didn't want to miss it.

She listened as the prosecutor asked that the indictment be impounded. It took a moment to understand what that meant. She held back tears, wondering if the killer had really been found.

A few minutes later, the district attorney met briefly with Judy and the Botelho family. He didn't tell them who was indicted. He didn't give them an answer. A detective later hinted the name on the indictment was Kenneth Ponte.

Judy and the Botelho family left the courthouse quickly. Judy didn't want to be seen crying.

JOSE AND MARYANN stayed in the office when the indictment was handed up. The two investigators had felt uneasy at that earlier meeting when the case against Kenny was presented to the staff. There wasn't enough evidence to convict. There was no "smoking gun"; they had no eyewitness to any of the murders; they had nothing to link Kenny directly to any of the killings. They had talked with Diane Doherty and didn't believe her claims were credible. Her stories shifted. They had interviewed so many people since 1988 who had made wild claims, who alleged they knew who the killer was, where bodies were. The teams of investigators had followed so many leads, so many suspects, so many paths leading to dead ends. They knew a person's word wasn't enough — they needed evidence. Sometimes people were mistaken, sometimes people misheard a conversation, sometimes people exaggerated, sometimes people simply lied.

There were other suspects, potentially better suspects, in the case even if there wasn't any proof to charge them with murder. Why Kenny and why now?

The troopers stayed in the office and waited for the families to call, uncertain about what to say.

THOMPSON'S CLAM BAR IN HARWICH WAS BUSY. It was a popular eatery and one of Kevin Reddington's favorites. A few hours earlier, he had been sixty miles away in New Bedford, over the bridge connecting Cape Cod to the mainland, fielding reporter questions and trying to figure out why his client wasn't arraigned. He was telling his friends about the day, how strange it was, probably the strangest so far in his legal career. It was interesting dinner conversation. Then they moved on to other subjects.

A few days later, he would be told someone had been listening to that conversation. Someone was saying he was joking and laughing about the case. Kevin was a bit unnerved and annoyed. "I was talking about how he was indicted and what a piece of crap case it was and someone is sitting there listening. Someone went so far as to go to a restaurant I was at and get a table near where I was sitting," he recalled.[14] It was, he suspected, going to be a long, arduous trial.

THREE DAYS LATER, the relatives of the dead women jammed the conference room at the district attorney's main office. Judy listened as Ron Pina told them what would happen in court later that morning. The defendant would enter a plea. The prosecution's case would be outlined and they would ask for a high bail. The defense attorney would likely ask for a lower bail, maybe even no bail. The judge would make a decision and the case would be continued to another date. There would also be a lot of media.

Only one murder case was being prosecuted, she remembered him saying. It was better to go with the one they could prove. If they didn't have a conviction on that one, they had others to fall back on. Judy knew her sister's murder was the "fall back" death. All of the seven of the victims represented by families in the room that day were in the "fall back" category. The death of Rochelle Clifford Dopierala was the case being prosecuted.

Judy held back tears as she looked over at Madeline Perry.

This doesn't feel like justice, Judy thought.

It is the little things people often remember in grief and crisis: the person at the wake or funeral, the card sent, the dinner made, the lawn mowed, the children entertained. Those are the things that can ease that crushing pain, if only for a moment. The slights are remembered years later just as deeply.

For Judy, the walk up the hill from the district attorney's office to the courthouse is what she remembers most.

There were too many relatives and too few vehicles available to drive the families to court, they were told.

Judy again turned to Madeline Perry. "Let's go," she told her.

The two got up and walked out of the district attorney's office. They walked through the front lobby, they went down the elevator, they walked out the front door and up the street that August 20, 1990, morning until they got to the courthouse. Behind them, a line of other families followed.

KEVIN REDDINGTON made sure his client was waiting at court early. He also gave him clear instructions on what not to do during the arraignment. No eye rolls. No head shaking. No grunting. No glaring. No grinning. No smiling. No deep exhales. No face making. No waving. No talking when the prosecutor is talking. No talking at all except to enter a plea of not guilty.

The first-floor courtroom, the same courtroom where the indictment had been handed up three days earlier, was crammed with relatives of the victims, reporters, lawyers, and court personnel. Kenny's teary-eyed mother and sister sat in wooden chairs along a courtroom wall, waiting for the case to begin.

Kevin could see the families of the victims, some crying, clustered on one side of the courtroom. He could see Kenny's mother on the other side, shaken, watching her lawyer-son now a murder defendant.

CHANDRA SAT ON ONE SIDE of her Uncle Wayne, her grandmother sat on the other. All three stared at the man the prosecutor alleged was a killer. She wanted to believe the DA was right; they all did. This man, this alleged killer, was big but her mother was a fighter, a tough fighter, and would never give up, Chandra thought. How did he do this?

She didn't pay any attention to the people filling the courtroom. She kept her focus on the man charged with murder, the man they said likely also killed her mother.

Judy sat in the third row, waiting for the arraignment to begin. Next to her sat her niece, Jill. In the second row was the district attorney's wife, Sheila Martines-Pina. Behind Judy and Jill were rows filled with twenty relatives of the dead women. Judy surveyed the courtroom. She saw Kenny's family sitting with their backs to the wall. She saw the reporters she knew. She saw court officers and lawyers. In one row, Robert St. Jean, the chief investigator for Pina's office, sat. In another row, there were people from the victim/witness office.

She scanned row after row. Jose and Maryann were not there. Neither was Richie. Neither were any of the state police or New Bedford investigators she knew.

In that instant, she feared there was a problem.

"Maryann and Jose had always said to me, if we feel we have the right person, we will be in that courtroom, but if you look around and don't see us there, we don't believe this is the right person," Judy recalled.[15]

THE INDICTMENT WAS READ by the court clerk: Kenneth C. Ponte, on or about the twenty-seventh day of April in the year one thousand nine hundred and eighty-eight, at New Bedford, in the County of Bristol, aforesaid, did assault and beat Rochelle Clifford Dopierala with intent to murder her and by such assault and beating did kill and murder the said Rochelle Clifford Dopierala.

How did he plea?

Kenny stood straight and answered in a loud and clear voice.

"Absolutely not guilty, your honor."

The relatives gasped. His lawyer wanted to smack him on the head. The district attorney didn't skip a beat and asked the judge to set bail at $50,000 cash or $500,000 surety.

District Attorney Ronald A. Pina told superior court judge George N. Hurd there were compelling reasons for setting bail. It was a serious crime and the defendant was and still is an intravenous drug user.

Kenny's eyes bulged at the words intravenous drug user. His attorney stood emotionless.

Ron then argued the defendant was a lawyer and knew better than anyone about the law. "As a member of the bar, Attorney Ponte crosses the line from the legal community and became a member of the drug community," he told the judge.

"He used these women because he was an attorney and afraid to go buy the drugs himself. He recruited different women at different times. He brought them to his home."

The district attorney said the defendant was pressuring Rochelle not to testify against him in a gun case, began pursuing her, and threatened to kill her.

Then it was the defense's turn to talk.

Kevin asked the court to free his client on personal recognizance — essentially a personal promise to come back to court without posting any bail. "He has no intention of taking flight," he told the judge. "He needs a trial to clear his name."

His client knew he was the focus of a grand jury investigation for seventeen months but never tried to hide or flee. He was living in Florida but returned to Massachusetts voluntarily whenever he was needed. He even passed two private polygraph tests (although polygraph tests can't be used as evidence in Massachusetts).

There was also an "outpouring of public support" for the defendant, he said.

The sister of Sandra Botelho, Liz Tavares, widened her eyes. "Tssss," she quietly hissed.

The judge sided with the prosecution. Bail was set at $50,000 cash or $500,000 surety. Most murder defendants are held without bail. Kenny's mom posted a house she owned on Austin Street as bail.

Two hours after pleading "absolutely not guilty," Kenny walked out of court.

"I just want to say, it's been a two-year-long nightmare for me so far, and I greatly look forward to the trial to be acquitted to end the nightmare once and for all," he told reporters.[16] Then he got into the passenger seat of his lawyer's Porsche and the two drove off.

ACROSS THE STREET from the courthouse, Gwen Andrade held a homemade sign and a painful vigil. The sign read

No. 1
What About???

Joanne Andrade.

Possibly #1 victim of the highway killings remains still forgotten.

And her 9 yr old daughter still lives day by day not knowing

what happened to her mother

Gwen's sister, Joanne Andrade, was found drowned off State Pier on October 25, 1987. Joanne, a recovering heroin addict, had been hit on the head several times and choked before being thrown into the water. Was she one of the uncounted highway killing victims? Were there more?

The deaths of Joanne and three other women murdered between 1986 and 1988 had been examined in connection with the highway killing case. Two different suspects were looked at in two of the cases.

But in the cases of Joanne Andrade and Dorothy Danelson, the nineteen-year-old woman found brutally raped along railroad tracks in New Bedford on July 16, 1986, some people still wondered if there was a link. Those were the same two cases that got now-retired John Dextradeur wondering if there could be a serial killer in the area.

Joanne's sister was convinced the answer was yes.

"I believe she was the first victim," Gwen told reporters outside the courthouse. "I believe she was number one."[17]

A YELLOW SCHOOL BUS idled in the lot reserved for court personnel at the front side of the courthouse. After the arraignment, the families were escorted to the bus and brought to the district attorney's office for a meeting.

Chandra, Debra Greenlaw's teenaged daughter, leaned out the window of the bus as reporters reached up with microphones to catch her words.

"I want him hung," she said bluntly.

AFTER THE ARRAIGNMENT, after meeting with the district attorney yet again, Madeline Perry went to Melrose Cemetery in Brockton and stood at her daughter's gravesite.

She couldn't bear to come here four days earlier, on what would have been her Deb's thirty-sixth birthday. She had nothing to say to the heavens. She had nothing but tears to leave on the soft grass. Now, on this day, she could say it was over, she could rest.

13 THE CAMPAIGN

IT WAS TIME TO CRANK UP the campaigning. The primary was less than a month away, and everyone in the Pina camp feared it would be a close vote. Whoever won in September would take the seat; there was no general-election challenger. Ron's closest advisors were worried — and convinced he was in big trouble. There was a chance he could lose. A very real chance. Ron shrugged off their concerns. He would win. He always won. He was a good DA and people knew it. They would vote for him. He was sure of that.

He made some campaign stops, debated his opponent, and figured when the votes were finally counted he would slide back into his downtown office. There was no doubt in his mind.

THE BEER WAS FLOWING and the cheers were loud when the election results were announced at LeBeau's Tavern in the city's North End where hundreds of Paul F. Walsh Jr. supporters were gathered on September 18, 1990.

As the votes from each ward and precinct in the cities and each town came in, cheers went up. Walsh won Dartmouth. Walsh won Fairhaven. Paul refused to get his hopes up. He was up against a twelve-year incumbent, and this was his first election. It would be close but there was a good chance he could lose. "The conventional wisdom was he would win Fall River and I would do well in New Bedford and then it would be a street fight," Paul recalled.[1]

When results came in from the Niagara section of Fall River, a neighborhood where 99 percent of the voters were Portuguese, he knew he had won. "We won, 2-to-1, and we knew Ron was in trouble," Paul said.

With each ward and precinct, with each town and city, the news continued to be good. The thirty-six-year-old, in his first bid for elective office, trounced the incumbent in all twenty communities in the county by a 62 to 38 percent margin. People crammed the building, backslapping and laughing as they celebrated the victory. Some supporters in the street raised brooms bought at a nearby store and shouted "sweep, sweep" until Paul's father, the campaign veteran, told them to stop, saying it was disrespectful. Paul moved easily through the crowd, thanking supporters and praising his opponent for a good campaign.

Across the city, in the waterfront restaurant Twin Piers, Ronald A. Pina was solemnly giving his concession speech at 10:15 p.m. before grim-faced supporters. His daughter, Kari, could see him tearing up.

Kari, aged sixteen, suspected this was how the election would turn out. She could see the Walsh signs on the lawns of former Pina supporters. She heard people talking about being disillusioned. She could feel that rumble of discontent. So did others in the campaign, but they all hoped the years of work would pay off with the electorate somehow.

"I've never lost in my life so I'm not used to it," Ron said that night.[2]

The party at the restaurant overlooking the fishing fleet this primary night was now over. The one in the middle-class neighborhood in the North End was just starting.

A FEW MEMBERS of the staff gathered in Pina's office in October of 1990 figuring out what needed to be done before January when the district attorney would be leaving office. It would likely be one of the last times — if not the last time — those in Pina's inner circle would be together there. When the incoming prosecutor came in, he would handpick his own staff. A few, maybe, would be asked to stay after officially "applying" for a job and undergoing an interview with the new boss. Out with the old. In with the new. That was how politics worked. That was how it always worked.

Lance Garth listened to what Pina was saying and wondered what would happen to him. He weathered politics well up until now as an assistant district attorney. He'd worked under four different district attorneys in Bristol County and had seen, firsthand, the housecleaning after each election. Some pending cases, upon review, got dropped. Some cases that had languished got prosecuted. The top staff, those closest to the outgoing DA, nearly always got the boot. Garth had started as a prosecutor in 1969, a year after passing the Massachusetts bar. It was the same year Senator Edward Kennedy drove an Oldsmobile off the narrow Chappaquiddick Bridge, killing twenty-eight-year-old staffer Mary Jo Kopechne. His boss then was Edmund Dinis, whose district at the time included the island of Chappaquiddick. Dinis knew politics. Dinis's father was the first Portuguese-American elected to the state senate, and his godfather was the legendary Boston mayor James Michael Curley. But it was clear he didn't know politics enough to know what would happen in the Kennedy case. Ed Dinis oversaw the grand jury in that case and the outcome — Kennedy pleaded guilty to leaving the scene of an accident and got a suspended sentence — failed to satisfy either the Kennedy lovers or haters. Dinis lost the election the next year.

Now, as Lance sat in the office, listening to Ron Pina, he wondered if his time as a prosecutor was finally coming to a close.

The meeting was wrapping up when the DA turned to him. "You're going to prosecute the Ponte case," the outgoing DA told him.[3]

Lance was quiet. He wasn't sure if Ron was doing him a favor, thinking this would secure him a spot with the new administration, or if it was a final way to stick it to him. Lance never felt part of the true inner circle in the office. He was a holdover from previous administrations, not one of Pina's handpicked young turks on the way up the political ladder. He was one of the prosecutors watching from the sidelines during the highway killing investigation. He wasn't privy to what investigators were doing. He wasn't involved with the grand jury presentation. His caseload was often filled with the heavy-hitting and headline-making murders, but this was not one of them. He wasn't sure why, but he knew not to ask. Now, he was tasked with prosecuting one of the biggest cases in the office, and the trial clock was ticking. In Massachusetts, a case must be tried within a year unless there are special circumstances or court-approved delays. It is called the speedy trial rule. Nearly two of the twelve months had already passed since Ponte was arraigned on the murder charge. Lance was now left with less than a year to try one of the most complicated and scrutinized cases in the county — and he knew little about the evidence.

Why didn't you give it to me eight months ago, he thought

Instead, he nodded. Okay, he told the lame-duck prosecutor.

As he left the office, he started a mental list of things to do to prepare for a trial.

I can do this and win, he tried to convince himself.

14 OLD SUSPECT BACK

IN THE MONTHS leading up to the indictment of Kenny Ponte and the district attorney's loss in 1990, the Freetown man accused of attacking prostitutes, Tony DeGrazia, was trying to start fresh and get back to work. The time behind bars trying to make bail took a toll on him financially and emotionally. It would be hard to get someone to hire him after the arrest and ensuing news coverage linking him to the murder case. Starting his own business seemed the only alternative. Tony once worked in the stone business with his father and figured he could do that again on his own. There were a few problems with that plan: he had no credit, and he had no truck. He turned to his parish priest for help.

The St. John Neumann Catholic Church overlooked Long Pond and was next to a popular church youth camp called Cathedral Camp. Tony would often come by the church to talk with Father George Harrison during the week and would be at Mass every Sunday. Sometimes the priest would see him in the pew, quietly saying the rosary. "He had a lot of spirituality," Father Harrison recalled. "He was always in church, praying."[1]

The priest knew about Tony's personal and legal problems — everyone did — and tried to counsel him. When police first searched Tony's house, he told the young man to go with the police and give honest answers. When Tony was later charged and held pending bail, the priest talked and prayed with him at the jail. He had nothing to fear if he was innocent, the priest told him. Eventually, Tony asked the priest if he could help him get started in his business. Would he be the guarantor on some rental trucks? Could he also be an officer of his company, at least temporarily, so he could rent the trucks? Please? The priest reluctantly agreed with the caveat that his name be removed as quickly as possible.

By March of 1991, Tony had created a new company called Colonial Stone Supply, leased a 1990 red Ford pickup truck and a Mack dump truck, and started to work. There were three people, including Tony, listed as corporation officers. By June of 1990, only Tony was listed. "Once he got off on the business, he was busy, busy all summer long," the priest would later testify.[2]

For Tony, things were changing personally and on the legal front, too. After years of self-consciousness about his appearance, Tony had surgery to repair the nose everyone described as "boxer-like." He wasn't considered a murder suspect anymore after that lawyer from New Bedford was indicted in the highway killings case. He still had the rape charges pending but he was feeling good about how those cases would turn out. He had a new attorney, an up-and-coming aggressive Boston lawyer named Robert George, whom he first met with in April of 1990 and officially hired by August, and Tony felt the charges would either be dropped or he would be acquitted. "He struck me as a young man who was deeply upset by the allegations against him and desperately wanted to be cleared," Robert George recalled.[3] "It was like he was caught up in a whirlwind he couldn't get out of."

Tony's demeanor surprised the attorney, too. "I was impressed what a gentle kid he was. He was gentle and he was very polite. I was touched by it."

There was still one rough spot in Tony's life, though. More than a year earlier, his high school sweetheart had broken up with him a month after they got engaged and was now dating someone else. She told him they would always be friends but she was in love. Tony took it hard. He had seen the new couple together one night at the Eagles Club in Lakeville and began to cry. When the couple noticed and left, he followed them outside, tears still in his eyes. He told her new boyfriend to take good care of her. People told Tony it would get easier and he would meet someone else. He still wasn't sure.

Other than his love life, the dark days for Tony seemed to be coming to a close. He was feeling good about his looks, his work, and, it appeared, his life.

The good times didn't last. By the fall of 1990, work had slowed down, there was little money coming in, and Tony couldn't pay his rent. He needed a place to stay. He sought a refuge at the church rectory.

Father Harrison had encouraged and counseled Tony over the years, just as he had other parishioners. Tony was now asking for more help. He wanted to stay at the rectory. The priest said no. Tony asked again. And again. And again. Finally, the priest relented. It would be a temporary arrangement, Tony was told. He could stay in a small room in the back of the rectory. But it had to be a short stay, just until he got on his feet. It was not permanent. "He was moving through," the priest recalled. "He was getting out. He didn't want to stay there. I mean, he just needed a temporary place to stay. And he was [saying] just, like, 'Can I stay here?' I was hoping he'd get out any day."[4]

Tony went to work early, went to Mass, and helped with church readings. Sometimes he ate in the rectory, often in the den. He would get anxious when a court date neared and he would talk with the priest and pray beforehand. The priest said there did not seem to be anything to suggest a problem at the time, other than the pending court case. Between church services, the youth ministry, parish business, and related events Father Harrison was very busy. Tony was focusing on work, church, and upcoming court dates.

A year earlier, Tony had been in jail, accused of beating and raping women. Now, he was hoping his new lawyer could convince a judge or jury he was innocent.

IT WAS A CLEAR NIGHT, around thirty degrees, when the woman on Purchase Street in New Bedford's Weld Square hopped in the red truck after midnight on November 2, 1990. Her boyfriend was nearby, taking note of what the truck and the driver looked like. The first two numbers on the license plate were 99, and there were three letters on the side of the truck, CSS. The truck had what appeared to be oversized tires, and the vehicle was sitting higher off the ground than most. It seemed new. He got a good look at the driver and knew, if anything happened, he could identify him.

Once in the truck, the woman and the driver agreed on a price for sex. She tried to chat with him but he was quiet as they drove to a spot behind a waterfront bar and stopped. The driver slid toward her. Then he grabbed her neck with one, then two hands and began squeezing. Tighter and tighter. "I was saying to him, 'What are you doing?'" the woman recalled.[5] She fought back. She could feel herself losing consciousness. She began to kick. The doors were locked. Each time she tried to unlock them, the man would lock them again using the automatic lock. She kept pushing and kicking and fighting until she reached the driver's side door. "Why are you doing this to me?" she cried.[6] She opened it slightly and then, gripping the door handle, pushed herself out of the truck. The inside door handle broke off as she toppled out.

Then she ran. First, she hid in a field, and then began banging on trailer trucks parked near the waterfront tavern. One of the truck drivers, sleeping in his cab, woke and called the police.

When police arrived to Herman Melville Boulevard at quarter to one in the morning, they spoke with the frightened woman and searched the area. New Bedford Officer William Perry, the first on the scene, later found the door handle on the ground.

Detective Paul LeClair on November 5, 1990, separately showed the woman and her boyfriend a photo array of men to see if they recognized the attacker. They both picked out an old photo of Tony DeGrazia, saying it looked similar to the man they saw. The nose, they both noted, looked different in the picture. A few days later, on November 8, Detective Tommy Thomas interviewed the couple and developed a composite drawing based on their descriptions. The drawing looked like Tony.

When Detective Richie Ferreira, who worked on the highway killing case, heard about the attack, he called the Chamber of Commerce to see if Tony registered a business with the group. The answer was yes: Colonial Stone Supply. C.S.S.

Richie called the state police. You're not going to believe this, he told them.

The same New Bedford and state police investigators who once wondered if Tony was tied to the highway killings were now looking at the Freetown man in yet another attack.

Trooper Lorraine Forrest, who, along with Trooper Kevin Butler, had interviewed Tony in the earlier cases, found Tony's truck parked at Cathedral Camp next to the church. It was a red 1990 two-door Ford pickup truck with silver gray strips on the side. The letters C.S.S. were painted on the doors. The first two numbers on the license plate were 99. Richie checked a local Ford dealership and found the handle recovered the night of the attack was one used for four years in full-sized trucks. One of those models was a 1990 Ford full-sized truck.

ON NOVEMBER 20, Tony was in the church rectory, preparing for his sister's wedding the next day. He would be doing the readings at the Mass and was making sure it was perfect. Father Harrison was eating spaghetti in the den and was about to head out in a few minutes to perform a wedding at four thirty, followed by a wedding rehearsal at six, and a Mass at seven. The wedding rehearsal for Tony's sister was at eight.

Tony said he would be at the seven o'clock Mass and at the rehearsal for his sister's wedding.

As the priest left, he told Tony to help himself to the leftover spaghetti on the coffee table.

RICHIE AND THE TEAM of state troopers were waiting near the Freetown rectory on Middleboro Road, an arrest warrant in hand for Anthony De-Grazia. Maryann and Jose went to a payphone down the street. Posing as a reporter, Maryann called the house and asked for Tony. She chatted with him for a bit then radioed the others. It was a go. Tony was there.

It was raining when the other investigators moved in. Richie went to the back of the building; Lorraine went to the front. More troopers arrived. They knocked on the door. No one answered. They didn't have a search warrant so they couldn't force their way into the house. Richie decided to walk over to the church to ask the priest to let them in.

Father Harrison had just finished officiating the four thirty wedding at the church. The bride, groom, and the guests were in the foyer, and the priest, still wearing his vestments, was headed to the sacristy when he saw a man in the hallway.

"Father, I would like to speak to you in private," Richie said.[7]

The priest noticed what appeared to be a wallet in the man's hand. He thought the man was giving the church a donation.

Richie looked at the priest. "Father, I have a warrant for Anthony DeGrazia's arrest."

The priest was flustered. "Okay, I'll go down there. He's at the rectory," he told Richie.[8]

Father Harrison got in his car and started to drive the 350 yards through the parking lot to the rectory next door, driving past Richie. He stopped and the detective got in. "I know you're upset about this," Richie comforted the priest.

As they pulled up to the rectory, the priest could see the police gathered outside. He asked to go in first so he could talk with Tony and bring him out. The officers agreed.

Inside, the priest went through the rooms, calling for Tony. There was no answer. He came back out and told the investigators Tony was gone. He is there, they answered. We spoke with him. The priest went back in, calling for Tony. "Anthony you gotta come out," he hollered.

When the priest came back out a second time, the investigators were skeptical. A trooper spoke with Tony. He was there. The priest invited the cops inside to see for themselves.

As they started in and began to search, one trooper asked about a plate of food and a cold drink on a table in the living room.⁹ The police later said the priest at that point suggested they needed a search warrant. The priest said he panicked and was worried he could get in trouble with the diocese for letting them in without a warrant.

"Stop," Richie told the investigators when the priest mentioned a search warrant.

Jose took the priest aside. He was a parishioner at St. John Neumann Church and knew Father Harrison well. He explained they would get a search warrant from the court if needed. Did he want that? The priest paused then told them to keep searching.

Tony was gone. There was a door on the southeast side of the house the police didn't know about.

The priest went back to the church for the next two wedding rehearsals as the police searched. He had to break the news to Tony's sister that he likely wouldn't be at her wedding.

Father Harrison walked around the property that night with his dog, calling for Tony. Later, Tony called the rectory; he wanted the priest to know he was safe. He wouldn't say where he was.

The next night, Tony called again. He would turn himself in to the authorities on Monday. Tony told the priest how he eluded arrest. He heard the police outside the rectory talking on the radio, saying they needed to notify

Freetown police they were making an arrest in town. Tony crawled out the guestroom window and onto the roof. He crawled along the roof, jumped off, then ran into the woods. Again, he wouldn't say where he was. He would only tell the priest that he had spoken with his attorney, that he was safe, and that he would surrender to authorities on Monday.

That Monday Tony was in New Bedford District Court with his lawyer to surrender. He was arraigned on charges of attempted murder and assault with intent to murder.

He was brought back, shackled, to the Bristol County Jail and House of Correction on Ash Street. There would be no bail.

When the attorney for Kenny Ponte heard about the arrest, he said police might have been too quick to eliminate Tony as a suspect in the murder case. "Mr. DeGrazia was linked a lot to this investigation in the past year," Kevin Reddington said.

KENNY PONTE read the news about Tony's latest arrest with interest. Why aren't they focusing on this guy as a suspect, he repeatedly asked. Why am I in the crosshairs? Why am I under indictment? Those were the same questions his lawyer, Kevin Reddington, had been asking publicly for months. The Freetown man had a history of sexual-assault arrests, was under indictment in a series of attacks on prostitutes, and revealed deep-seated mental health issues during court-ordered evaluations. The decision to indict Kenny was puzzling to the defense attorney when, based on the evidence he was seeing, Tony DeGrazia was a better suspect.

"DeGrazia kind of slipped by the wayside," Kevin recalled. "For some reason, the DA's office focused on Kenny. It seemed almost like a vendetta."[10]

It was now one month after the primary and two months before a new district attorney would take over. The defense attorney was waiting for the next move after the first of the year. He was hoping that move would be to drop the charges against Kenny.

PAUL WALSH closed the door of the conference room and then sat across from Jose and Maryann. The conference table was clean. He wanted every meeting with the troopers to start that way. Clean table. Fresh start.

Just two weeks earlier, he had been sworn in by his father, Paul Walsh Sr., in the second-floor courtroom at New Bedford Superior Court as the new Bristol County district attorney. After his swearing in, there was a bit of political handshaking, backslapping, and congratulations. Then there were, as always, the quiet "do-you-have-a-second" requests: Do you have a job for me? For my kid? For my wife? For my brother? He expected that and knew how to answer. He would smile; he would review the names, the résumés, the backgrounds. He might say it was too soon to make any decisions, or he might say he was still settling in. He always answered people with a smile. He had grown up with election days, election nights, and political parties. He knew which political events to attend, how long to stay, how to be polite but noncommittal. He knew the language of politics and subscribed to the adage of Boston politician Tip O'Neill: "All politics is local." Now, with the election over and his team in place, Paul knew it was time to get down to the business of the office: prosecuting bad guys. At the top of the list was the highway killing case.

The new district attorney knew he couldn't move forward without looking back. He needed to make a decision quickly. The legal speedy-trial clock was ticking in the murder case against Kenneth C. Ponte. In Massachusetts, a defendant must be tried within 365 days after arraignment unless a judge approves an extension. It was now month five in the case of *Commonwealth v. Ponte*. Hard decisions needed to be made. If he prosecuted and lost, Ponte could not be tried again if new evidence surfaced. If he dropped the case, his predecessor's supporters would claim the "kid," the "new guy," didn't have the balls to take on the tough cases. He wondered if this indictment of Kenny Ponte in the waning days of the campaign was a land mine, a political "FU" from his predecessor when polls suggested a Walsh primary win.

Walsh knew a little bit about the highway killing case. As a defense attorney, he had represented a cab driver, Arnold "Goldy" Goldblatt — who would sometimes shuttle girls to Kenny Ponte's house — on drug charges, and a woman who claimed to have a porn tape that never materialized. At the time he was representing the cab driver accused in 1989 of conspiring with Kenny Ponte to buy drugs, Paul wasn't impressed with the evidence the prosecution provided in that case. He knew, though, that most of the prosecutors in the office were the best of the best: sharp, ethical, hardworking. The previous district attorney could have screwed up the case, but his staff would have walked those errors back. They wouldn't let a bad case move forward — or would they? He needed to know what was in the files, what led to the laser focus on Kenny Ponte, and why he was the prime suspect. It would start here, in this conference room, on a clear table.

Jose pulled out a folder and started at the beginning. And the new district attorney listened.

For nearly two months, three times a week, from nine thirty in the morning to twelve thirty in the afternoon, Walsh met with the state troopers and, eventually, New Bedford detective Richard Ferreira. They showed him photos of the scenes, gave him details about the victims, told him stories about prostitutes who survived beatings, rapes, and being choked. He learned more about drug deals, hole-in-the-wall bars, and how cheaply sex was sold. He learned about real people unable to escape drug addiction. He learned the list of suspects was very long at times: there was the Coast Guard petty officer caught picking up a hooker; the two guys in a van who raped another prostitute; a guy who lived in Rhode Island and later in Fall River who let the girls stay in his house; the sex offenders out on furlough; fishermen up from the South; Neil Anderson, accused of rape. And, of course, there was Tony DeGrazia. He was impressed by the thoroughness of the reports, the minutiae gathered by teams of state police and local detectives. The investigation was deeper and broader than he initially thought. He recognized the places in the reports: the stores, the bars, the streets. He even recognized some of the names from his childhood days shooting hoops at Clasky Common Park, the Boy's Club, and the YMCA. He listened and later read the police reports, realizing this was a part of the city he didn't recognize from either his days on the basketball court or from his neighborhood Catholic school less than a mile from Weld Square. This was a different community. How did he not know this? "The thing that hit me like a two-by-four in the face was that entire, separate universe was going on down there," Paul later recalled. "It was that second universe. It was almost like storm clouds coming towards you."[11]

He learned about other suspects who were commercial truck drivers delivering frozen seafood throughout New England, members of the Coast Guard, doctors, cops, businessmen. He learned about the distribution of porn videotapes and the people who rented them. He learned about drug sales, about the street sex trade. The new DA and the investigators went through every document, every theory, every witness, every interview. They noted every vehicle used by which suspect. They looked at theories, at motives, at lack of motive. They looked at serial-killing cases in other parts of the country.

Each session on a specific suspect and segment in the investigation would start the same: with a clean table.

Each session would end the same: clear the table, pack the file box.

Jose, Maryann, and Richie gave him facts, not opinion. He would have to reach his own decision. Paul knew what he should do, what he wanted to do, what was the ethical thing to do. To prosecute a person without evidence, to prosecute a person if you have a reasonable doubt as to his guilt, to wonder if someone really did it, would be a violation of the code of ethics for prosecutors, he knew. But he also worried whatever he decided would appear as political, not as justice. He wanted the case to be examined on its merits, outside the Bristol County circles. He wanted another set of eyes on the case. He wanted a second clean table.

PAUL F. WALSH JR. looked for advice about what to do next with the indictment against Kenny. The new district attorney talked with cops, lawyers, and his advisors in the office about the strength of the case. Should it go to trial? Could it go to trial? In the post-election office reshuffling, Paul had let go Lance Garth, the longtime assistant district attorney his predecessor had tapped to prosecute the case. In the meantime, Paul needed to find someone to take his place.

The highway killing case posed so many problems for his office, both ethically and politically. When he was a defense attorney, Paul represented at least three people involved in the case. When he was a candidate for the office, he was a harsh critic of how his predecessor handled the murder case and made Pina's appearances in the media one of the central issues in the primary fight.

Now, after a two-month review and with five months to prepare for a trial, Paul had a clearer perspective and knew the detailed work that went into the investigation. He was impressed. Dozens of suspects were looked at, hundreds of witnesses were interviewed, federal forensic experts had been brought in, and FBI profilers had even offered suggestions on interviewing techniques and information on possible suspects. Plus, he could see, state and local police put in thousands of hours searching for witnesses and evidence in the case. It wasn't the investigation that was flawed. This was a case with weathered crime scenes, no eyewitnesses, and fuzzy timelines. A lucky break — or someone with a guilty conscience — is what was needed from the start. He still wasn't sure indicting Kenneth Ponte had been the right move, based on the evidence he saw. Was he missing something? Would they learn more as a trial date moved closer? Would witnesses — credible witnesses — come forward then? Should they even think that way with a case this serious, with a person's liberty on the line?

A few people suggested he bring in a special prosecutor. It was a good idea, Paul thought, but who would be best? One person suggested a former prosecutor named Paul Buckley from the Boston area, a man who had probably never even visited New Bedford, let alone have any political stake in the case. The new DA had started off as a prosecutor in the Boston area and was familiar with Buckley's work. Buckley was gone from the prosecutor's office and was in private practice by the time Paul started work in Boston, but he remembered seeing the more experienced attorney in the courthouse, offering advice and compliments to younger colleagues. "I never met a classier, more professional guy," he recalled.[12]

The fifty-five-year-old Buckley was experienced, well liked, and respected. When he was younger, he worked with the Massachusetts Defenders Committee representing poor defendants, from 1964 to 1967, before becoming a prosecutor. He served as a first assistant district attorney in Suffolk County, which included Boston, from 1979 to 1981. He prosecuted murder cases and supervised more than a hundred assistant prosecutors. Serving as a special prosecutor was nothing new to him. He was the special prosecutor in the highly publicized murder trial of Myles J. Connor Jr., a former rock musician and art thief. (Connor was convicted of murder in 1981 and then acquitted in a 1985 retrial on charges of orchestrating the killing of two eighteen-year-old women who, prosecutors said, witnessed another man fatally shoot someone outside a Boston bar.)

Paul quietly asked around: Do you think Paul Buckley would take on the job as a special prosecutor if I asked?

PAUL BUCKLEY was acquainted with the new Bristol County district attorney professionally, but he didn't know too much more about him, even though they had been adversaries in a few district court cases. He knew the new DA was young, politically connected in Bristol County, and once worked as a prosecutor in the Suffolk County prosecutor's office. When he got the call in his Milton office, asking if he would be interested in being the special prosecutor in the highway killings case, he was intrigued. Other than read-ing a couple of news stories, he didn't know much about the case, about the defendant or the evidence. He also understood why the new DA might want to hire an outside prosecutor. The case had become hot on several levels.

Sure, he told the new district attorney. Sure, I'll take the case.

On March 7, 1991, nearly three years after eleven women had gone missing, the district attorney announced he was appointing a special prosecutor in the case. "He had this wealth of knowledge," Paul Walsh recalled. "I thought he would be the perfect choice."

Even the former DA praised the appointment, saying he was relieved the case wasn't dropped and offered to do whatever was needed to help the effort. "This has been a two-year effort. . . . It's very difficult to walk away from," Ron Pina said at the time.[13]

WHEN SHE SAT IN THE COURTROOM in August of 1990, watching as Kenny pleaded "absolutely not guilty," Judy DeSantos could see the beginning of the end. Here, before her, was the man charged with murder. It may not be her sister's murder, but it was close enough. She knew she would sit through the trial, she would listen to the witnesses, she would finally get an answer to why her sister, Nancy Paiva, was killed. Judy had had faith in Ron Pina. She trusted him.

She didn't know this new guy, Paul Walsh. She worried he would drop the case, leaving all of the families back where they started. She felt slightly relieved when he named a special prosecutor. At least the case was moving forward — for now. She still couldn't shake the feeling it would eventually be dropped, that the only person charged in the killings would go free. She talked with Jose and Maryann, sharing her concern. They tried to reassure her, telling her this new prosecutor was looking closely at the case. That was a good thing, they told her. She wanted to believe them. Her life was finally getting back to normal, sort of, after the indictment was handed up. She was back at work full-time, no longer taking long breaks from work to sit in the courthouse hallway during the grand jury sessions. She found herself laughing, seeing the joy in everyday things again. Death and those who kill were not always at the forefront of her mind.

Now, dread coursed through her. What would this district attorney do? Would he care as much? Would he work as hard?

What if this wasn't the end?

CARDBOARD BOXES OF REPORTS and grand jury testimony were stacked on the lower shelves in the conference room doubling as a law library in the Milton law office Paul Buckley shared with four other attorneys. Every week for four months, starting in early March of 1991, Jose, Maryann, and Richie hauled boxes to Milton then meticulously went over what was inside, just as they had done earlier with the new district attorney. Every piece of paper, every report, every piece of evidence, was explained. They talked about the suspects, about issues with witnesses, about the interlocking relationships in a small-city drug world. Then, they brought witnesses up to the office for the special prosecutor to interview, to weigh firsthand their credibility. At night, Paul Buckley would bring reports home to read as he tried to reconstruct the investigation in his mind. When he was done with one set of reports, the investigators would bring more boxes. "They were very, very helpful," he said. "They never expressed an opinion one way or the other. They were professional and proud of the work they did."[14]

He was surprised at the depth of the investigation and the number of state troopers and local detectives working the case. "I remember thinking: this is a good job," he recalled. "It was detailed, very detailed."

As he went through each box and reviewed each report, as he examined each suspect, the special prosecutor searched for evidence tying someone to a murder. Some of the suspects were better than others. He wondered why Tony DeGrazia wasn't considered a better suspect by the former district attorney, based on the information gathered by police. He wondered why the grand jury investigation took this fork in the road.

When he took the case, he was prepared to prosecute Kenneth Ponte. He went into the case prepared to prosecute. Now, after reviewing the evidence, he wasn't so sure.

JUDY WAITED A LITTLE BIT then decided to write the special prosecutor, to make sure he knew the families needed answers. This was not just a case. This was not a political issue. She wanted him to know they were all counting on him to do the right thing, to find justice for the dead and give some comfort to the families through that. She didn't expect he would answer, so when a letter came in mid-May with a return address from the Law Offices of Buckley, Haight, Muldoon, Jubinville & Gilligan in Milton, Judy was encouraged.

"I know only too well the frustrating and angry feelings you and the families of the other victims continue to experience," Paul V. Buckley wrote in the three-paragraph May 15, 1991, letter. "I am not in a position to answer all of your questions and I may never be able to answer some questions to your satisfaction. However, I can advise you that the State Police investigators have been most helpful and cooperative. The material to review is voluminous, but I can assure you I have been able to keep to the schedule that I originally established."

As she kept reading, Judy could detect signs that the case had problems. "District Attorney Paul Walsh and, in turn, myself have been dealt a very difficult hand," the special prosecutor noted in the letter.

THE FIRST CALL was to Paul F. Walsh Jr., the new Bristol County district attorney.

The second call was to Ronald A. Pina, the man Walsh defeated.

Paul Buckley, the special prosecutor hired to handle the prosecution against the only person charged in the highway killing case, knew the second would be an uncomfortable call. He also knew it was the professional thing to do. Ron Pina spent two years trying to identify who killed at least nine women — most likely eleven — and he deserved to know what the next step would be in court. Buckley had gone through boxes of police reports and grand jury minutes. He talked with the investigators, including Maryann, Jose, and Richie. He was brought to the body dump scenes. He looked at the evidence with the eye of a prosecutor. He looked at what he would present at trial.

When the former district attorney got on the phone, Buckley identified himself.

"You're not going to like what I'm going to tell you," he told Ron Pina.[15]

The murder charge against Kenneth C. Ponte would be dropped on July 29, 1991, the following Monday. The charge would be formally *nolle prosequi*, Latin for "we shall no longer prosecute," also called *nolle prossed*. What it meant in practice was the prosecution could still bring the charge back if more evidence was found.

"What? You can't do this," he remembers Ron answering.

The rest of the conversation was short and curt.

When he finally hung up, Paul Buckley realized the ex-DA, the man who spent years on the case, never asked him why the charge was being dropped.

JUDY WANTED TO SCREAM when she heard the news. She couldn't cry; she had no tears left. The only person charged in the murders would soon go free, leaving her and all of the families stuck in justice limbo. She had faith in the district attorney, she had faith in the police, she had faith in the system. Kenny Ponte was a killer, she was certain. That was why he was charged with murder. Now, he would be on the street, living his life while her sister and eight others were dead.

The special prosecutor hired by the new guy was saying there was no evidence against Kenny, and a gun-assault charge would also be dropped because it wasn't prosecuted fast enough. How could that be, she wondered.[16]

The special prosecutor was emphatic in his conclusion: there was nothing tying Kenneth Ponte to murder or to the disposing of a body. If the case did go to trial, a judge would throw it out.

Judy didn't believe him. She called the only people she now had faith in: Maryann and Jose. They answered on the first ring.

She posed the question bluntly: Did he do it?

She was surprised by their answer.

This was the right decision.

She hung up. It was just Thursday. She wondered how she would get through the rest of the week until the court hearing on Monday.

ATTORNEY BOB GEORGE did not like this latest development in the highway killing case. With charges against the main suspect to be dropped, did this mean they would look at his client, Tony DeGrazia, anew? Tony was in a tough spot, but the defense attorney was mapping out a good trial strategy to win on the rape charges, both those lodged in 1989 and the one pressed in 1990. He felt pretty confident about that. The prosecution witnesses likely would be weak on the stand, if they appeared at all, he believed. He would hit their credibility, their memories, and their backgrounds as drug addicts. If they were high, could they really remember? If they were high, how sure could they be that they identified the right person? Did they swap stories with other prostitutes? Did they make up their stories? These were all issues he could raise if the case went to trial.

On the flip side, Tony was a hardworking, churchgoing young man who was heading to college, who was well liked, and who was devastated by the allegations. He kept insisting he was innocent. This was the portrait of a young man Bob George planned to show the jury when the rape cases went to trial.

The defense attorney thought his guy was eliminated as a suspect in the highway killing case but it appeared that wasn't quite true. He knew he needed to go on the offensive if the DA shifted gears and focused on Tony. He hoped it wouldn't happen.[17]

IT WAS 3:30 in the afternoon on Friday, July 26, 1991, and Father George Harrison was rushing out the door when he saw Tony on the rectory deck. The priest didn't have time to talk for long but he could tell something was wrong. Tony seemed very depressed. Earlier, Tony tried yet again to convince his ex-girlfriend to come back after more than a year apart. He was planning to go to college in Boston, he told her. His life was changing. Let's try again, he pleaded. She said no. Not now. Not ever. She was in love, engaged, and pregnant, she told him. She would always love him as a friend but they would never be together. She was starting a new life without him. "I just can't believe it," Tony told the priest.[18]

Father Harrison said they could talk more later; he had an appointment, and he was running late.

The news that the special prosecutor planned to drop the murder charge against Kenneth C. Ponte was never brought up. Tony never asked for the Sacrament of Reconciliation — commonly called confession. The two just parted.

Two and a half hours later, his ex-girlfriend's parents left their Pawnee Court home in Freetown for a spaghetti dinner at the Lakeville Eagles Club, a community hall one town away. They stayed until midnight then stopped at the Freetown VFW for a nightcap before returning home.

It was one in the morning when they slipped the key into the front door and headed to bed. No one saw anyone come by the house while they were gone.

When the couple rose the next morning and looked out the back window, they saw a motionless figure on the picnic table and called police.

AS HE ROUNDED THE BACKYARD of the house, Jose Gonsalves could see Trooper Kevin Butler and Freetown cops clustered near a picnic table. On the ground, at the end of the table, was the body of a man. He knew, even before pulling up to the Pawnee Court house in Freetown, what he would find.

Tony DeGrazia was already cold to the touch. His body was already stiff, in full rigor mortis. Kevin Butler, the trooper who interviewed Tony two years earlier and later charged him in a string of sexual assaults, was taking detailed notes on what was at the scene.

Tony was wearing a gold chain and cross around his neck. He had a rosary in his front jeans pocket. In his wallet were ten dollars and two business cards. One was from the Wentworth Institute of Technology housing director in Boston. The second one was from a doctor at McLean Hospital in Belmont.

There were two sixteen-ounce bottles of Diet 7-Up, one empty, one partially full. Nine feet from Tony there was a capsule of the anti-anxiety medication Mylan 5410.

In his right breast pocket, there was an empty prescription bottle for 100-milligram capsules of the antidepressant Doxepin HCL, filled five days earlier. Tony was supposed to take three capsules before bed. Trooper Butler surmised 85 of the 100 capsules were unaccounted for. The medical examiner, Dr. William Zane, would later tell the trooper that Tony had more than ten times the minimum fatal level of Doxepin in his blood.

The medical examiner officially ruled the death a suicide.[19]

That Saturday morning, the second call by the ex-girlfriend's parents was to Father Harrison. When the priest arrived, he knew Tony was gone and there was only one thing left to do: pray.

"Heavenly Father, have mercy on him," the priest prayed over the body. "Give him eternal rest."[20]

By Monday, two days later, the murder charge against Kenneth C. Ponte was set to be dropped. The reason: lack of evidence.

Months later, all of the charges against Anthony DeGrazia were dismissed in court. The reason: defendant deceased.

KENNY STOOD NEXT TO HIS LAWYER in the first-floor courtroom, beaming, while the families of the dead watched and cried.

Three years earlier, in July of 1988, the first of the bodies was found along the highways circling New Bedford, launching one of the largest criminal investigations in the region. Now, it was ending the way it started: with tears, frustration, and questions.

Sandy Botelho's mother bowed her head. Nancy Paiva's sister wiped away tears. Dawn Mendes's mother said a silent prayer. Debra Greenlaw DeMello's mother scowled; Deb's sixteen-year-old daughter looked puzzled.

Judy DeSantos looked around the courtroom crammed with reporters and saw Maryann and Jose sitting in a row behind her and remembered what they had told her from the start: if you see us there in the courtroom, it is the right decision.

The investigators initially planned to skip the court hearing and the media scrum that day; they preferred to let politicians take center stage and liked staying out of the media glare. Then, while in the office, Jose remembered what he told Judy and how their absence would be perceived not only to the families, but the public. The two — and many, but not all, of the investigators — agreed with the decision to dismiss the murder charge. There wasn't enough evidence to convict Kenny, they believed. There wasn't even enough evidence to charge him. They had shared those concerns with the former district attorney, Ronald Pina. Jose had told the district attorney before the indictment was sought that he believed it was the wrong thing to do. There were other suspects they could look at, both Maryann and Jose calmly told him several times. But the case against Kenny moved forward. When the new district attorney and special prosecutor reviewed the evidence, the trio presented the facts and tried not to give their opinions. They went over the investigation, the suspects, the witnesses — and let the prosecutors decide the next step. Now, by their simple presence, the troopers could let all the families — and the public — know they agreed with this new decision.

Paul Buckley, the special prosecutor, rose from his seat and asked Judge Richard Connon that the murder charge lodged against Kenneth C. Ponte — the only murder charge pressed in the highway killings case — be formally closed by a *nolle prosequi*. It was not a total vindication but close. Within a half hour, the case was over, the courtroom emptied, and Kenny was standing outside the courtroom, addressing reporters in the same spot the former district attorney once held press conferences.

"It has been a long, terrible nightmare that is finally ending here today," Kenny told reporters outside the courthouse.[21] "There was no case and there never was. . . . I'm just looking forward to picking myself up and dusting myself off."

His attorney, Kevin Reddington, praised the decision to drop the charges. "This is an opportunity to highlight what can happen to an innocent man . . . when a grand jury hands up an indictment as a result of a prosecution which was biased and in fact improper," he told reporters.

And then they walked away.

"I'm glad you can go home to your family. I have to go to the cemetery to see mine. Why don't you talk about your relationship with the girls?" Judy yelled at Kenny, tears in her eyes.

Shaking, she turned and walked to the other families gathered at the side of the courthouse. They hugged and sobbed. Then left.

"We were misled," Wayne Perry, Debra Greenlaw DeMello's brother, said.

"All you can do is hope and pray," Dawn's mother, Charlotte Mendes, said.

The special prosecutor, Paul Buckley, would later say, based on his review of the case, that his key suspect was Tony DeGrazia, even though there was no evidence linking him to the murders. The timing of Tony's death, shortly after the announcement that the murder indictment would be dropped, was "just too coincidental."[22]

Tony's lawyer, Bob George, later said prosecutors were "dancing on the grave of Mr. DeGrazia," and "taking pot shots at a person who can no longer defend himself."

At the district attorney's office, Trooper Kevin Butler was finishing his report on Tony's death.

In the *Standard-Times,* the four-paragraph obituary for Anthony R. De-Grazia, twenty-nine, was published that afternoon. The photograph accompanying it was taken in court.

It was July 29, 1991. The next day would mark the third anniversary of the day Nancy Paiva was found dead.

THE SNOW WAS COMING DOWN HARD when Kevin Reddington passed the run-down former Coca-Cola factory that once served as a bus terminal on Route 6 in New Bedford. It was December, Christmas was just around the corner, and the defense attorney was feeling the holiday spirit. Kenny Ponte had opened his new office in this dreary building at the base of Route 140 hoping to jump-start his life and his career after the murder charge was dropped. It was tough going, Kevin suspected. He knew his former client was struggling to get his law practice running, and people likely weren't lining up to hire him. Kenny had name recognition but not quite the type would-be clients were looking for. Kenny was still angry at the former district attorney, Ronald A. Pina, and bitter at how his life had been upended.

Kevin pulled into the lot and drove to the back of the building, the tire tracks quickly covered by the falling snow. He planned to say a quick hello to Kenny, slip him a hundred as a holiday present, then head up the highway home. Kenny broke into a wide smile when he walked in. The office wasn't much, Kenny admitted, but the building was historic. You have to see some of the odd things in the building, Kenny insisted. He escorted Kevin through the structure then opened a door that led to the top floor. Snow was coming through the roof. It was cold. Reddington heard a gasp and a shuffle. Kenny leapt to the heavy metal fire door, grabbing the corner just before it could slam shut. He could see the relief on Kenny's face. It would have locked behind us and there is no other way out, Kenny told him. *No one would have found us this snowy evening,* his lawyer thought. *No one would have found us for days.*[23]

It was one of the last times the two saw each other. Over the years, Kenny would call or drop a short note to Kevin Reddington to touch base, but when the former murder suspect was later arrested for drunken driving, shoplifting, or marijuana possession, other attorneys would represent him.

15 UNANSWERED QUESTIONS

CHRIS DEXTRADEUR AND HIS BOSS, Lt. Thomas DaCosta, were heading the unmarked narcotics cruiser to a Portuguese restaurant on Belleville Avenue for a quick bite to eat before an hours-long surveillance. Chris loved his assignment in narcotics: the guys he worked with were a tight group, reliant on each other as they strapped on bulletproof vests, kicked in doors, fished heroin out of toilet traps, and searched cockroach-infested apartments. His colleagues were funny, smart, and made the days and nights pass quickly. Surveillances could be tedious, but, overall, the work was an adrenaline rush. It was, as far as police work went, fun.[1]

Chris was now twenty-four and could boast nearly six years on the police department. He started at eighteen, as a cadet, then became a full-time officer at age twenty. His dad and mentor, John Dextradeur retired in May of 1989 under the so-called heart bill, where cops who suffered job-related heart problems could retire with a full disability pension. As an adult, he found himself closer to his father than any other time in his life. They played golf together, they would share an occasional beer, and his dad would some-times give him some tips to follow up on. These days, his dad was working as a private investigator, sifting through court records and tracking down information for attorneys, but he always harbored the hope his last case, the highway killings, would eventually be solved.

Even though the stress of police work was out of his father's life, Chris knew his father's health was not good. In the six years since leaving the New Bedford force, the twice-divorced John Dextradeur suffered another heart attack outside a Fall River courthouse, and his doctor told him that his heart was badly damaged. He needed surgery. He declined. Instead, he kept busy as a private investigator, played a little golf and tried, overall, to enjoy retirement. He kept telling his son to take the department promotional exams to advance on the job. Chris, though, was enjoying his work in the narcotics division, and studying really wasn't how he wanted to spend his free time. Sitting behind the wheel of the unmarked cruiser, with his boss in the passenger seat, preparing for a surveillance or raid was how he wanted to spend his days.

Chris knew the night in the city would be busy. It always was. This afternoon and evening, they would watch some of the street dealers, send an undercover in to make some buys, then make some arrests. Maybe they would get enough information from these street dealers to secure a search warrant and hit a house. He was always amazed by the drug subculture — and its business infrastructure — in the city. It was a big business where some people made big money destroying lives. That was clear to him when they raided apartments with bare mattresses on the floor and tens of thousands of dollars hidden in the refrigerator.

Chris knew the schedule tonight, and in the days to follow, would also be a bit relaxed and unstructured for his boss. The lieutenant's daughter was pregnant and the call from the hospital that she was going into labor could come at any time. His boss planned to be at the hospital when that happened.

In the unmarked cars of the 1990s, detectives relied on a bulky phone with an antenna stretched toward the windshield for phone calls. Sometimes they had to move the antenna to catch a signal. The signal was strong as they drove along. The phone rang and the lieutenant looked serious after he answered. Sgt. John Silva was on the other end.

"Is Chris with you?" the sergeant asked.[2]

"Yeah, he's right here."

The lieutenant turned to Chris. They just took my daughter to St. Luke's, he told him.

Chris turned the cruiser around and headed south, toward the hospital. His boss kept directing him down other streets, avoiding Cottage and Robeson Streets where there had been a car accident.

As they pulled up to the hospital emergency entrance, within eyeshot of an ambulance, the lieutenant put his hand on Chris' shoulder. It's not my daughter. It's your dad. He had a heart attack. He got in an accident. Chris could see the paramedics pulling his father out of the ambulance, performing CPR as the stretcher was wheeled into the hospital.

John Dextradeur was pronounced dead at St. Luke's Hospital on March 4, 1994. He was fifty-two.

At his wake, the line of mourners queued through the funeral home to pay respects. At his funeral the next day at St. Mary's Church on Tarkiln Hill Road in the city's far North End, six of his former police colleagues in dress blues carefully carried his casket.

WHEN THEY WERE PROMOTED, both Maryann Dill and Jose Gonsalves left the Bristol County District Attorney's Office. Maryann left first in 1992 and eventually went to the state police unit at Logan Airport; Jose left later and eventually went back to the Dartmouth barracks. Both finally retired in 2009, both with the rank of lieutenant. Richie Ferreira remained a detective for a few more years then was transferred to the traffic division before retiring in 2006.

Bob St. Jean wondered for years what he could have done differently in the case. He still believes Kenny had something to do with the case but knows there was no hard evidence to convict him. The persistent stories of the locally produced pornographic — and possibly snuff — films nag him to this day. What was the seed to that story and was it related to the killings? When, as expected, he was let go from the district attorney's office in the post-election purge of Ron Pina hires, Bob returned to work in the family excavation business in Acushnet and got involved in town government. As a civilian, he watched from afar as others tried to solve the case. He quietly sympathized with their frustration.

A series of commanders led the state police unit in the DA's office in the following decades and each one would field calls and tips about the highway killings. One of those commanders would be Nelson Ostiguy, who returned to the unit for about a month, then moved on to a job in state police headquarters and a series of promotions. Each new commander would first call Maryann and Jose to confer when something about the case came up, years after the two had moved on. With each improvement in forensic science and the ability to pull DNA from smaller evidence samples, investigators quietly checked to see if anything they had could be tested anew. They checked and rechecked for fibers and hair. They cross-checked what was gathered at the scenes, then examined it again when new, improved tests came out. Lt. Joseph Costa, one of the commanders in the following years, sent evidence to the FBI laboratories to see if something — anything — could be gleaned to finally identify the killer, alive or dead. Nothing substantial came back.

Paul Walsh asked both FBI profilers and also the lab to give the case another look in the 1990s, hoping new developments in the field could yield a new perspective on the killer. "They thought it was significant none of the bodies were found in New Bedford proper," he recalled, referring to the profilers.[3] "If you put pins on a map, you can see all of the bodies are just outside New Bedford. The bodies seemed to be dotted right around the city border. It was as if the person didn't want New Bedford police investigating, that by doing this it would keep New Bedford out of it. They thought it was very significant."[4]

Walsh said profilers raised the possibility the killer was familiar with law-enforcement techniques, that a few of the bodies may have been left in what might be considered sexually suggestive positions intentionally and that whoever was responsible could have sexual problems. The intriguing theories had been raised before, but theories weren't evidence.

The stuff investigators quietly examined in the years after the single murder indictment against Kenny Ponte was dropped was interesting but had "no legal significance," Paul said, without elaborating.

Paul Walsh would eventually face his own upstart challenger in 2006, another candidate promoting that familiar political mantra of change. Walsh lost to C. Samuel Sutter, an attorney both Ron Pina and Paul had hired as a prosecutor at separate times over the years. This newest DA met with the highway killing families, pledged to do whatever he could to solve the case, but made no promises. Some items, including those already tested by the FBI, were sent to the updated state police crime-lab facilities to be examined. Nothing new was announced.

When a bank took over Kenny's former home on Chestnut Street in New Bedford, investigators decided to resolve a rumor that the body of one of the still missing women, Christina Monteiro, was buried beneath a backyard concrete slab. They brought in heavy equipment and dug up the yard. No bodies were found.

By the late 1990s, Kenny Ponte was living in a single-story home on Austin Street owned by his mother and trying to eke out a living as an attorney in his hometown. He sued Ronald Pina on behalf of Tony DeGrazia's mother who claimed the prosecutor hounded her son to death. The case was dismissed. He had some minor run-ins with the law, including arrests for shoplifting and driving under the influence, and tried unsuccessfully to sell the film rights for his story. He never published his book, "Presumed Guilty." It was unclear if he ever finished it. Kenny's neighbors on Austin Street didn't like him and often complained to police about trash, traffic, and his demeanor. He had a lot of cats and fed the strays.

16 MOVING ON

NEW BEDFORD OFFICER JACK INDIO didn't recognize the man standing outside the Shirley Street apartment. The guy was disheveled and smelled bad. Jack figured he was homeless. It was a mid-September afternoon in 2003 and near the end of his shift when the call came in about a disturbance on the street. Based on what Jack was seeing, he figured he would be done with the situation fairly quickly and would be heading home.

Then the man gave his name: Kenneth Ponte.

Jack knew in that second it would not be an easy call. The young officer had been on the force since 1993, five years after the first woman went missing off the streets of the city, but he knew the story of the highway killing investigation and he knew the stories about the lawyer who became a central character in the probe.

In the decade since the charges against Kenny were dismissed, the drug addict turned lawyer turned addict still occasionally popped up in the headlines when he was arrested for shoplifting or drunk driving — short news briefs this time instead of the front-page eye-catching articles from a few years back. He briefly considered running for office but never followed through. Stories surfaced again about his drug use. He was disbarred in 1997 for stealing clients' funds and mingling his personal account with his clients' money. And he continued to obsessively write letters, sometimes handwritten, sometimes typed, still railing against Ron Pina, the man he blamed for ruining his life. Kenny did not fade into obscurity.

Here, outside the Shirley Street apartment on September 18, 2003, Jack was dealing with the latest drama in Kenny's life.

Kenny was telling the officer he went to the house to check up on a friend whom he routinely drove to the methadone clinic. Instead, he was punched in the face then shoved out the door by a man.[1] Those inside the apartment had a different story.

As the officer walked in, he saw a twenty-three-year-old woman on a bed. She was so still she appeared lifeless. Another woman was on the telephone, calling drug-treatment centers. Scribbled notes with the names and numbers of programs and hospitals were scattered next to her. Kenny was a problem, the woman told the officer as she put down the phone. He was part of her friend's drug problem and, when he showed up, she asked him to leave. When he didn't, she asked a male friend to get him to leave.

Jack leaned over the woman on the bed and spoke with her privately. What's going on? he asked. She was a drug addict, she told him. She met Kenny a few months ago and partied with him quite a bit. He would buy a hundred-dollar bag of cocaine and the two would do it, she told him.

"Did he ever assault you?" Jack asked. "No, but," she answered.[2]

He pressed her for more information. Kenny gave her the creeps, and she had an uneasy feeling about him. The sliding door lock in her apartment was broken and he would sneak in, she said. Sometimes she would wake up in the middle of the night and find him standing over her in the bedroom. Kenny told her about the book he had written about a man who picks up prostitutes, kills them, and then leaves their bodies along the highway.

Until that September day, she did not know the bodies of nine women who vanished in 1988 were found along the local highways. She did not know that two women — Christina Monteiro and Marilyn Roberts — remained missing. She did not know Kenny had been charged with murder in one of the cases. She did not know the charge had been dismissed.

The next day, she was in a treatment program.

THE NEIGHBORS WERE FED UP. The stench of cat piss was overwhelming. The yard at the 336 Austin Street house was overgrown. There were rats. There was trash. People would drive up, go to the door then leave quickly with something in their hands. Sometimes Kenny would scream obscenities. Sometimes it would be veiled threats, like the time he yelled "Nice car? But not for long" at a neighbor whose vehicle was later found to be vandalized. He left a note scrawled in crayon for one person, saying "Please do not leave your trash on my lawn." There was no running water in the house, so Kenny had taken to using the back yard as a "cesspool."[3]

But the nudity was the last straw.

The heavy-set Kenny would stand in the front doorway naked just about every morning. It was not a pretty sight.

Every time police went to the house, he wouldn't come to the door.

THE STENCH hit New Bedford detective Claudia Sampson in the gut as she walked up the driveway. It drilled up her nostrils and into her throat so deeply she could taste it. Cat urine mixed with decomposition. The veteran cop, who worked narcotics and vice before eventually taking over as evidence officer, stepped carefully through the back door of the Austin Street house, over empty boxes of food and soup cans. There were papers and bags and bottles littering the floor. There were needles and prescription bottles tucked in corners and on chairs. She looked down and could see the trash moving. She hoped it was a cat.[4]

She moved forward into the living room, through ankle deep trash. The odor was overpowering and all too familiar. It was the smell of death. By the front picture window, she saw two mattresses stacked. The bloated body of a man was on top. There were flies everywhere: on the body, on the mattress, on the windows. She held her breath.

A young man who said he did yard work and odd jobs at the Austin Street house had called police around 2:30 in the afternoon on January 26, 2010, to say he was worried about his employer. He noticed the guy was sleeping on the mattress in front of the living room window whenever he drove by. The guy seemed to be in the same spot for the past couple of days and he was afraid he was dead.

Uniformed patrol officer Mark Giammalvo was faced with the same scene as Detective Sampson encountered a few minutes earlier when, as the first officer to the scene, he choked back the smell, walked into the house, and saw a body partially covered with a thick bedspread. He had an idea who the man was. He had been to the house before. He noticed, as he carefully stepped away into the kitchen, that the oven was set to high and the oven door open. He turned it off and closed the door. He wondered if that was how the homeowner was heating the house.[5]

Teams of New Bedford and state police detectives soon converged on the house. Each investigator carefully stepped in, then a few minutes later ducked out to breathe. Sampson gave up trying to hold her breath inside the house as she took photographs to document the scene, instead pushing through the harsh stench. She took photos of the body, the needles, the black plastic bags filled with garbage. She took photos of the flies on the window, the empty bottles of water and juice. She took photos of the bottles filled with urine, the box of Frosted Flakes on the floor, the hundred-dollar bill sticking out of the mattress beneath the body. She took photos of the D-Con box, the window shade on the floor, the jacket slung over the lamp. She took photos of the bare mattresses, stacked atop each other, in front of the living room window, the body still on them. She took note of the hole cut on the bottom of the back door, a space just big enough for a cat to squeeze through. Sometimes she had to walk outside to take a deep breath, fill her lungs with clean air, before plunging back into the fetid house.

Next to the bed, Claudia saw several crack pipes and needles. She wasn't surprised.

The medical examiner arrived and determined there were no signs of foul play. The body was removed by Le Beouf Livery Services.

Kenneth C. Ponte, the former attorney once so desperate for companionship and drugs he would feed desperate female addicts cocaine to stay with him, had died alone on a bare mattress at age sixty. His death certificate listed chronic substance abuse as the cause of death.

IT HAD BEEN EIGHT YEARS since Richie Ferreira worked in the detective division and four years since he retired after thirty-two years on the New Bedford police force. He was now working part-time as a private investigator, doing much the same thing he had done for years without the added stress of crime scenes. He kept in close touch with the guys on the job, though, and sometimes stopped in to one of the three stations in the city. On this day, he parked his two-toned green 2005 Kia Sorento on the street, just up from the South End station and walked in.

"Hey Richie, your buddy died," Officer Lenny Motta told him.[6]

Richie paused. "Who?"

"Kenny Ponte. He was found dead in his house yesterday."

Richie took a deep breath and shook his head.

Jose Gonsalves was home, eating dinner, when his son, who was a New Bedford police officer, called. "You're not going to believe this," he told him. "That guy, Kenny Ponte, was found dead in his house."[7]

Maryann Dill, retired for nearly a year, was driving to her parents' home, listening to the radio, when she caught a familiar name in the news report: Kenneth Ponte, one-time suspect in a series of killings in the New Bedford area, was dead.[8]

Bob St. Jean was in Acushnet, working in the office at the family business, when he heard on the radio that the former lawyer was dead. He wondered what secrets died with him.[9]

Judy DeSantos was in Florida where she had moved a few years earlier, joining her sister Nancy's daughter, Jill, when she got a call from New Bedford. Kenny Ponte was found dead, her daughter, Jessie, told her. Death usually came with a sense of finality, but Judy found herself left with that open-ended grief of unanswered questions.[10]

She thought back to a letter she once sent to Kenny during the height of the homicide investigation, pleading with him to cooperate with authorities. "It is not my wish to make you feel harassed, I just want to end this continual nightmare and maybe be able to pick up the remaining pieces of my life," she wrote in the typed letter.[11]

At the bottom, in a handwritten postscript, she added: "I'm looking forward to hearing from you."

EPILOGUE

AT AN UNDISCLOSED WAREHOUSE along the south coast of Massachusetts, boxes of evidence in the case are locked up. Some have been unboxed over the years, the contents sent to yet another laboratory for testing, and then packed up again. The FBI has examined the evidence at least twice; the state police laboratory at least once. A private laboratory was also used several times. Fibers have been compared and examined; DNA examinations have been done; evidence has been compared for similarities at the nine crime scenes. The investigative reports compiled by dozens of detectives over the years are massive. They are stuffed in cardboard boxes and file cabinets in the state police offices at the Bristol County District Attorney's Office. The cold-case unit is now officially in charge of the case; if there is a new lead, it will go there.

On the streets of the city, there are still addicts. Many more are now from the suburbs, the young adults who snorted OxyContin or popped Percocet or the next pharmaceutical opiate painkiller turned party drug only to find themselves addicts scrounging for cheap heroin. City narcotics detectives still arrest the dealers and the addicts, hoping at least a handful will get clean and survive. There are overdoses here, just as there are in nearly every city and town in the country, as opiate addiction is proclaimed a national crisis.

The city's downtown is now vibrant, sporting two college satellite campuses and specialty restaurants along the cobblestoned streets. Tourists prowl those streets, photographing the historic nooks and landmarks. Along the waterfront, fishermen head out to sea as they have for centuries, braving the elements and now battling tighter federal fishing regulations.

Life in New Bedford moves on in the shadow of history.

THERE WERE FIFTEEN CHILDREN left behind when their mothers disappeared in 1988. At least two had brushes with the law, two wound up briefly in the custody of social services, and two died, one just a teenager in a car crash. The other children are now adults, most with children of their own. Some went to college. Some moved out of state. They are working, they are paying taxes, they are paying bills, paying rent, paying mortgages, paying insurance on cars and homes. They have crafted lives in the shadows of death, getting married, going on vacations, working, going to school. Some are still in New Bedford, a few are scattered along the East Coast. Some were too young to remember their mothers. Some still remember what they lost.

Two of the women reported missing in 1988 were never found: Christina Monteiro, aged nineteen, and Marilyn Cardoza Roberts, aged thirty-four.

For years, Christina's mother, Shirley Monteiro, would stop into the state police barracks in Dartmouth to talk with Jose and pass on any information she heard that she prayed might help solve the case or, at the very least, find her missing child. She held out hope — it was a slim hope, she knew — that her daughter just left the area to get away from the drugs, that she would be back some day. She told him it was that glimmer that kept her going. She held onto it until the day she died.

A SMALL, STORE-BOUGHT ROCK PLAQUE leans against the tombstone in Cushing Cemetery in Mattapoisett, Massachusetts. "No farewell words were spoken, no time to say goodbye, you were gone before we knew it, and only God knows why," it reads. Marilyn Roberts' parents placed it there after her brother died of cancer, a simple reminder in the cemetery of their only daughter. They cannot bear to etch her name in stone yet. For years, Marilyn's parents imagined she was living out of state, unaware she was being grieved. They knew, though, even in those early days of the investigation, that she would not have left them in this heart-wrenching limbo. She would have come back, she would have called, she would at the very least have sent a card to say she was alive, she was well, she was happy. They know she is not coming home.

The cemetery is a place to pay respects, to mourn, to remember. It is where, with this gray-rock plaque, her parents can remember that Marilyn lived.

THE LARGE OAK DESK that once belonged to her grandmother sits in the living room corner of the suburban Massachusetts home Chandra shares with her husband and children. The drawers are brimming with mementos of the past: photographs, letters, holiday cards, death certificates. There are the photos of a young Debra Greenlaw DeMello clutching a doll, standing next to her brother; grinning on Christmas Day as a child; smiling next to her own children. There are the letters to her family, apologizing for a past misspent and promising a future of change. On the wall is the large framed photograph of Deb in her wedding gown. It is the same portrait that hung for years in the Brockton apartment Chandra grew up in with her grandmother. Chandra brought the photograph to her own home after her grandmother died, a memory of a different time. It was her grandmother's favorite photo. It was an image of hope.

IMAGES OF THE LIVING adorn Judy DeSantos's third-floor New Bedford apartment walls. After living in Florida for four and a half years, she moved back to New Bedford, where her children now live. Photos of her nieces and their children, her own children, her grandchildren, her great-grandchildren. Photos of the dead — her sister, her parents, her grandparents — are tucked away in albums and boxes. Out of sight but not forgotten. A tradition celebrating life has quietly evolved in the family: grandchildren, great-grandchildren, nieces, nephews, all with the middle name of Lee, all in memory of Nancy Lee Paiva. "You have to go on, you have to survive and keep going, but you never forget," Judy says. "A part of my sister lives on in all of us. In all of the children and grandchildren. I see Nancy in all of them."

THE SCENTS of cooking *bacalhau* and *carne de vinhoa d'alho* waft in the summer night air as people nudge through the tight crowd. On one stage, a band is playing "Sweet Caroline"; on another stage the band Grupo Folclorico Madeirense performs traditional Portuguese dances. It is the Feast of the Blessed Sacrament, a century-old tradition in New Bedford, reenacting a feast day celebrated in the Catholic parish of Estreito da Calheta on the southwest coast of Madeira island roughly four hundred miles off the coast of Morocco. One story about its origins says four immigrants from the island began the "festa" back in 1915 after a hazardous ocean trip to the United States. At its heart, this four-day festival is a religious celebration honoring the Blessed Sacrament. In its soul, it is the rousing cheer of a region overcoming adversity, whooping for joy at another day lived, another year survived.

On this first evening of the festival decades after the highway murders, the old-timers sit in lawn chairs near one of the main stages to watch the traditional dances. Rabbit, codfish, goat, pork butts, and marinated tuna are sizzling on the grills at the food stands. And there is the traditional Madeira wine, that sweet drink that goes down a bit too easily. There are the children begging parents to win giant stuffed bears at kiosks. There are grinning teenaged boys with stiff-brimmed baseball hats passing teenaged girls, some with shorts too short and met by the clucks of the old. There is the smell of cigarettes mixed with the scent of cooking meats and the sounds of music jumbled with caws of laughter. It is the place where new meets old and traditions grow stronger for another year.

Ric Oliveira, the founder of the group Magik Squirrel, is on stage with his five-member rock band while men with straw hats emblazoned with the word "Madeira" stroll by. Ric and his band sing to the crowd about Madeira wine, the blues, and life.

"Whether you are a city, region, or a country, don't let anyone tell you what you can't do," Ric tells the applauding crowd.

Then the band begins to play Ric's original song, "No Limits."

"They will hold you down if they can't take your dreams," he sings.

"I won't forget, won't forget what he said.

"He said there may be a sky but there are no limits to you. There may be a sky but there are no limits to you."

Three days later, thousands line the streets in the North End of New Bedford for the Sunday parade marking the end of the Feast of the Blessed Sacrament. Some people watch from the porches of the two- and three-family homes; others sit on blankets on the street curbs or on folding chairs just off the sidewalk line. They cheer as the Feast Committee members and children holding the light-blue banner saying Future of the Feast pass. As people atop floats toss candy to the children. As the Clydesdale horses pull an orange wagon for Hallamore Crane Services. As the man following the horses in a golf cart shovels up the droppings. As the Dartmouth high school marching band plays. As the dancers leap. As the politicians prance. As the Sons of

St. Patrick playing bagpipes stroll. As the local chapter of Vietnam Veterans of America and World War II veterans march by and some, usually fellow veterans, salute.

The people on the street applaud and cheer for more than an hour, just as they do every year. There is promise today, as they stand along the streets, and gratitude.

There is life.

ACKNOWLEDGMENTS

SOME STORIES HAUNT YOU. They burrow into your soul, peering out at odd moments in your life. Sometimes they return as you drive along the highway. Sometimes when you pass a wooded spot or a neighborhood corner. Sometimes it happens when you catch the scent of waterfront air. Sometimes it just happens. What happened in New Bedford, Massachusetts, in 1988 is one of those stories that has haunted me for decades. It is a story people should never forget.

My interest in drug addiction, and the struggles faced by drug-addicted women in particular, started in 1985 when I was working on a story and interviewed a woman named Doreen on the streets of New Bedford. It was in the dead of summer, and her cotton shirt was neatly pressed, a sharp crease along the long sleeves. She was telling me about how two acquaintances arrested that week had been treated. "Just because we're drug addicts, just because we're on the street, that doesn't mean we aren't people," she said. "We're human." Since that day, I have met a series of women who battled and ultimately overcame both the streets and their addiction to heroin. Some eventually died of AIDS-related illnesses, some are living quiet lives appreciating every day. I have learned much from them.

This is a work of nonfiction written in a narrative style. All direct quotes in the book are taken from court records, news accounts, or police reports, were based on the direct recollection of one or more parties to the conversation, or were heard directly by me. In cases where the exact words were in question, but not the spirit of the conversation, quotation marks are not used.

I am forever grateful to all of the families of the victims who were so patient with me and other reporters during the worst moments of their lives at the height of the murder investigation in New Bedford. Their grace during that period should serve as an inspiration to us all. The families of Nancy Paiva, Debra Greenlaw DeMello, and Marilyn Roberts were especially gracious as they relived that painful time years later for this book.

This project would not have been possible without the continued support of my husband, Kevin Kalunian — who was there when this story first broke and has encouraged me every day to write this book — and my son, Christian Kalunian.

Heartfelt thanks to Maryann Dill, Jose Gonsalves, and Richard Ferreira for patiently taking me back in time to relive the investigation. The hours they spent making sure I understood the intricacies of the investigation were invaluable, and the work they, and others, put into the case was extraordinary. My deep appreciation to Robert St. Jean for both his honest appraisal and the hours spent sharing his insights of that time.

Also, thanks to William Delaney, Kevin Butler, Lorraine Levy, and Alan Alves, as well as retired New Bedford detective Gardner Greany — who also investigated earlier New Bedford homicides — for sharing their experiences. The behind-the-scenes help by Robert Jones and Curt Brown, a former *Fall River Herald News* reporter now at the *Standard-Times* of New Bedford, helped get this project off the ground. The assistance from the staff at the *Standard-Times,* past and present, including the current editor-in-chief, Beth Perdue, is greatly appreciated. Special thanks to Jim Nelson, manager of the New Bedford Port Authority; Joe Thomas, local historian extraordinaire; James Sylvia and Ronald Cabral for their insights into the drug culture of the 1970s and '80s; Richard Lauria for sharing his expertise on fingerprinting in the 1980s; Kenneth Martin for patiently detailing field forensics; and Andy Rebmann for making sure I thoroughly understood search work. Also, Bruce Machado, Paul Boudreau, Louis J. Pacheco; New Bedford capt. Steven Vicente, head of the New Bedford detective division; Claudia Sampson, one of the best undercover female detectives around; Dick Phillips, retired Dartmouth police officer; David Wordell; Paul Fitzgerald, whose amazing memory for detail was greatly appreciated; Christopher Dextradeur for sharing memories of his late father; also Paul Buckley, Lance Garth, Paul Walsh, Kari Pina Barcellos, Nelson Ostiguy, and the many police officers in southeastern Massachusetts — to all my gratitude. Thanks also to retired Connecticut trooper Kevin Rodino, who helped in the search. Thank you to Natalie White for her early reading and suggestions; Cannon Labrie for his detailed editing and patience; and my colleagues at Stonehill College, especially Maria Curtin, who offered support for this project.

It all would not have happened, of course, without my editor at University Press of New England, Stephen Hull, who had faith in the project, and my dear friend Elaine McArdle, whose referrals and unwavering encouragement led me to this wonderful publishing house.

There are many people I have likely forgotten and, to them, please accept my apologies.

NOTES

PROLOGUE

1. The description of what an individual experiences while being strangled is based on reports, studies, and presentations by Dean Hawley, Candace Heisler, Dinesh Rao, and Kelsey McKay.

1 MISSING

1. Dextradeur 1988.
2. Greany, Baron, et al. 1986.
3. Vosburg 1987.
4. J. D. Thomas et al. 2013, 29.
5. whalingmuseum.org, n.d.
6. J. D. Thomas et al. 2013, 198.
7. Ibid., 56.
8. J. Thomas 2016.
9. Oliveira 2007.
10. Fishermen's Memorial Service program 2016.
11. Dextradeur 1988.
12. DeSantos 2015a.
13. Ibid.
14. DeSantos 2015b.
15. Ibid.
16. DeSantos 2015c.

17. DeSantos, n.d.(a)
18. DeSantos 2015c.
19. DeSantos 2015b.

2 BODIES

1. Alves 2015.
2. Ibid.
3. Delaney 2015.
4. Wordell 2015.
5. DeSantos 2015a.
6. Ibid.
7. Muntzel 1988a.
8. Delaney 2015.
9. G. Greany 1989.
10. Boyle 1989n.
11. Commonwealth of Massachusetts 1989g, 92.
12. Ibid. 1989f, 163.
13. Ibid. 1989c, 6.
14. Ferreira 1988.
15. Commonwealth of Massachusetts 1989i, 49.
16. Ibid., 50.
17. Boyle 1988a.
18. St. Jean 2016a.

19. St. Jean 2016b.

20. Boyle 1988a.

3 SEARCHING

1. J. Levin 1982.

2. St. Jean 2016b.

3. Fitzgerald 2016.

4. Phillips 2016.

5. Fitzgerald 2016.

6. Gonsalves 2015c.

7. Rebmann 2015.

8. St. Jean 2016b.

9. Rebmann 2015.

10. Rebmann, David, and Sorg 2000.

11. Ibid.

12. Rebmann 2015.

13. Ibid.

14. Butler 2016; Rebmann 2015.

15. Martin 2016.

16. Commonwealth v. Jose Cintron 2003.

17. Lauria 2016.

18. Commonwealth of Massachusetts 1989a, 19.

19. Boyle 1988b.

20. Cunha 1989.

21. Machado 2016.

22. Sylvia 2016; Machado 2016.

23. Cardoza and Cardoza 2016.

24. Sylvia 2016.

25. Morgado 1989.

26. Ibid.

27. Boyle 1988c.

4 THE STREETS

1. Gonsalves 2015a.

2. Gonsalves and Dill, 2016

3. Ibid.

4. Ibid.

5. Personal observation by Maureen Boyle 1987–88.

6. Gold 1989.

7. Urbon 2016.

8. Prostitute 1988.

9. Commonwealth of Massachusetts 1989e.

10. Ibid., 184–88.

11. St. Jean 2016b.

12. St. Jean 2016a.

13. Dill 2015b.

14. Martin 2016.

15. St. Jean 2016a.

16. Ibid.

17. Ibid.

18. Machado 2016.

19. Boudreau n.d.(b).

20. Boudreau 2015.

21. Ibid.

22. Machado 2016.

23. Gonsalves 2015a.

24. Paiva 2015b.

25. Paiva, 2015a.

26. DeSantos 2015c.

27. C. Dextradeur 2015.

28. Ferreira, 2016.

29. Paiva 2015b.

30. Spinner 2016.

31. Dill 2015c.

32. Gonsalves 2015b.

33. Costa-Crowell 1988.

34. Dill 2015c.

35. W. Perry 2016.

36. Kolata 1987.

37. *Brockton Enterprise* 1975.

38. Boyle 1988f.

39. Hardin 2016.

40. C. Gregory 2016.

41. S. Perry 2016.

5 THE INVESTIGATION EXPANDS

1. Muntzel 1988a.

2. Ferreira 2015.

3. White 1988

4. Boyle 1989d.

5. W. Perry 2016; C. Gregory 2016.

6. Boyle 1989c.

7. Gonsalves 2016.

8. Boyle 1989e.

9. Commonwealth of Massachusetts 1989g, 96.

10. Ibid., 129.

11. Ibid. 1989b, 95–96.

12. Gonsalves and Dill 2016.

6 IN THE CROSSHAIRS

1. St. Jean 2016a.

2. Ibid.

3. Boyle 1989b.

4. Ibid. 1989f.

5. Ibid. 1989a.

6. Ellement 1989.

7. Ressler, Burgess, and Douglas 1988, 113.

8. Ibid., 15.

9. Ibid., 122.

10. Pacheco 2016.

11. McCabe 2016.

12. Pacheco 2016.

13. Boyle 1989g.

14. Massachusetts State Police 1989a.

15. Butler and Greany 1989.

16. Starkey 1990, 25.

17. Ibid., 27.

18. Ibid., 24.

19. Butler 1989a.

20. Starkey 1990, 24.

21. Ibid., 25.

22. Ibid., 13.

23. Commonwealth of Massachusetts 1989g, 92.

24. Starkey 1990, 29.

25. Commonwealth of Massachusetts 1989e, 29.

26. St. Jean. 2016a.

27. Boyle 1989h.

28. Commonwealth of Massachusetts 1989b, 192.

7 "CATCH THIS GUY"

1. Dill 2015b.

2. C. Dextradeur 2015.

3. Boyle 1989i.

4. Baeur 2016.

5. Boyle 1989j.

6. Karen Sunnarborg Consulting 2010.

7. Boyle 1989k.

8. Boyle 1989l.

9. Ostiguy 2016.

10. Ferreira 1990.

11. Gonsalves 2015a.

8 NEW SUSPECT

1. White 1989.

2. Boyle 1989m.

3. Massachusetts State Police 1989b

4. *New Bedford Standard-Times* 1982.

5. Forrest 1989a.

6. Ibid.

7. Commonwealth of Massachusetts 1989h, 148–50.

8. Ibid., 150.

9. Ibid., 151.

10. Ibid., 153.

11. Ibid. 1989e, 97.

12. Ibid. 1989a, 129.

13. Forrest 1989b.

14. Butler 1989a.

15. Gonsalves 2016b.

16. Commonwealth of Massachusetts 1989g, 151.

17. Ibid., 151–52.

18. Jillson 1989.

19. Ibid.

20. Boyle 1989o.

9 LOOKING IN OTHER CORNERS

1. Bristol County District Attorney's Office 1989.

2. Pacheco 2016a.

3. Tink 1988.

4. Ferreira 2016.

5. Boudreau 2015.

6. Boudreau n.d.(c).

7. Ibid.

8. Boudreau, n.d.(a).

9. Boudreau, n.d.(b).

10. McArdle 1990.

10 THE CIRCLE TIGHTENS

1. Reddington 2016.

2. Boyle 1990a.

3. Boyle 1990c.

4. Ibid.

5. Ibid.

6. Walsh 2015.

7. Ibid.

8. Pina-Barcellos 2016.

11 FLORIDA FOLLIES

1. Commonwealth of Massachusetts 1990a.

2. Ibid., 31.

3. Ibid., 42.

4. Ibid., 60–64.

5. Ibid., 68.

6. Reddington 2016.

7. Mello 1990.

8. Reddington 2016.

9. State of Florida 1990a.

10. State of Florida 1990b.

11. Commonwealth of Massachusetts 1990a, 8.

12. Ibid., 5.

13. Pina-Barcellos 2016.

14. Veary 2015.

12 THE INDICTMENT

1. January 2015.

2. Powell 2015.

3. Commonwealth of Massachusetts 1990a, 114.

4. Ibid., 112.

5. Ibid., 133–35.

6. Ibid.

7. Ibid., 145.

8. Ibid., 166.

9. Ibid., 145–66.

10. Ferreira 2016.

11. Gonsalves 2015a.

12. Reddington 2016.

13. Ibid.

14. Ibid.
15. DeSantos 2015.
16. Boyle 1990e.
17. Ibid.

13 THE CAMPAIGN

1. Walsh 2015.
2. Boyle and Burt 1990.
3. Garth 2016.

14 OLD SUSPECT BACK

1. Harrison 2016.
2. Commonwealth of Massachusetts 1990b, 34.
3. George 2016.
4. Commonwealth of Massachusetts 1990b, 63.
5. Boyle 1990f.
6. Commonwealth of Massachusetts 1990b, 19.
7. Ibid., 37.
8. Ibid., 38.
9. Ibid., 12.
10. Reddington 2016.
11. Walsh 2015.
12. Ibid.
13. Boyle 1991a.
14. Buckley 2016.

15. Ibid.
16. DeSantos 2015a
17. George 2016.
18. Harrison 2016.
19. Butler 1991.
20. Harrison 2016.
21. Boyle 1991b.
22. Ibid.
23. Reddington 2016.

15 UNANSWERED QUESTIONS

1. C. Dextradeur 2015
2. Ibid.
3. Walsh 2016
4. Ibid.

16 MOVING ON

1. Indio 2003.
2. Ibid.
3. Cabral 2008.
4. Sampson 2015.
5. Giammalvo 2010.
6. Ferreira 2016.
7. Gonsalves 2016b.
8. Dill 2015b.
9. St. Jean 2016b.
10. DeSantos 2015a.
11. DeSantos n.d.(b).

BIBLIOGRAPHY

Alves, Alan. 2015. Interview by Maureen Boyle, October 16. Retired Freetown police detective.

Baeur, Robert. 2016. Interview by Maureen Boyle.

Boudreau, Paul. n.d.(a) "Bristol County Drug Task Force Supplemental Investigators Report, Business Dealings of Paul F. Ryley."

———. n.d.(b) "Bristol District Drug Task Force, Supplemental Investigator's Report."

———. n.d.(c) "Bristol District Drug Task Force Investigative Report."

———. 2015. Interview by Maureen Boyle, June 15. New Bedford detective, retired.

Boyle, Maureen. 1988a. "Fear Builds for Missing Women." *New Bedford Standard-Times,* October 3.

———. 1988b. "Skeleton Located in Freetown." *New Bedford Standard-Times,* December 2

———. 1988c. "Hooker Escaped Highway Rapist." *New Bedford Standard-Times,* December 3.

———. 1988d. "Remains Could Be Those of R.I. Woman." *New Bedford Standard-Times,* December 1.

———. 1988e. "Families' Hopes Fade with Each Grisly Find." *New Bedford Standard-Times,* December 5.

———. 1988f. "Denied Parole, Woman Walked Away from Prison — and to Her Death." *New Bedford Standard-Times,* December 30.

———. 1989a. "Lawyer Is Upset about Stories Linking Him, Victims." *New Bedford Standard-Times,* January 11.

———. 1989b. "Lawyer Won't Aid Body Probe." *New Bedford Standard-Times,* January 19.

———. 1989c. "DA Runs Out of Overtime for Probe." *New Bedford Standard-Times,* January 20.

———. 1989d. "In Death, Family Holds Memory of a Smile." *New Bedford Standard-Times,* January 22.

———. 1989e. "Costly Police Overtime Had Threatened Investigation." *New Bedford Standard-Times,* January 27.

———. 1989f. "Judge Denies Request for Hair Samples." *New Bedford Standard-Times,* January 28.

———. 1989g. "Pina Calls Special Grand Jury to Investigate Highway Killings." *New Bedford Standard-Times,* February 14.

———. 1989h. "Grand Jury Widens Probe of Highway Killings." *New Bedford Standard-Times,* March 3.

———. 1989i. "A Mother's Cry: I'll Never See Her Again." *New Bedford Standard-Times,* March 30.

———. 1989j. "Anonymous Letter to DA Hinted at Body Off Route 88." *New Bedford Standard-Times,* April 1.

———. 1989k. "Body Shakes Marion's Peace." *New Bedford Standard-Times,* April 27.

———. 1989l. "'Catch This Guy,' Family Pleads." *New Bedford Standard-Times,* April 28.

———. 1989m. "Abuse as a Child Haunts Rape Suspect. Psychiatrist Tells Court DeGrazia Is a Danger to Himself and Others." *New Bedford Standard-Times,* May 6.

———. 1989n. "Husband, Sons Yearn for Missing Woman." *New Bedford Standard-Times,* July 23.

———. 1989o. "Assault Suspect Charged in Threat against DA." *New Bedford Standard-Times,* December 20.

———. 1990a. "Ponte, 3 Others Accused of Conspiracy." *New Bedford Standard-Times,* March 31.

———. 1990b. "Attorney Wants DA off Ponte's Case." *New Bedford Standard-Times,* April 14.

———. 1990c. "Police Follow, Heckle Ponte, Lawyer Claims." *New Bedford Standard-Times,* April 14.

———. 1990d. "To Her, Sister's Death in '87 Is No. 1." *New Bedford Standard-Times,* August 21.

———. 1990e. "Ponte Free on Bail, Looks Forward to Murder Trial." *New Bedford Standard-Times,* August 21.

———. 1990f. "Woman Recounts the Horror of Hands Clutching Her Throat." *New Bedford Standard-Times,* November 28.

———. 1990g. "Ponte Lawyer: DA Should Focus on DeGrazia." *New Bedford Standard-Times,* November 30.

———. 1991a. "Highway Murder Probe Back on Track, Special Prosecutor Buckley Draws Peers' Accolades." *New Bedford Standard-Times,* March 8.

———. 1991b. "Pessimistic DA Plans Continuing Investigation." *New Bedford Standard-Times*, July 30.

Boyle, Maureen, and Jeffrey Burt. 1990. "Walsh Wins." *New Bedford Standard-Times*, September 19.

Bristol County District Attorney's Office. 1989. Telephone log, "Pay phone, Whispers." January 25.

Brockton Enterprise. 1975. "Miss Greenlaw Is Bride of Mr. DeMello." August 26.

Buckley, Paul. 2016. Interview by Maureen Boyle, June 23. Special prosecutor.

Butler, Kevin. 1989a "Massachusetts State Police Computerized Homicide Report Form," January 5.

———. 1989b. "Bureau of Investigative Services, Massachusetts State Police," May 1.

———. 1991. "Commonwealth of Massachusetts, Massachusetts State Police, Suicide — Anthony DeGrazia," July 29.

———. 2016. Interview by Maureen Boyle, February 4. Massachusetts State Police, retired.

Butler, Kevin, and Gardner Greany. 1989. "Massachusetts State Police Computerized Homicide Report Form." January 26.

Cabral, Emanuel. 2008. "New Bedford Police Report." June 18.

Cardoza, Robert, and Bernadine Cardoza. 2016. Interview by Maureen Boyle, July 19. Parents of Marilyn Roberts.

Commonwealth of Massachusetts. 1989a "Commonwealth of Massachusetts in the Matter of John Doe," March 2.

———. 1989b. "Commonwealth of Massachusetts in the Matter of John Doe," March 3.

———. 1989c. "Commonwealth of Massachusetts in the Matter of John Doe," March 6.

———. 1989d. "Commonwealth of Massachusetts in the Matter of John Doe," March 31.

———. 1989e. "Commonwealth of Massachusetts in the Matter of John Doe," April 5.

———. 1989f. "Commonwealth of Massachusetts in the Matter of John Doe," May 1.

———. 1989g. "Commonwealth of Massachusetts in the Matter of John Doe," May 2.

———. 1989h. "Commonwealth of Massachusetts in the Matter of John Doe," June 19.

———. 1989i. "Commonwealth of Massachusetts in the Matter of John Doe," June 20.

———. 1990a. "Commonwealth of Massachusetts in the Matter of John Doe," August 17.

———. 1990b. "Commonwealth of Massachusetts in the Matter of Anthony DeGrazia," December 5.

Commonwealth v. Jose Cintron. 438 Mass. 779 December 6, 2002–March 6, 2003 Hampden County. 438 Mass. 779 (Massachusetts Supreme Judicial Court, Boston, MA March 6). Accessed July 2016. http://masscases.com/cases/sjc/438/438mass779 .html.

Costa-Crowell, Carol Lee. 1988. "Waiting Ends for Victim's Family." *Fall River Herald News,* December 9.

Cunha, Carlos. 1989. "Woman's Father Feared Dangers of Street Life." *New Bedford Standard-Times,* March 2.

Delaney, William. 2015. Interview by Maureen Boyle, October 16. Retired state trooper.

DeSantos, Judy. 2015a. Interview by Maureen Boyle, May 20.

———. 2015b. Interview by Maureen Boyle, June 9.

———. 2015c. Interview by Maureen Boyle, October 23.

———. n.d.(a). Interview by Maureen Boyle.

———. n.d.(b). Undated correspondence from Judy DeSantos.

Dextradeur, Christopher. 2015. Interview by Maureen Boyle, December 11. New Bedford police, retired; son of detective.

Dextradeur, John. 1988. Interview by Maureen Boyle. New Bedford detective

Dill, Maryann. 1989. "Massachusetts State Police Report."

———. 2015a. Interview by Maureen Boyle, November 17. Massachusetts State Police, retired.

———. 2015b. Interview by Maureen Boyle, December 8.

Douglas, John, and Mark Olshaker. 1997. *Journey Into Darkness.* New York: A Lisa Drew Book/Scribner.

Ellement, John. 1989. "Probers Say Lawyer Not Key Suspect in Killings." *Boston Globe,* January 10.

Ferreira, Richard. 1988. New Bedford Police Report.

———. 1990. "Bristol District Attorney Computerized Homicide Report Form," January 9

———. 2015. Interview by Maureen Boyle, July. New Bedford detective, retired.

———. 2016. Interview by Maureen Boyle, August 13.

"Fishermen's Memorial Service Program." 2016. New Bedford Port Society Fishermen's Memorial Service, May 30. New Bedford: New Bedford Port Authority.

Fitzgerald, Paul. 2016. Interview by Maureen Boyle, June 22. Massachusetts State Police, retired.

Forrest, Lorraine. 1989a. "Bureau of Investigative Services, Massachusetts State Police," January 23.

———. 1989b. "Bureau of Investigative Services Massachusetts State Police," August 22.

Garth, Lance. 2016. Interview by Maureen Boyle, March 4. Former assistant district attorney, retired judge.

George, Robert. 2016. Interview by Maureen Boyle, April 22. Former defense attorney.

Giammalvo, Mark S. 2010. "New Bedford Police Report," January 26.

Gold, Allan R. 1989. "New Bedford Journal: For Troubled City, All-America Lift." *New York Times,* May 23, http://www.nytimes.com/1989/05/23/us/new-bedford-journal-for-troubled-city-all-america-lift.html.

Gonsalves, Jose. 2015a. Interview by Maureen Boyle, August 27. Massachusetts State Police, retired.

———. 2015b. Interview by Maureen Boyle, December 8.

———. 2016. Interview by Maureen Boyle, August 16.

Gonsalves, Jose, and Maryann Dill, 2016. Interview by Maureen Boyle, February 23.

Greany, Gardner. 1989. "New Bedford Police Report." New Bedford, Massachusetts, May 1.

———. n.d. "New Bedford Police Report."

Greany, Gardner, Gary Baron, John Dextradeur, Ernest Frechette, and William Perry. 1986. "New Bedford Police Department Incident Report," July 16–31.

Gregory, Chandra. 2016. Interview by Maureen Boyle, March 15. Daughter of Debra Greenlaw DeMello.

Gregory, Chandra, and Wayne Perry. 2016. Interview by Maureen Boyle. Daughter and brother of Debra Greenlaw DeMello.

Hardin, Gail, 2016. Interview by Maureen Boyle, March 24. Sister, Debra Greenlaw DeMello.

Harrison, George, the Rev. 2016. Interview by Maureen Boyle, August. Roman Catholic priest.

Hawley, Dean. n.d. "Death by Strangulation." Accessed November 2016. http://www.markwynn.com/wp-content/uploads/death-by-strangulation.pdf.

Hawley, Dean, and Candace Heisler. 2012. "Strangulation and Suffocation." Phoenix, AZ: National Adult Protective Services Association. Accessed November 2016. http://www.napsa-now.org/wp-content/uploads/2012/11/102.pdf.

Indio, Jack. 2003. "New Bedford Police Department Investigative Report," September 18.

January, Charles. 2015. Interview by Maureen Boyle, November 30.

Jillson, Bruce. 1989. "Bureau of Investigative Services, Massachusetts State Police," December 18.

Karen Sunnarborg Consulting. 2010. "Town of Marion, Massachusetts Housing Production Plan." Accessed July 3, 2016. www.marionma.gov/pages/marionma_bcomm?housprodplan.pdf.

Kolata, Gina. 1987. "15 Percent of People with AIDS Survive 5 Years." *New York Times,* November 19, http://www.nytimes.com/1987/11/19/us/15-of-people-with-aids-survive-5-years.html.

Lauria, Richard, 2016. Interview by Maureen Boyle, August. Massachusetts State Police, retired.

Levin, Alan. 1982. "Pina Banishes Pro-Lowney Staff." *New Bedford Standard-Times,* September 30.

Levin, Jack, and James Alan Fox. 1988. *Mass Murder: America's Growing Menace.* New York: Plenum Press.

Machado, Bruce. 2016. Interview by Maureen Boyle, January 22. New Bedford Police detective, retired.

Martin, Kenneth. 2016. Interview by Maureen Boyle, February 21 Massachusetts State Police, retired.

Massachusetts State Police. 1989a. "Computerized Homicide Report Form," January 26.

———. 1989b. "Computerized Homicide Report Form," October 6.

McArdle, Elaine. 1990. "Lawyer Withdraws from Case." *New Bedford Standard-Times,* January 17.

McCabe, Dan. 2016. Interview by Maureen Boyle, August 18. Taunton police captain and former intern.

McKay, Kelsey. 2014. "A closer look at strangulation cases." The Prosecutor (Texas District County Attorney's Association) 44 (1). Accessed November 2016. http://www.tdcaa.com/journal/closer-look-strangulation-cases.

Mello, Leslie. 1990. Interview by Maureen Boyle. New Bedford resident.

Morgado, Victor. 1989. "New Bedford Police Memo," May 17.

Muntzel, Patty. 1988a. "Trooper Searches for Clues to Mystery of Unidentified Bodies." *New Bedford Standard-Times,* August 13.

———. 1988b. "R.I., Mass. Police Study Possible Link in Murders." *New Bedford Standard-Times,* December 21.

New Bedford Standard-Times. 1982. "Victim's Mother Punches Suspect Charged in Rape," July 23.

Oliveira, Ric. 2007. "Fishing's Deadly Dark Side." *New Bedford Standard-Times,* March 12.

Ostiguy, Nelson. 2016. Interview by Maureen Boyle, May 31. Massachusetts State Police, retired.

Pacheco, Louis J. 2016. Interview by Maureen Boyle, January 28. Bristol County Drug Task Force leader; Raynham police; retired.

Paiva, Jill. 2015a. Interview by Maureen Boyle, July. Daughter of Nancy Paiva.

———. 2015b. Interview by Maureen Boyle, October 5.

Perry, Suzanne, 2016. Interview by Maureen Boyle, June 17. Sister-in law, Debra Greenlaw DeMello.

Perry, Wayne, 2016. Interview by Maureen Boyle, March 19. Brother, Debra Greenlaw

Phillips, Richard. 2016. Interview by Maureen Boyle, February 16. Dartmouth, Massachusetts, police officer, retired.

Pina-Barcellos, Kari, 2016. Interview by Maureen Boyle, July 21. Daughter of former district attorney Ronald A. Pina.

Powell, Beverly, 2016. Interview by Maureen Boyle, December 4.

Prostitute. 1988. Interview by Maureen Boyle, New Bedford.

Rao, Dinesh. n.d. "Ligature Strangulation." Accessed November 2016. http://www .forensicpathologyonline.com/e-book/asphyxia/ligature-strangulation.

Rebmann, Andrew. 2015. Interview by Maureen Boyle, November 9. Connecticut State Police trooper, retired.

Rebmann, Andrew, Edward David, and Marcella H. Sorg. 2000. *Cadaver Dog Handbook: Forensic Training and Tactics for the Recovery of Human Remains.* Boca Raton, Florida: CRC Press.

Reddington, Kevin. 2016. Interview by Maureen Boyle, July 1. Attorney.

Ressler, Robert, Ann W. Burgess, and John E. Douglas. 1988. *Sexual Homicide: Patterns and Motives.* Lexington, MA: D. C. Heath and Company.

St. Jean, Robert. 2016a. Interview by Maureen Boyle, January 14. Former chief investigator, Bristol County District Attorney's Office.

——— . 2016b. Interview by Maureen Boyle, July 20.

Sampson, Claudia. 2015. Interview by Maureen Boyle, October 28. New Bedford police.

Spinner, Linda. 2016. Interview by Maureen Boyle, March 26.

Starkey, Carol A. 1990. "Factual Report of the Indictable Offenses of Kenneth C. Ponte," February 9.

State of Florida. 1990a. "State of Florida v. Kenneth Ponte." Deposition of Diane Doherty, Pasco County Government Center, June 15–18.

——— . 1990b. "State of Florida v. Kenneth Ponte." Advisory hearing, Pasco County Government Center, June 15.

Sylvia, James. 2016. Interview by Maureen Boyle, January 10. New Bedford Police narcotics sergeant, retired.

Thomas, Joseph, 2016. Interview by Maureen Boyle, August. New Bedford historian.

Thomas, Joseph D., Marsha L. McCabe, Alfred Saulniers, Natalie White, Jay Avila. 2013. *A Picture History of New Bedford, Volume One — 1602–1925.* New Bedford, MA: Spinner Publications, Inc.

Tink, Ian E. 1988. "Massachusetts Treatment Center, memorandum." August 9.

Urbon, Steve. 2016. "40 Years of Change: For Fishing Industry, the Spring of 1976 Was the Start of a New Era." *New Bedford Standard-Times,* August 15.

Veary, Raymond P. Jr. 2015. Interview by Maureen Boyle, December 10. Former first assistant district attorney.

Vosburg, Mark. 1987. "Caller Warns He'll Kill Again." *New Bedford Standard-Times,* July 18.

Walsh, Paul. 2015. Interview by Maureen Boyle, December 9. Former Bristol County district attorney.

Warren, Cat. 2013. *What the Dog Knows: Scent, Science and the Amazing Way Dogs Perceive the World.* New York: Touchstone/Simon & Schuster.

whalingmuseum.org. n.d. New Bedford Whaling Museum. Accessed January 5, 2016. whalingmuseum.org.

White, Natalie. 1988. "Vigil Message: 'People Do Care.'" *New Bedford Standard-Times,* December 28.

———. 1989. "Divorce Records Portray Abused Boy, Parents' Pawn." *New Bedford Standard-Times,* May 11.

Wordell, David. 2015. Interview by Maureen Boyle, December 7. Massachusetts State Police, retired.